Received on

MAR 30 2022

Green Lake Library

PRAISE FOR *Carceral Con*

"This is an important intervention in bringing prison and police abolition together in a way that provides both theoretical underpinnings and practical advice for organizers."

—Alex S. Vitale, author of *The End of Policing*

"In *Carceral Con*, Kay Whitlock and Nancy A. Heitzeg expose the misleading, superficial gambit of so-called bipartisan criminal justice reform. Drawing on a range of writers organizations working against the inequities and barbarities of racial capitalism, carceral logic, and militarized policing, they offer us clear thinking and transformative action for change. *Carceral Con* is a critical resource for all progressives."

—Lisa Duggan, Professor of Social and Cultural Analysis, New York University

"*Carceral Con* is a must-read for activists and scholars alike working to abolish the interlocking systems of punishment, racial capitalism, and structural inequality. In clear, trenchant prose, this book lays out why criminal justice reforms not only fail but often strengthen the very penal institutions they seek to ameliorate. Kay Whitlock and Nancy A. Heitzeg have written a movement book that reflects the wisdom of many years of abolitionist organizing and dares us to think expansively about the true origins of transformational change."

—Donna Murch, author of *Living for the City: Education, Migration, and the Rise of the Black Panther Party in Oakland, California*

D1604157

Carceral Con

Carceral Con

THE DECEPTIVE TERRAIN OF CRIMINAL JUSTICE REFORM

Kay Whitlock
and
Nancy A. Heitzeg

UNIVERSITY OF CALIFORNIA PRESS

University of California Press
Oakland, California

© 2021 by Kay Whitlock and Nancy A. Heitzeg

Library of Congress Cataloging-in-Publication Data

Names: Whitlock, Kay, author. | Heitzeg, Nancy A., author.
Title: Carceral con : the deceptive terrain of criminal justice reform / Kay Whitlock and Nancy A. Heitzeg.
Description: Oakland, California : University of California Press, [2021] | Includes bibliographical references and index.
Identifiers: LCCN 2021005243 (print) | LCCN 2021005244 (ebook) | ISBN 9780520343467 (cloth) | ISBN 9780520343474 (paperback) | ISBN 9780520974807 (epub)
Subjects: LCSH: Criminal justice, Administration of—United States—21st century.
Classification: LCC HV9950 .W534 2021 (print) | LCC HV9950 (ebook) | DDC 364.60973—dc23
LC record available at https://lccn.loc.gov/2021005243
LC ebook record available at https://lccn.loc.gov/2021005244

Manufactured in the United States of America

30 29 28 27 26 25 24 23 22 21
10 9 8 7 6 5 4 3 2 1

Dedicated to

Keeley Schenwar
1990–2020

Stephen "Stevie" Wilson

and

All those, living and dead, past, present, and future,
who, in the fight for abolition,
help bring a more just, generous, and compassionate
world into being—first in our imaginations
and then into the material realm

Contents

Illustrations

Acknowledgments

For many years, our individual work and activism have focused largely on the structural violence—raced, classed, gendered, ableist—of policing, prosecution, and prisons. A decade ago, together, we began following the money of an emergent wave of "bipartisan criminal justice reform." This concise book distills much of what we have learned over time, always with the help and insight of so many others whose work has, in varying ways, illuminated a murky and troubling reform landscape. We express special gratitude here to organizations and individuals whose work has been especially helpful, often inspirational, to us. At the same time, no one else is responsible for the analysis and conclusions in this book. The responsibility for any errors and shortcomings is also ours.

Our deep respect and gratitude go to a number of organizations whose organizing and insight is at once visionary and practical: Critical Resistance, California Coalition for Women Prisoners, Incite!, Californians United for a Responsible Budget (CURB), Black and Pink, Southerners on New Ground (SONG), the National Bail Fund

Network, Survived and Punished, Project NIA, and—a rarity in bar associations—the abolitionist National Lawyers Guild. We honor the work and voices of #BlackLivesMatter, the #SayHerName campaign, and The Movement for Black Lives (M4BL). They have all played key roles in the emergence of a powerful, Black-led movement against police violence and carceral expansion. Dreaming Freedom, Practicing Abolition, a project led by incarcerated people in Pennsylvania, with an outside network of support, is invaluable.

Several online blogs and independent news-and-analysis sites have encouraged and supported our work in interrogating the deceptive nature of the bipartisan reform consensus. We are indebted to the Prison Culture blog, an excellent abolitionist resource created by Mariame Kaba, and to Angola 3 News, founded by Hans Bennett to educate about and campaign for the release of three Black men who—framed for a murder they did not commit when they began to expose the racism, systemic corruption, and horrific violence inside a Louisiana prison—were buried alive in solitary confinement for decades. Ten years ago, we removed our weekly Criminal Injustice series from a well-known blog with which we no longer wished to affiliate. It found a wonderful home in the then-new Critical Mass Progress site, founded by the remarkable Seeta Persaud, where it continued for several years. Truthout, a nonprofit, independent social justice news organization, took a lively interest in our analyses of bipartisan criminal justice reforms and amplified the reach of our writing on same. Beacon Broadside, a Beacon Press blog, and Political Research Associates, a social justice think tank, also deserve our thanks.

Other individuals have helped us along the way. We extend heartfelt thanks to Leslie Thatcher, who first published our work in Truthout. In 2014, Leslie and Maya Schenwar, Truthout's editor-in-chief, created a special series for some of our takes: "Smoke and Mirrors: Inside the New 'Bipartisan Prison Reform' Agenda." Maya and Victoria Law generously permitted us an early read prior to publication of their groundbreaking book, *A Prison by Any Other Name: The Harmful Consequences of Popular Reforms.*

We also express our profound appreciation to Dan Berger and Craig Gilmore, without whose support this book would not be possible. Craig, Dan, Jordan T. Camp, Alex A. Vitale, Donna Murch, and Sharlyn Grace, variously read and commented on the book proposal, the manuscript, or portions of it. James Kilgore and Michael Cox generously responded to questions. Su'ganni (Aaron Lester) Tiuza provided us with important information he compiled while imprisoned. Others, too numerous to mention here, helped call our attention to useful material or otherwise offered encouragement and support. We thank them all. Finally, we express profound gratitude to the terrific people at the University of California Press: Niels Hooper, Robin Manley, Madison Wetzell, Teresa Iafolla, and all those in the design and marketing departments. Claudia Smelser of UC Press and Charles Brock Design conjured a remarkable cover. We are grateful to copyeditor Gary J. Hamel and indexer Laurie Prendergast for their indispensable work.

KAY WHITLOCK'S PERSONAL ACKNOWLEDGMENTS

As I grew into and deepened my abolitionist commitments, the work of three radical queer organizations helped shape my own vision and analysis, and to them I offer eternal gratitude: The Audre Lorde Project, Queers for Economic Justice, and the Sylvia Rivera Law Project. Among the individuals whose work and insights have greatly expanded my own justice vision are Fay Honey Knopp, Ejeris Dixon, Joey Mogul, Mariame Kaba, Andrea J. Ritchie, Aishah Shahida Simmons, Kenyon Farrow, Stevie Wilson, and Kelly Hayes. I had been learning from Ruth Wilson Gilmore's work long before I interviewed her for a bipartisan reform critique I was writing at one time. She has been consistently generous, helpful, insightful, and candid. In very different ways, I am equally grateful to two wise friends, Anita Doyle and Carol Heer, who help me navigate the journeys into the underworld of carceral inhumanity while keeping my heart intact and open. So many friends and colleagues have offered ongoing encouragement and support. But special thanks are due three people. The first is Nancy A. Heitzeg, friend and co-conspirator. We are both stubborn and opinionated, and we share a "ride or die" commitment to each other and to a different, better world. This is a book we had to write together. I want to honor Bette Whitlock, my mother, long deceased, who taught me about the interdependence of humans, trees, and critters. Finally, Phoebe Hunter, my partner of more than thirty years and best friend, deserves thanks for all of it. She challenges, helps, supports, and understands why this work is important, heart, mind, and spirit. And she makes me laugh, which is worth everything.

NANCY A. HEITZEG'S PERSONAL ACKNOWLEDGMENTS

Thanks are due to many who have made this book and all my work possible. First of all, special thanks to Kay Whitlock, my colleague and comrade, whose vision and generosity bring forth the best. Special thanks too to St. Catherine University, my academic home and a place where my work toward justice has always been encouraged. I am especially grateful for St. Kate's support of my abolitionist work as Endowed Chair in the Sciences, for my colleagues in the Sociology Department, and for my long-standing friends and colleagues—Sharon Doherty and Deep Shikha of St. Catherine University, and Rose Brewer of the University of Minnesota.

A world without cages has always been my aim, long before I knew the term *abolition*. My scholarship and activism have been inspired by many along the way: Angela Davis, the Black Panther Party, old Karl Marx, John Brown, Eugene V. Debs, AIM and the case of Leonard Peltier, Joy James, Mumia Abu-Jamal, and more. But the freedom to imagine a different world was/is made possible by my family: my grandparents; my parents, Louie and especially my late mother Barbara; my brother Steve, Gwen, and Zadie; and my partner, William W. Smith IV—who did and does still trust me to pursue the hardest questions. And that freedom is nurtured and sustained by that place I call "the farm," where the broad embrace of nature and so many extraordinary species shines as a beacon for how it should be.

Introduction

WORLD MAKING AND "CRIMINAL JUSTICE REFORM"

> Everywhere I look I see sleepwalkers under the spell of the prison. What counterspell is powerful enough to break the prison's stranglehold on our imaginations?
>
> —Jackie Wang, *Carceral Capitalism*, 2018

From the beginning, evasions, hedging, deceptive rhetoric, trap doors, backroom reversals, hidden agendas, and slippery "success" indicators have been built into the misleading and false promises of sweeping criminal justice reform. The detritus is scattered, often within the inspiring razzle-dazzle of well-funded promotional campaigns, and most of it is not visible at first glance. But it's been there all along.

Philanthropic funding consolidated the first public stirrings of the contemporary wave of "bipartisan criminal justice reform,"* just barely visible in the early 2000s, into a "strange bedfellows" crusade amassing increasing political support. By 2010, the institutionalization of a self-perpetuating reform industry was well underway. By

* Throughout this book, the authors use *criminal justice reform* when referring to agendas utilizing this term or quoting individuals, organizations, and publications who use it. We prefer the term *criminal legal system* for our own references to the collective processes of policing, prosecution, and punishment because, as readers will learn, there is little that can be collectively recognized as "justice" to be found within them.

mid-2020, as videos made clear, racist vigilante and police violence blended seamlessly in public view. In response to the police murders of George Floyd, a Black man in Minneapolis, Minnesota, and Breonna Taylor, a Black woman in Louisville, Kentucky, and the vigilante murder of Ahmaud Arbery, a Black man in New Brunswick, Georgia, hundreds of thousands of people in Minneapolis, Louisville, Atlanta, and throughout the United States took to the streets protesting racist structural violence and declaring that #BlackLivesMatter. Police, National Guard units, and other law enforcement agencies predictably responded to the uprising with counterinsurgency tactics originally designed for military suppression of global, anticolonial rebellions.[1] Throughout the nation, many activists and groups took up the call to #DefundThePolice. As noted organizer and abolitionist Mariame Kaba emphasized, they intended to do exactly that, despite the efforts of mainstream reformers to suggest it didn't mean that at all.[2]

The uprising occurred against a backdrop of well-publicized criminal legal system reforms. The fuse was lit centuries ago by the relentless criminalization—the presumptive and baseless attribution of criminality to entire groups—and routine state and vigilante violence directed against Black people and other marginalized communities. Urban uprisings in response to police abuse and killings are not new, but, as pent-up rage and grief exploded, it became clear that this was a watershed moment.[3] And in this moment, powerfully opposing visions of the world "as it should be," already on a collision course, met in the streets. One vision showcased the violence that upholds white supremacy in service to political and economic elites, while the other sought its dissolution in the name of justice.

In the wake of the 2020 uprisings, many people seek to better understand why contemporary reforms have not produced more justice, especially justice for Black people. This book tells the story of the smoke-and-mirrors nature of those reform agendas and their ongoing failures to dismantle the entwined harms of structural racism and poverty so foundational to the criminal legal system. These failures are deeply rooted not only in the histories of US prisons and policing, but in the neoliberal world making of its architects. In telling this story, *Carceral Con* also takes note of the decades-long gathering of activist forces, within and without prisons, arrayed to advance different visions of world making that no longer rely on organized violence—policing, prosecution, and prisons—to produce justice, safety, and community well-being.

THE BIPARTISAN CRIMINAL JUSTICE REFORM CONSENSUS

In his State of the Union address to Congress on February 5, 2019, President Donald Trump lifted up passage of the First Step Act, featuring a set of federal sentencing reforms, as a "groundbreaking" achievement in criminal justice reform and bipartisan cooperation across a presumptive Republican-Democratic divide. "Together," he said, "we can break decades of political stalemate. We can bridge old divisions, heal old wounds, build new coalitions, forge new solutions, and unlock the extraordinary promise of America's future." For some people, this stirring call to unified action sounded disingenuous, even ludicrous, coming from a president whose initial campaign for public office was rooted in racist dog-whistling and whose trademark response to disagreement is publicly humiliating, vilifying, and criminalizing opponents and enemies, both real and imagined, often in vulgar, racially coded, and misogynist terms. But not, perhaps, to many others, including two of Trump's guests for the evening. They were Alice Marie Johnson, who had served twenty-two years in prison before Trump commuted her life sentence for a drug-related offense, and Matthew Charles, sentenced to thirty-five years for selling drugs and related offenses. Charles was the first person released from federal prison under First Step reforms. These people and their stories, Trump said, underscored sentencing disparities that have "wrongly and disproportionately harmed the African-American community."[4] Johnson and Charles deserve their good fortune, however long delayed it was in arriving. But the implication of a resonant bipartisan commitment to systemic racial justice inherent in their presence and visibility is highly misleading. Feel-good snapshots of "reform in action" often tell pleasing public relations half-truths while less palatable, more complicating realities of the same story remain in the shadows.

Drawing almost exclusively on prepared talking points promoting the First Step Act, mass media response to its passage, with Trump's support, was ecstatic. When Trump first announced support for First Step, CNN pundit, putative liberal, and celebrity reformer Van Jones tweeted, "Give the man his due: @realDonaldTrump is on his way to becoming the uniter-in-Chief on an issue that has divided America for generations" (@VanJones68, November 14, 2018). Even as political polarization over such issues as immigration policy, police violence, and climate crisis deepened, Trump and Jones played to the last frayed—but not yet completely destroyed—nerve of hope in the body politic. Whatever their views of Donald Trump, many people wanted to believe that reform could halt the brutalities and injustices bundled under the rubric of mass incarceration. What better proof of progress than the sight of politicians reaching across the aisle to reject—or so people are led to believe—the decades of raced, classed, gendered, and ableist "tough-on-crime" policies that they had jointly produced?

In support of such reforms, civil rights advocates have joined with conservative-Right counterparts who virulently oppose or seek to limit the rights of women, migrants and immigrants, LGBTQ people, people with disabilities, homeless people, and more. Notable First Step supporters included such strange bedfellows as the corporate-Right policy mill ALEC (American Legislative Exchange Council) Action and the American Civil Liberties Union (ACLU); Americans for Tax Reform, a libertarian-Right antitax group, and the National Association for the Advancement of Colored People (NAACP); Right on Crime, a self-proclaimed one-stop source for conservative-Right reform analysis, and the Leadership Conference on Civil and Human Rights; and the virulently anti-LGBTQ Faith and Freedom Coalition and the Center for American Progress, a Clintonian think tank. Similar state-based unlikely alliances also exist. Their shared agendas and policy templates are identified and often referred to in this book as "the bipartisan consensus."

Under the celebratory bipartisan surface, the terrain is murky and untrustworthy. Erroneous assumptions about the nature, scope, and impacts of criminal legal reforms abound. For example, while many people assumed all US prisons were covered by the First Step reforms, that legislation applies only to those in federal Bureau of Prisons (BOP) custody, less than 10 percent of all people confined in US prisons and jails. And while First Step reform makes it possible for some federal prisoners to be considered for early release, many others were convicted on charges that make them ineligible for such consideration. Beyond that, First Step mandated the creation and system-wide deployment of a data-based analytics tool utilized to predict and address the risk of recidivism (being arrested for a new offense following release) for every federal prisoner. This and other predictive profiling tools, linchpins of bipartisan reforms, purport to erase racial and other forms of bias in assessing the "dangerousness" of arrested and incarcerated people. Yet so-called "risk assessment" tools have attracted controversy and criticism for years because, as readers will learn, they reinforce rather than erase bias while creating vast new databases. First Step is one example of similar kinds of bipartisan consensus work carried out at state and local levels.

The rhetoric and public relations campaigns used to market bipartisan reforms are often misleading. For example, promises to end "overcriminalization" litter bipartisan talking points. But that's a word as deceptive as quicksand. The bipartisan consensus intentionally sidesteps the matter of explosive growth in immigrant detention. Even though being in the United States without the required authorization is considered a civil, not a criminal, infraction, various major coalition members and funders disagree on the issue, and a decades-long fusion of immigration policy with processes of criminalization and aggressive policing—"crimmigration"—has been an expansive bipartisan project. Symbiotic relationships among US jails, prisons, and immigrant detention centers define the terrain. The bipartisan silence surrounding that symbiosis is unconscionable, particularly in a time of intensified policing of migrants and immigrants, closing doors for refugees, workplace raids, and ever more draconian detention and deportation policies primarily targeting Latinx peoples and Black immigrants. *Carceral Con* also takes note of the increasing criminalization of protest; political dissent; and efforts to document industrial practices that are cruel, exploitative, and harmful to the public, another issue that elicits only silence from the bipartisan consensus.

The bipartisan consensus also provides some degree of cover for criminalizing sleights of hand. While many reform coalitions officially endorse reinstatement of the right to vote for formerly incarcerated people under various conditions, some of the same conservative-Right actors active in those coalitions utilize the lens of criminalization to legitimize suppression of voting rights more broadly. In 2018, Florida voters overwhelmingly approved Amendment 4 to the state constitution, reinstating voting rights for as many as 1.5 million persons with felony convictions—disproportionately Black—who were released from prison. Florida's Republican-dominated state legislature then acted swiftly to roll back the full reach of the amendment by adding definitions of the crime convictions that would disqualify a person from re-enfranchisement. In a move that evoked the earlier use of poll taxes to suppress the votes of Black people, they also instituted a requirement that formerly incarcerated people pay any remaining court costs, fines, or fees before reinstatement.[5] A flurry of legal challenges and appeals ensued; weeks before the November 2020 election, the Eleventh Circuit Court of Appeals ruled that fines and fees must be paid before people with former felony convictions could vote. A combination of advocacy, organizing, and charity determined the matter for thousands of those people as the Florida

Rights Restoration Coalition, with the help of high-profile athletes, celebrities, and philanthropist Michael Bloomberg, raised $25 million to cover as many fines and fees as possible.[6] But charity is not justice, and many thousands more continue to face exclusions based on offense convictions as well as financial and procedural hurdles to re-enfranchisement.

Despite such hypocrisies, contradictions, and omissions, the public is encouraged to believe that any reform packaged and sold as bipartisan serves the public good. Yet bipartisanship is a mixed, inconsistent, and unreliable quality at best, often harnessed toward oppressive ends. It produced legal racial segregation and opposed efforts to end school segregation long after *Brown v. Board of Education*. It launched and escalated devastating wars in Vietnam and Iraq. It produces massive—and racialized—financial hardship through the deregulation of financial institutions engaged in predatory practices that target lower-income—predominantly Black—households. Over the course of four decades, it built the machinery of mass incarceration and technological control, expanding the reach and capacity of an already violent and unjust carceral system. Under the guise of reform, it decimates social welfare programs even as it undermines public school systems and labor unions through privatization. Such material impacts only reinforce structural racism, economic exploitation, and poverty.

We may well ask whether the affluent producers of nightmare are best equipped to preside over hopes of substantive change for the better. Especially for the hardest hit, most vulnerable communities, who are simultaneously subject to the violence of criminalization, vigilante assault, policing, punishment, and militarization. But abandoning the myth that bipartisanship is inherently virtuous is difficult for many people who want to believe that even flawed agreements are better than nothing, that we must never ask for more than what entrenched political and economic elites can be persuaded to approve. Some of the reformers themselves exhort anyone who questions their agendas to "not let the perfect be the enemy of the good." Those who do raise substantive concerns and objections to new reform proposals are often scolded as "unrealistic" or "extreme," and admonished to not be "spoilers." Characterizing dissenters as irresponsible and outside the presumptive "stable, reasonable center" is a tactic commonly used to discredit legitimate critiques and discourage critical analysis. It's useful, then, to take a closer look at the larger context that frames this critique.

KEY CONCEPTS AND TERMS

Several concepts and terms are utilized throughout the book to help describe the purported "stable, reasonable, center" and the results of its actions. *Carceral Con* argues that it is not possible to fully grasp the implications of various reforms without inquiring more deeply into multiple forms of *structural inequality and* violence that are foundational to the United States and its systems of policing and carceral control. That is to say, racial, gendered, economic, and ableist hierarchies and discrimination are structured into the everyday workings of political, legal, and economic systems. Their impacts are destabilizing, severe, and far-reaching. Indeed, *Carceral Con* also regards policies and practices that have produced environmental devastation and destruction of the biodiversity so essential to the earth's well-being as forms of structural inequality and violence.

The terms *carceral state* and *carceral systems* are frequently used throughout this book. As historian Dan Berger notes, these terms are often used as shorthand for prisons and policing or interchangeably with *mass incarceration*, and *prison-industrial complex*.[7] But while the carceral state indeed includes the workings of the formal criminal legal system in the United States, it is also far more expansive. There is no single definition that all scholars and organizers agree upon; moreover, systems of control evolve and expand over time. For the purposes of this book, then, discussions of the carceral state, carceral systems of control, and carceral power refer to repressive, punishing means of social and economic control and surveillance within the formal criminal legal system and its many public/private institutional proxies.

All of this unfolds within the structures of *racial capitalism*, an analytical concept advanced by political theorist Cedric Robinson in his groundbreaking book *Black Marxism: The Making of the Black Radical Tradition*. Robinson argues that capitalism is a global system that evolved from and requires racialized hierarchy, inequality, exploitation, and violence. Racism is not a by-product of capitalism; it is intrinsic to it.[8] Throughout *Carceral Con*, readers will find myriad examples of ways in which the co-constructive nature of racial and class hierarchies shapes criminal legal reforms.

In the United States, whiteness stands at the apex of racial hierarchy, or at least the institutionalized political construct and cultural mythos of whiteness. Here, racial capitalism is buttressed by a particularly virulent current of *anti-Blackness*. This refers to the structural refusal of US society to fully recognize the humanity of Black people while conflating their collective existence with the active presence of social disorder, danger, and criminality.[9]

Another key concept informing this book is *intersectionality*. Race, class, gender, sexuality, disability, age, and other characteristics cut across and through people's lives in overlapping and co-constructive ways that affect how they see themselves and how they fare within a society's legal, political, and economic systems. In 1989, legal scholar Kimberlé Crenshaw introduced the concept of intersectionality as a way of recognizing the dynamic complexity of these interrelationships and their structural impacts. In the United States, severe inequalities historically have been and continue to be visited primarily upon groups of people who live at the intersections of race (not white or not white enough), class (working class, low-income, and impoverished), gender and sexuality (cisgender women, transgender women or men, gender non-conforming or nonbinary, queer, intersex), and disability. Age, too, complicates the picture, for both children and elders. These groups experience a systemic, lifetime disadvantage in terms of health, economic well-being, and vulnerability to a myriad of harms. The geographer Ruth Wilson Gilmore, whose work analyzes the political economy that produces, sustains, and expands systems of carceral control, defines racism as "the state-sanctioned or extralegal production and exploitation of group-differentiated vulnerability to premature death."[10] By paying attention to these vulnerabilities and harms—experienced collectively as well as individually—*Carceral Con* shifts discussion away from the popular but erroneous notion that the massive harms and injustices of the criminal legal system can be reformed as a standalone project.

This book looks at some of the ordinary workings of racial capitalism through the prism of carceral control and bipartisan consensus reforms. The strategic choices and "unlikely allies" nature of the bipartisan consensus are explained by the bipartisan turn globally and in the United States toward *neoliberalism*. Rooted in a long and complex theoretical history, and in response to the waning of industrial capitalism, neoliberalism began to emerge as a dominant force in the 1970s and 1980s, gaining momentum since that time. In brief, neoliberalism can be understood as a particular set of economic and social practices and relationships between the political state and late racial capitalism marked by the aggressive elevation of private property rights, free markets, and free trade. These go hand in hand with the pursuit of "entrepreneurial freedoms" (deregulation, privatizing, union-busting, and the rise of the gig jobs economy). Within the neoliberal context, says economic geographer David Harvey, the role of the state, "is to create and preserve an institutional framework appropriate to such practices," including establishing "those military, defence, police, and legal structures and functions required to secure private property rights and to guarantee, by force if need be, the proper functioning of markets."[11] In the United States, neoliberalism has created a redistributive framework for weakening and dismantling programs that return state revenues directly to working people in the form of basic, stabilizing supports. These include Social Security, health care, public education, housing, food assistance, environmental protection, and more. Monies once used for these "public good" expenditures are redistributed to the ultra-wealthy: to private sector corporations and entities. Tax policy accomplishes the same redistribution goal, favoring corporations and the already-wealthy at the expense of working people and those on low and fixed incomes. Many politicians, foundations, and advocacy organizations who consider themselves liberal, moderate, or centrist either support or fail to challenge this framework.

The concept of *political economy* is important here. Briefly, this refers to the dynamic relationship between political and economic systems and the resultant distribution of income, wealth, power, and other resources in a particular society. In order to advance the restructuring of the political economy, neoliberalism relies on a manufactured politics of scarcity to institutionalize its policies. The political solder that fuses diverse elements of the bipartisan reform agenda is fiscal *austerity*. This refers to mandated policies put in place by national governments in the late twentieth and early twenty-first centuries to reduce debt and restructure economies in response to demands from such international financial institutions as the World Bank and the International Monetary Fund (IMF) and unified regional trade and monetary bodies, including the European Union. In the United States, austerity politics are pursued through perpetual but highly selective claims of "budget crisis" at all levels of government, together with equally selective calls to reduce the national debt by slashing spending for public services and social welfare programs. By contrast, public spending for police and military forces usually increases. Tax cuts for the wealthy proliferate.

Processes of *organized abandonment* characterize the bleak heart of neoliberalism. This refers to the results of neoliberal economic and industrial restructuring: massive losses of jobs, health care, homes/rental residences, and farms, and livelihoods in communities and regions already struggling for survival. In a sense, organized abandonment can be seen as a systemic, profit-oriented destruction of the possibility of life-giving social, economic, and ecological relationships. Extractive industries—fracking, mining, drilling for oil—together with the polluting practices of Big Agriculture, and the routine cruelty of factory farms—continue to produce long-lasting environmental and ecological harms. Many of those harms remain long after industry has left the area. Civic infrastructure deteriorates. Public services and resources are privatized. While corporate profits and tax breaks for the wealthy rise, poverty expands everywhere, but most intensely among Black and Brown populations. Rural and small-town populations shrink, along with tax bases. Severe contractions of already minuscule investments in public well-being follow. Hospitals, no longer sufficiently profitable, are closed, taking essential health care accessibility and more jobs with them. The loss of economic stability and community coherence produces other forms of precarity: increasing homelessness, substance abuse, and psychological stress. Policing intensifies, and particularly in rural areas and in small towns, a carceral economy develops or expands through the growth of county jail capacity, the placement of newly sited prisons, and explosive growth in immigrant detention. Such an economy never fulfills its munificent promises.[12] But in the midst of abandonment, almost any possibility of employment can seem hopeful to people who, understandably, are frightened about their own futures, and those of their children.

The ethic of *individualism*, enshrined within the neoliberal framework, shatters the notion that governance bears responsibility for providing for societal well-being, ensuring collective justice, and remedying structural inequalities. By exalting only the individual and casting aside collective justice commitments to one another, the isolationist scarcity frame of austerity begins to influence how many people redefine themselves and their relationship to their labor, to culture, to other people, to the society, and to the earth. Indeed, neoliberalism depends on the dramatic expansion of quasi-governmental *public-private partnerships* to carry out functions once considered core public responsibilities. An example is privatization of public schools through the transfer of public revenue to charter schools and voucher programs. By blurring the lines between the operations of government and the private sector, neoliberalism essentially opens up public revenue and even governance itself as a new—ultimately unregulated—market. Core public responsibilities and monies are ceded to private designees with less or no public accountability. Not surprisingly, most criminal legal reforms are focused on the administration of a system obsessed with individual offenses, attributing the incarceration of those individuals not only to individual crimes, but also to purported individual moral failings and so-called "criminogenic factors." These values, beliefs, and "cognitive-emotional states" that purportedly correlate with "criminal conduct" include such risk factors as feelings of anger and rage, defiance, "the expression of negative views about conventional institutions and authorities," and "criminal identity"—an essentially eugenic idea.

By contrast, as readers will see, the exclusion of structural law enforcement violence is a strategic imperative that runs like a major artery through mainstream reform agendas. In its place, philanthropy-driven reforms establish an intricate branching system of procedural and managerial tweaks, training modules, technological innovations, and facilities redesign that shifts attention away from the pandemic of mass criminalization, routine police and prison violence, and carceral expansion.

INEQUALITY

"The criminal justice system," Dan Berger says, "is an index of inequality."[13] But that inequality doesn't originate within jails and prisons. The product of racial capitalism, it defines US society, determining who is likely to be incarcerated and who isn't, just as it defines the society that is awaiting people when they are released from custodial confinement. A quick glance at just a few indicators of widening structural inequality along the fault lines of race, class, and gender, helps establish a material context for understanding the false and distorting promises of many reforms.

Researchers for the Institute for Policy Studies, together with the Poor People's Campaign, examined the terrain of inequality in 2018, fifty years since Rev. Dr. Martin Luther King Jr. launched the first Poor People's Campaign. Their report, *The Souls of Poor Folk*, underscores the urgent need to recognize and address the complex interrelationships that produce and amplify injustice:

> These issues demand that we dispel the notion that systemic racism, poverty, ecological devastation and the war economy hurt only a small segment of our society. More than 40,600,000 Americans subsist below the poverty line; this report additionally shows that there are close to 140 million people dealing with some combination of these crises every day. Nearly half of our population cannot afford a $400 emergency, which presents a structural crisis of national proportion that ties poverty to things like healthcare and housing. The devastation cuts across race, gender, age, and geography. It has carved a dangerous and deepening moral chasm in America.[14]

The United States is home to an always severe and now deepening racial wealth divide. Wealth refers to the monetary value of all assets (homes, stocks, possessions, land) owned by a person or household, minus debts that are owed. For households, that value is a marker of greater stability or precarity. A great deal of US wealth is heritable, passed on from one generation to the next. For Indigenous peoples, massive theft began from the point of colonial contact. As Roxanne Dunbar-Ortiz points out, "A rich, ancient agricultural civilization was appropriated. The Europeans appropriated it and then created agribusiness, capitalized, monetized the land, created real estate."[15] She describes the founding of a state based on the ideology of white supremacy, settler colonialism, and a policy of genocide and land theft, linking it with the institution of chattel slavery. "The quality of life in US society depends on the personal accumulation of wealth," says African American studies scholar Keeanga-Yamahtta Taylor, and home ownership is the largest single investment that most families make to accrue this wealth." Yet for one hundred years, even past the time when legal forms of housing discrimination were banned, the housing market remains "fully formed by racial discrimination."[16] A violent record of Black farm family dispossession and displacement also stains US history.[17] In the 1930s, Great Depression-era mass repatriation and anti-employment laws targeting people of Mexican descent, many of whom were US citizens, meant dispossession and loss of livelihood and property for perhaps as many as one million people.[18] The World War II–era incarceration in concentration camps of more than one hundred twenty thousand people of Japanese ancestry—at least two-thirds of whom were US citizens—who had violated no laws, meant the mass loss of homes, businesses, livelihoods, and personal belongings.[19]

The Institute for Policy Studies examined a widening divide from 1983 to 2016: while the wealth for median white households was rising, that of Black households was plummeting. The same period also saw enormous and growing concentration of wealth at the top. The number of households with wealth of $10 million or more "skyrocketed by 856 percent," and the Forbes 400 richest plutocrats alone held more wealth than all Black households plus one-quarter of Latinx households.[20] Single Black and Latinx mothers—and their children—bear the brunt of wealth inequality. While Indigenous peoples are seldom represented in studies of wealth inequality, 2018 data from the US Census confirms that at least one-quarter of Indigenous households are impoverished, a higher percentage than other racial and ethnic groups. But since the federal poverty line is widely recognized as underestimating economic precarity, the real measure of severe economic hardship among Indigenous peoples is undoubtedly significantly higher. Rising home prices are not sufficiently matched by rising wages in a majority of US housing markets; more people are renting. But rents, too, are rising beyond the ability of many people to keep up with them, and processes of gentrification serve as ruthlessly efficient forms of urban clear-cutting, displacing longtime poor and low-income residents and making it impossible for many long-standing small businesses to survive. Decreases in federal funding for public housing subsidies over years has taken a severe toll on housing availability and affordability.[21] In 2019, the federal Department of Housing and Urban Development (HUD), found that about five hundred sixty-eight thousand people are homeless on a given night. Black people represented about 40 percent of all people who are homeless and about 52 percent of homeless people who were members of families with children.[22] But these numbers underestimate the situation. For the 2017–18 school year, according to the National Center for Homeless Education, the number of homeless public school students—prekindergarten to twelfth grade—was about 1.5 million, a 15 percent increase from the previous school year. This number includes children and youth whose nighttime residences are unstable: shelters, transitional housing, awaiting foster care, unsheltered (cars, abandoned buildings, campgrounds), doubled up with others, or cut-rate motels/hotels.[23]

Despite statistically low employment rates in 2019, Brookings reported, prior to the massive worker furloughs and permanent job losses that accompanied the COVID-19 pandemic, that fifty-three million US workers, ages eighteen to sixty-four, are low-wage workers, with median annual earnings of $18,000. That means 44 percent of the workforce, pre-pandemic, earned about $10.22 per hour, with no health insurance, sick leave, vacation, other benefits, or even employer-provided workplace safety equipment. Most of these workers are in their early and middle adult years; many are raising children. Black workers, especially Black women, are far more likely to earn low wages than white workers. Latinx workers also fare worse than white workers. And women, people of color, and people with low levels of education are most likely to remain in low-wage jobs.[24] Official job and income mapping omits countless—often criminalized—people whose survival comes from participation in "street" or underground economies. By late 2020, a COVID-weakened US economy was hemorrhaging hardship. The Center on Budget and Policy Priorities noted that many public job losses were in education; in the private sector, most losses affected low-wage workers, disproportionately people of color.[25]

This backdrop is essential for understanding who is—and always has been—most likely to be swept into the criminal legal system. The answer has less to do with "crime" than with raced, classed, gendered, and ableist processes of criminalization, the policing of criminalized communities, and the organized abandonment of peoples, communities, and regions. Without understanding the racial capitalist and neoliberal paradigms in which bipartisan reform agendas have emerged, we stand on shifting sands, unable to recognize and respond effectively to what is happening underneath the enticing rhetoric of reform. Unless we address the structures—not simply the procedures, technologies, and remodeling projects—that create and shape the US carceral state, "reforms" will only advance its expansion. The stakes could not be higher. At the end of 2020, we are in a political moment marked by the growth, in the United States and globally, of anti-democratic movements—white nationalist, fascist, authoritarian—that rely on a fusion of state-sanctioned violence and the rapid expansion of systems of surveillance, monitoring, and tracking. Such movements have the potential to outpace the efforts of mainstream reformers and politicians to control them.

SHIFTING REFORM TERRAIN AND THE PLAYERS

Generations of criminal justice reforms always beget new ones, few of them liberatory in any collective, sustainable way. Almost all of them allocate more funding resources for law enforcement agencies while expanding processes of criminalization and increasing the number of people under some form of carceral control. The bipartisan reform tsunami of the 2000s unfolds against a backdrop of federal and state reforms, beginning in the 1960s, that transmuted powerful momentum for civil rights and systemic anti-poverty measures into anti-crime measures, racist in implementation if not in legislative wording, meant to contain so-called "urban disorder"—rebellions and riots in major US cities that exploded as the US failed to address the intersections of structural racism and poverty.[26] In the following decades, through the 1990s, both Republican and Democratic politicians, embraced "tough-on-crime" measures.[27] Many of those same politicians on both sides of the aisle now vie for accolades as reformers.

The terrain of criminal legal system reform is never fixed. It shifts and expands rapidly, according to demographic, political, economic, environmental, and other factors and conditions. The histories of prisons in the United States, along with the systems of criminalization and policing that are foundational to it, are histories of reform. Mass incarceration is the result of criminal legal reform. On the terrain of reform, different interests compete to shape the final outcomes. Given this always-evolving, contested landscape, it can be difficult to sort out both the players and impacts of reforms on offer. To help readers navigate this complexity, *Carceral Con* identifies several sectors of institutional actors and social justice activist interests in the mix, all seeking to leverage change. None of these sectors is monolithic, but while disagreements exist within them, agendas generally agreed upon are put forward by major partners.

Broadly speaking, *the bipartisan consensus* was forged by public-private partnerships that not only promote but benefit politically and/or financially from reform. Partners and coalition members include philanthropic organizations and major donors, foundations, think tanks, influential advocacy and nonprofit organizations, corporations, universities and research institutes, and governmental agencies and boards. As this book notes, while bipartisan consensus agendas are well advanced, some of the initial unity among major players shows definite signs of fraying in specific areas. To further complicate the picture, there are also scores of actors engaging in various sorts of prison/policing reform advocacy who are not formally allied with the major reform organizations and coalitions. But sometimes their interests mesh with specific bipartisan agendas or reforms. They include international, federal, state, and local human rights/civil rights groups, legal defense groups, organizations of families of prisoners and others who provide direct aid to incarcerated people, prison education programs, and more. While the primary focus of this book is on the architects of the bipartisan consensus, these actors often influence reform outcomes, especially at state and local levels.

Law enforcement lobbies constitute another powerful sector: law enforcement officials and correctional officers; their unions and professional associations; prosecutors; judges; commercial bail bond agencies; and suppliers of technologies and services for policing, carceral control, community supervision, and surveillance. When conflicts arise among the bipartisan consensus and law enforcement lobbies, they are usually resolved by preserving the veneer of reform while accommodating law enforcement demands.

Abolitionists comprise the third sector, a movement that arises from the Black radical tradition. Abolitionist perspectives and practices seek to ensure that poverty and social and political problems and inequalities are addressed not through processes of criminalization and policing, but by approaches designed to dismantle the structural conditions that produce them. Profound political and economic shifts are necessary in order to replace civic reliance on policing and prisons with robust public investment in education, health care, social services, housing, jobs, and ecological/environmental well-being—the things that help both individuals and entire communities thrive.

Since the 1970s, centering the experiences of the communities most heavily policed and incarcerated, a myriad of activists and advocates inside and outside of prisons, grassroots organizations, scholars, and defense campaigns have educated about, exposed the violence of, and addressed the catastrophic impacts of the US carceral state. Such abolitionist organizations as Critical Resistance, the California Coalition of Women Prisoners, INCITE!, Survived & Punished, and Black and Pink argue that it is impossible to dismantle structural racism and class, gender, and ableist violence within the criminal legal system by treating it as a standalone issue, confined to policing, US courtrooms, jails, detention facilities, and prisons. Abolitionists seek to reduce reliance on, defund, and dismantle systems of criminalization, policing, and carceral control. And simultaneously, they work to replace those systems with more life-giving approaches that emphasize community and ecological well-being; that focus on accountability, repair, and healing over retribution.

Finally, outside of the bipartisan consensus, *hybrid coalitions* exist that bring together both abolitionists and various reformers to work to steadily shrink and defund the carceral capacity of while increasing public funding for community supports and services not linked to the criminal legal system.

The impacts of every major new wave of criminal justice reform remain with us for generations. Even though some observers argue that neoliberalism has already begun to collapse of its own weight, the reality is that these reforms affect what is happening now and will happen in the near future, and they establish the foundation for what comes next. The world-making efforts of bipartisan reform reaffirm racial, class, gender, and ableist hierarchies (and their intersections), strengthen structural inequality, and increasingly replace social welfare and the concepts of civil and human rights with privatized philanthropy, advocacy, and services. Writer and longtime anti-prison activist James Kilgore calls this era of reform "carceral humanism."[28] *Carceral Con* provides an overview and analytic framework for understanding how reforms serve this world-making project, both within and beyond prison gates. But another world is possible.

CHAPTER SUMMARY

Utilizing an abolitionist lens, this book asks readers to think differently about public safety, community well-being, and the purpose of justice. Chapters are organized to provide readers with basic information foundational to the subject, and then to follow the reform trail through the carceral funnel as most people are swept into the criminal justice system. While it is impossible to cover the entire universe of contemporary reform initiatives, *Carceral Con* identifies some of the main elements of bipartisan reform and, by placing the discussion within a larger social, economic, and environmental context, notes their probable impacts and consequences. Since the reform terrain is fraught, its evolving nature cannot be predicted with certainty. But this book is also intended to help readers critically interrogate new proposals as they arise.

The first chapter introduces readers to the decentralized, maze-like reality of carceral control in the United States, a sprawling, often confusing tangle of jurisdictions, political interests, and systems of confinement and supervision. Drawing on the experience of California, *Carceral Con* illustrates myriad ways in which reforms produce tangles of dead ends and mixed results, sometimes functionally expanding systems of correctional confinement and supervision. Chapter 2 focuses on "following the money" in order to understand how billionaires, think tanks, large foundations, research institutes, and influential advocacy organizations brokered and benefit from the philanthropy-driven bipartisan consensus. It takes note of basic policy and rhetorical frameworks.

Chapter 3 describes the complexity of law enforcement agencies and actors, addressing ways in which intrinsically violent, race-and-class-based processes of criminalization, policing, and profiling drive not only mass incarceration, but the expansion of systems and technologies of carceral control into more and more arenas of public life. Major reform efforts over the past three decades and their failures are noted. Chapter 4 accompanies readers down a slippery slope of pretrial reform, considering campaigns to reform/abolish money bail and reduce pretrial detention amid increased political backlash by law enforcement lobbies and their enablers. The increasing use of algorithm-based risk assessment instruments in determining pretrial outcomes is addressed along with increased imposition of onerous "conditions of supervision" and "e-incarceration," or the use of varied forms of electronic monitoring.

Chapter 5 reviews sentencing reforms, including reclassification of offenses and revised sentencing guidelines as well as prosecutorial and court-based methods of widening rather than permanently shrinking the net of carceral control. Reforms include decriminalization, the creation of specialty courts, a growing "alternatives to incarceration" industry of private and nonprofit providers who remain within the orbit of the criminal legal system, and reliance by local governments on "fines and fees" citations as a source of revenue. Chapter 6 examines the violent conditions that characterize US jails, prison, and detention centers, and reforms said to address them in such areas as solitary confinement, sexual and gender violence, health care, environmental harms, and economic exploitation. Looking toward eventual release for most people, *Carceral Con* takes note of selected reforms intended to prepare them "for success."

The book's conclusion invites readers to choose a radically different way forward that confronts the harms and structural violence of the carceral state and works to dismantle the prison industrial complex through organizing that restores and gives tangible meaning to the concepts of the public good and community well-being. *Carceral Con* encourages readers to make necessary paradigm shifts beyond the structures of racial capitalism and neoliberalism and to reject, or at least question, the notion that jails, prisons, and the policing that fill them are indispensable to the good society. *Carceral Con* also invites readers to reject reformism as an adequate response to the inequalities and brutality of the criminal legal system. That does not mean rejecting every reform measure out of hand: some reforms can help reduce immediate harm without putting more resources into an expanding system. But those are decisions that should be made with great care. Sometimes, as readers will see, it is better to withhold support, better to regroup and redefine the fight, than to embrace proposals that will make things worse.

And so the journey commences. Where do we start? Perhaps by recognizing that we are entering territory that is a desolate and dark Wonderland of sorts, where things aren't always what they seem, and words do not always mean what we assume—or what we hope—they mean.

1 Correctional Control and the Challenge of Reform

> The most difficult and urgent challenge of today is that of creatively exploring new terrains of justice, where the prison no longer serves as our major anchor.
>
> —Angela Davis, *Are Prisons Obsolete?* 2003

Carceral control is a multitiered and never-ending labyrinth. Increased criminalization; local, state, and federal jurisdiction; expanding options for incarceration; public-private partnerships; community-based and technological extensions; and an escalating series of citations, fines, and fees constitute this maze. Those who enter are selected to do so, primarily due for their perceived disposability under a regime of racial capitalism, and however carefully they may try to navigate this terrain, the labyrinth offers no real way out.

The view from the outside is not any clearer. For the general public, much of this terrain is obscured—not by accident, but by design. This is precisely what makes the landscape of criminal justice reform so deceptive. It is difficult to find the way out of the spiraling patterns of policing and punishment. What seems like a pathway toward reform is often another dead end, or worse, a side road toward more expansion.

CALIFORNIA: THE COMPLEXITIES OF REFORM

There is perhaps no better example of carceral expansion and the limits of criminal justice reform than the case of California. As the epicenter of the rise of the prison industrial complex, California has been at the fore of proposed criminal justice reform as well as abolitionist organizing. And while the results of the latest reform efforts continue to unfold, it is clear that a massive policing and punishment apparatus is a monster that is much easier to build than to constrain.

In 2011, the Supreme Court of the United States (SCOTUS) ruled in favor of the prisoner plaintiffs in *Brown v. Plata*.[1] The case was a consolidation of two federal class action suits brought by prisoners—*Coleman v. Brown* and *Brown v. Plata*, filed in 1990 and 2001, respectively.[2] At issue was the access of California prisoners to both mental and physical health care, access that had been limited for decades, but was increasingly denied due to excessive overcrowding in the California penal system. The Supreme Court upheld a federal ruling that identified excessive overcrowding as the key contributor to unconstitutional denial of care and subsequently ordered California to reduce its prison population as remedy.

The 5–4 decision was a surprising one for a court not often sympathetic to prisoner rights, but the California situation was so egregious it was deemed a violation of the Eighth Amendment prohibition against cruel and unusual punishment.[3] At the time of the 2011 SCOTUS decision, California's prisons, which were designed to hold eighty thousand prisoners, were at nearly 200 percent of design capacity with a population of more than one hundred fifty-six thousand. The peak of overcrowding had been reached in 2007 with more than one hundred seventy thousand prisoners, many triple-bunked in gyms, quadruple-bunked in cells, and left for days in mobile telephone-booth-sized cells.[4] This extreme overcrowding resulted in horrific housing conditions that contributed to declines in both the physical and mental health of prisoners and then compounded their conditions with long delays for treatment. As a result, an average of more than one prisoner per week died due to medical neglect and/or suicide. The state was ordered to reduce its prison population by nearly forty thousand or to 137 percent of capacity by 2014, which is still overcrowded, but it offered prisoners some measure of relief.[5]

This crisis of overcrowding was three decades in the making as California led the way in the failed US experiment in mass incarceration. It was California—deemed the "Golden Gulag" by carceral geographer Ruth Wilson Gilmore—that most clearly exemplified the expansion of the modern prison industrial complex.[6] California engineered a prison-building and -filling project that was the "largest prison building program in the history of the world."[7] Beginning in the 1980s, bipartisan public policy shifts, dictated by both economic factors and political mood, resulted in expansion of criminal law—twelve hundred new criminal justice–related laws in the decades during the penal expansion, including the first and most restrictive three-strikes law, and the proliferation of gang legislation. Other factors included a state-sponsored boom in prison building and new jobs in depressed agricultural regions, correctional spending that far outstripped educational investments, a nascent influence of private correctional profit interests, and the escalating political power of the state's prison guards union, the California Correctional Peace Officers Association (CCPOA), which plays a significant role in advocating for pro-incarceration policies in California.[8]

The result is an overcrowded and racialized correctional population. In California, Black people are still incarcerated at a rate 6.5 times greater than whites, and Latinx people at nearly two times the rate of whites, rates higher than national patterns of racial disparity. Collectively, people of color comprise more than two-thirds of the state's outsized prison population. They are overrepresented in the state's draconian web of solitary confinement units, as the "gang" designation is carceral code for race-based segregation and punishment.[9] One of the prisons constructed during this building binge was the notorious supermax at Pelican Bay, designed to hold prisoners in long-term solitary confinement. While overcrowding characterized most California prisons, the state also heavily relied on solitary confinement for certain prisoners, particularly those designated as "gang" members. This practice largely continues, despite two major prisoner hunger strikes, legal challenges, a settlement agreement, and ongoing litigation in *Ashker v. Governor of California.*[10]

California's response to the court-mandated prison population reduction was a series of legislative reforms and ballot measures. All of these measures centered public safety as a primary consideration and promised both reduced recidivism rates and lower correctional costs. Collectively, these measures intended to reduce the state prison population by providing alternatives for "non-serious, nonviolent and nonsexual" offenders. These options included a shift to the county level, early release, and reduced sentencing for certain crimes. All initiatives—Realignment and Propositions 36, 47, and 57 had at least some bipartisan support, and in the end, mixed results.[11]

The Public Safety Realignment initiative (AB 109) was passed by the legislature in 2011. Realignment essentially moved large numbers of state prisoners to county jails or transferred them to out-of-state prisons or private prisons within the state.[12] The immediate impact was a reduction in the state's prison population, due to shuffling prisoners rather than outright release. The Three Strikes Reform Act of 2012 (Proposition 36) rewrote the harsh 1994 law that mandated life imprisonment for a third felony conviction, even if the third strike was a nonviolent crime. Under the revisions, a life sentence for the third strike is available only if the crime is "serious or violent." Approximately half of third strikers became eligible for resentencing.

California Proposition 47, the Reduced Penalties for Some Crimes Initiative, was passed by voters in 2014. Referred to as the Safe Neighborhoods and Schools Act, the bill reduced several property crimes and possession of most illegal drugs to misdemeanors. This allowed for retroactive resentencing of possibly ten thousand prisoners serving time for offenses now reclassified as misdemeanors.

One of the major selling points of the bill was the establishment of a fund to allocate saved monies to reduce truancy, support trauma centers, and provide mental health and substance abuse treatment.[13]

Proposition 57, The Public Safety and Rehabilitation Act, passed in 2016, allows for nonviolent offenders to be considered for early release via credits earned through participation in educational, vocational, and self-help programs. Prop 57 also allows judges rather than prosecutors to decide whether certain juveniles should be tried as adults. The stated goal of Prop 57 is rehabilitation and reduced recidivism, as some youth are diverted from the adult system, and incarcerated adults are encouraged to prepare for reentry.[14]

These initiatives enjoyed a degree of bipartisan support. Propositions 47 and 57 were supported by the ACLU, NAACP, most labor unions, many prominent Democrats, and a host of conservatives associated with Right on Crime. They were opposed by the California GOP, a few law-and-order Democrats, and the usual associations of sheriffs, police, prosecutors, and crime victims. All opponents cited fear of rising crime and added risks to public safety with increased prisoner releases. The prominent progressive coalition, Californians United for a Responsible Budget (CURB), while in strong support of Props 36 and 57, remained neutral on Prop 47, out of respect for the varied positions of coalition members. Several grassroots abolitionist groups, including Critical Resistance and Justice Now, opposed Proposition 47, citing concerns over the expenditure of justice reinvestment dollars and the notion that only nonviolent offenses should be considered for release.[15]

Following the Supreme Court order of 2011, California reduced its overall incarceration rate to a twenty-year low by 2019. The state successfully met the Supreme Court mandate for reduced population and, as of 2019, held approximately one hundred twenty-five thousand prisoners.[16] Yet California prisons remain over capacity and increasingly populated by those who have been convicted of a violent felony. This reifies the notion that prisons are the only possible solution available for addressing violent crime, a fear expressed by abolitionist groups in opposition to Prop 47. This suggests, too, that the reduction in the state prison population is reaching a point of stasis, and California may remain saddled with a large and intractable prison population that is still among the highest in the nation and that continues to be characterized by persistent racial disparities.[17]

Aside from the reduced overall state prison numbers, other reform promises have yet to materialize. The health care concerns central to *Plata* and *Coleman* have barely been addressed. There has been some investment in prison health care at the state level, although prisoners still experience long wait times, and the COVID-19 pandemic resulted in a largely unattended explosion of cases and deaths in 2020.[18] The state correctional budget, $12.6 billion in 2019, continues to grow, and as of 2020, most justice reinvestment has been cycled back into corrections.[19]

The most significant outcome of California's reforms is increased pressure on community corrections and county jails. What was once a state-level issue has now been relegated to the county level, where elected sheriffs and other correctional officials exert control with little oversight and variation across California's fifty-six counties. County-level probation caseloads have increased and intensified, requiring probationers to pay a growing list of fees for the conditions they are required to meet.[20] Further, the bulk of the reduction in state prison populations via realignment came from shifting prisoners to county jails. "Nonviolent, non-serious, nonsexual" prisoners were now serving their sentences in jails designed for pretrial or short-term detention of less than one year. There is even less programming available here than in prison, and often these facilities are not capable of providing adequate health care to prisoners. Additionally, there is a reported rise in violence, neglect, and death in some of these facilities.[21] Ironically, the unconstitutional conditions in state prisons that realignment and other reforms were designed to relieve may have largely been shifted to the county level, leaving large classes of prisoners still in need of relief.

Exactly what that relief might look like also remains the subject of intense political debate. Supporters of bipartisan "reform" advocate for the construction of new jails to address the growing population, including a series of new specialty jails designed to address mental health and addiction needs. Conversely, abolitionist organizers such as Critical Resistance and others have successfully spearheaded several No New Jails! campaigns, arguing that funds are better expended on authentic and reentry options rather than continued investment in the carceral apparatus.[22]

THE RISE OF THE US CARCERAL STATE

With the entrenchment of neoliberalism in the late twentieth century, the preferred bipartisan approaches to creating public safety and controlling crime were expanded criminalization, policing, and punishment. Austerity regimes—tax cuts for the wealthy; a rise in crushing inequality; shrinking governmental budgets for social programming; and corresponding divestments from public resources such as education, housing, health care, anti-poverty and employment programs, and more—are accompanied by greater reliance on systems of carceral control. The preference for criminal legal responses is coupled with investment opportunities for private corporate interests and the emergence of a prison industrial complex whose reach ripples through networks of public and private institutions, and through halls of political and economic influence.

The result is a political economy largely built on the business of raced, classed, and gendered processes of criminalization that is largely intransigent to fundamental change.[23] While the United States tells a cultural story of success (and conversely failure) based on individual achievement or merit, the reality says otherwise. Racial capitalism and intersectionality shape the contours of institutional access and "success." Race, class, gender, sexual orientation, age, and physical/cognitive ability all are singularly correlated with both associated stereotypes and blocked structural opportunities. Because systems of inequality are intersectional in practice, those who occupy multiple disadvantaged statuses experience magnified oppression, in this case, disproportionate access to the structural violence inflicted by the carceral state.[24]

Within the space of several decades, the United States evolved into a vastly expanded carceral state that relies on ubiquitous processes of criminalization, policing, and punishment. The carceral state includes legislators who expand the scope of the law; law enforcement; and criminal justice administration at federal, state, and local levels—police, sheriffs, prosecutors, judges, criminal courts, jails, prisons, and correctional officials. It also includes the extension of surveillance, policing, and control into schools, homes, workplaces, and social services. It entails a political economy—a prison industrial complex—grounded in the political production of crime and punishment that is financially and politically rewarded. Both officially and informally, in prisons and in communities, tens of millions of people are subject to the expansion of policing and punishment in the United States.[25]

Criminalization and Policing

In the United States, criminalization, policing, and punishment have always served to protect literal property interests and whiteness as intangible property. As Gilmore notes, "Capitalism requires inequality and racism enshrines it," with policing and punishment as key features in the maintenance of unequal social, economic and political arrangements.[26] The criminal legal system also functions to enforce gendered forms—patriarchal and heteronormative—of social control. Structural inequality is supported by an array of criminalizing narratives and related laws and policies that target the poor, people of color, women, LGBTQ communities, youth, and disabled people. Race, class, gender, sexual orientation, age, and ability shape entry into the criminal legal system, and are greater predictors of criminal labeling than any actual participation in crime. In short, while the processes and procedures are neutral on the legal face of it, criminalization, policing, and punishment operate to enforce inequality by targeting groups that are already the subjects of structural violence.

The current carceral state is the result of system expansion at every turn. This starts with legislation that mandates prison time and long terms of correctional supervision, which has led to a tenfold increase in prison and probation populations over the past fifty years. This explosive growth is also linked to the proliferation of legislation that criminalizes additional aspects of everyday life: use of public spaces and, de facto, homelessness, poverty, protest, attire (via gang legislation and "sagging pants" laws), sexuality, reproductive options for women, struggles with substance use, student misbehavior at school, and more. Matters of personal choice, public health, or school discipline fall increasingly under the purview of criminal law, as other social institutions are subsumed by the carceral state.[27]

Enforcement of the laws is supported by a massive infrastructure. There are nearly eighteen thousand federal, state, county, and city law enforcement agencies in the United States; over four hundred twenty thousand officers and law enforcement agents.[28] The contemporary carceral state relies on heavily militarized policing and inevitably targets vulnerable and marginalized communities in ways that are intensely racialized, classed, and gendered, and geographically bounded.[29] This, coupled with the rise of public order policing increases the likelihood of police encounters, arrest, brutality, and even death for certain demographics, particularly poor people and communities of color.

Given the US tendency toward criminalization and heavy policing, it is not surprising that over seventy-three million, approximately one in three people, have a criminal record.[30] Any encounter with the criminal legal system leaves a mark, and again, race, class, and gender shape just how consequential that mark will be.[31] In criminal cases, the prosecutor has the power to make charging decisions, bail recommendations, and plea offers. Most prosecutions are carried out at the county level, where the overwhelming majority pf prosecutors are elected, and more than 90 percent are white and male.[32]

Even if arrests are for minor offenses that result in no charges, criminal records persist and can potentially trigger a range of collateral consequences such as barriers to employment, education, voting, and housing. Where expungement of certain records sometimes is legally possible, it is rarely automatic and often requires onerous paperwork and court processing.[33] For those who are charged with a crime, arrest becomes a portal into a criminal legal system filled with fees and fines, drug testing and electronic monitoring, onerous conditions of probation and community supervision, and possibly confinement in jail or prison.

COMMUNITY CORRECTIONS

Those arrestees who are charged and found guilty by plea bargain or trial are subject to longer-term supervision. Collectively, there are currently 6.7 million people under some form of correctional control in the United States. The majority of these—4.5 million—are under community supervision, such as probation or parole (see figure 1).[34] Probationers represent the overwhelming number of those in community corrections, and have been sentenced to community supervision as an alternative to prison, often for minor or first-time offenses. Parolees are those under supervised release into the community on their way out of prison. A growing number of defendants find themselves under correctional supervision in lieu of a conviction via the proliferation of "diversionary" special courts designed to address drug use, mental health, homelessness, and veterans.

While community corrections are considered diversion from prison, this is not to say that these options are without severe restrictions and sometimes setups for failure. Probationers and parolees are subject to intense surveillance and required to meet a growing series of conditions; various estimates suggest that people on

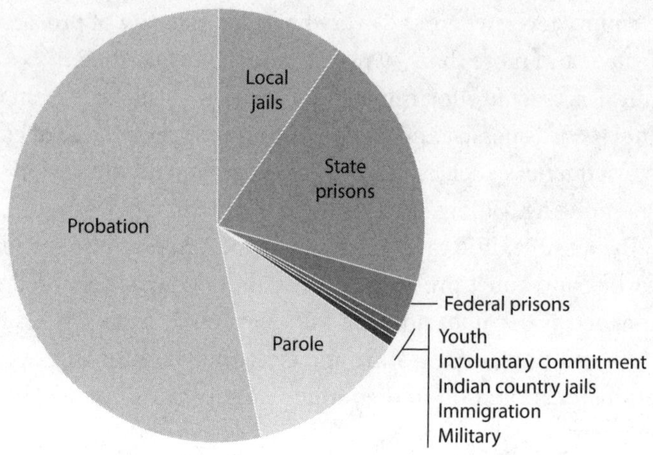

Figure 1: Pie chart of correctional control in the United States. Alexi Jones, "Correctional Control 2018: Incarceration and Supervision by State," Prison Policy Initiative, December 2018.

probation or parole must comply with eighteen to twenty requirements a day.[35] Violating any of these conditions can result in prison or jail time. Already marginalized populations are put at additional risk. The bulk of women under correctional control—more than 70 percent—are on probation.[36] The majority of these women have child- and eldercare obligations, and the conditions of probation and parole are often difficult for them to meet. Black people are subject to a disproportionate level of community correctional control; they represent 13 percent of the US population but more than 30 percent of those under community supervision.[37] Risk of revocation, which is highest for African Americans, is further compounded by an increase in probation fees, especially under privatized probation programs.[38]

Detention, Disparity, and Death

Incarceration represents the most extreme and total form of correctional control. Nonetheless, 70 percent of all convictions result in a

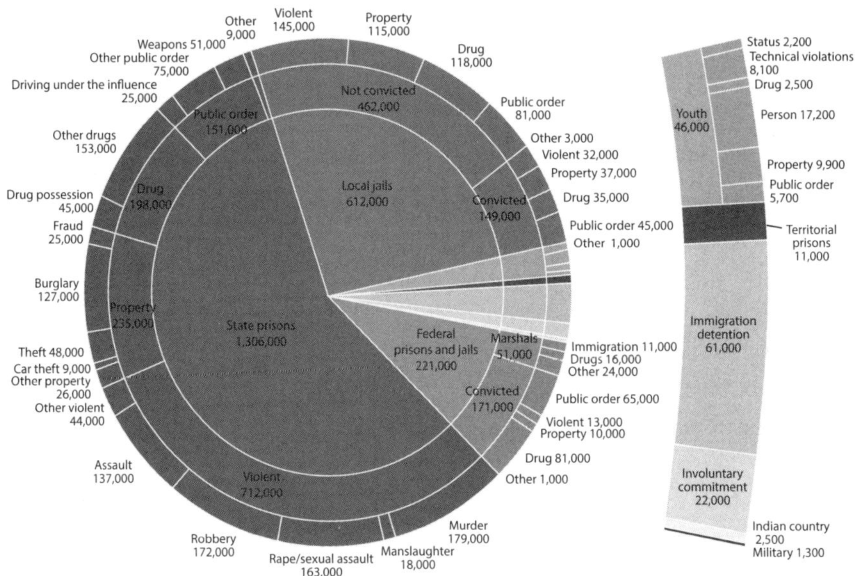

Figure 2: Pie chart of mass incarceration in the United States. Wendy Sawyer and Peter Wagner, "Mass Incarceration: The Whole Pie," Prison Policy Initiative, March 24, 2020.

sentence of imprisonment.[39] Since the 1970s, the US prison and jail population has exploded, increasing more than tenfold. While the draconian War on Drugs accelerated the expansion of policing, prosecution, and punishment, drug offenses account for a smaller percentage of people held in prisons and jails than many believe. The majority of people are imprisoned for violent or property offenses (see figure 2).[40] But many are held for increasingly longer sentences due to the reliance on mandatory minimum sentences with prison terms, three-strike legislation, penalty enhancements for gun and gang crimes, sentences of life without parole, and an increased tendency to try certain juvenile offenders as adults.[41]

The United States currently imprisons more people per capita than any other country in the world. With an incarceration rate of

698 per 100,000, the US imprisons at a pace of more than five times that of European nations. Even the most progressive states imprison people at a rate that exceeds that of more authoritarian regimes.[42] In 2020, "the American criminal legal system holds almost 2.3 million people in 1,719 state prisons, 109 federal prisons, 1,772 juvenile correctional facilities, 3,163 local jails, and 80 Indian Country jails, as well as in military prisons, immigration detention facilities, civil commitment centers, state psychiatric hospitals, and prisons in the US territories."[43] The vast majority of prisoners are held in publicly operated facilities at the state level, followed closely by local city and county jails.[44]

The Vera Institute of Justice reported that by the end of 2020, the *rate* of prison population decline continued from its peak in 2007.[45] The rate of incarceration, different from the actual number of people behind bars, is calculated by the number of people in federal/state prisons per 100,000 residents. While every decline and the lives it represents matter, Prison Policy Initiative points out that most of the decline was driven by lower sustained incarceration rates for federal prisons and in several states—notably New York and California—with extremely large prison populations.[46] The actual numbers of incarcerated people and a look at their uneven distribution tell a more nuanced story. At the end of 2020, more than 1.5 million people were imprisoned at the state or federal level.[47] Incremental declines since the late 2000s, PPI emphasizes, do not begin to significantly undo the explosive and sustained annual growth in prison populations during the 1980s and 1990s. Some states have closed or are closing prisons, both publicly and privately owned, without immediately moving to replace them with new ones, but others seek to expand existing facilities, repurpose closed ones, and open new prisons.[48]

Three-quarters of US residents live in the shadow of the prison and the political and economic implications of prison gerrymandering. Gerrymandering means dividing geographic areas into voting districts so as to produce some form of unfair demographic advantage; in this case, it means counting prison populations as if they are part of the permanent residential population. This affects redistricting processes at all levels of government: Inflated counts that influence everything from congressional districts to representation in state legislatures to county and municipal governments and boards. Prison Policy Initiative underscores the point: "Because prisons are disproportionately built in rural areas but most incarcerated people call urban areas home, counting prisoners in the wrong place results in a systematic transfer of population and political clout from urban to rural areas."[49] The result is not only inflated representation for some areas, predominantly white, but voter dilution in others, particularly, PPI says, "in the districts with the highest incarceration rates"—that is, in many predominantly Black, low-income communities.[50] In 2001, PPI launched a campaign against prison gerrymandering; by the end of 2020, a dozen states had enacted some form of legislation ending it, giving counties the authority to end it, or recommending that the US Census Bureau do so. More than two hundred county and municipal governments have adopted measures to end prison gerrymandering.[51] Prior to 2030, it may also be possible to bring pressure to bear on the US Census Bureau to permanently change its policy and count people who are imprisoned as residents of their home addresses. Earlier attempts to do so have failed.

Jails primarily detain those who have not yet been convicted of a crime and are unable to afford money bail to secure their own release. In 2019, more than six hundred thousand people were detained in these short-term correctional facilities, with the vast majority being held prior to trial and/or sentencing.[52] While many discussions of incarceration focus primarily on prisons, the role of jails and "jail churn" cannot be under-estimated: Over 600,000 people enter *prison* gates, but people go to *jail* 10.6 million times each year."[53] As of 2017, this meant that nearly five million people were jailed each year, with at least one in four of these jailed multiple times.[54] Some of this churn is accounted for by new crimes, but much is the result of warrants for outstanding fines or for technical violations of the conditions of probation and parole.

Vera Institute of Justice reports that as jail populations in large urban areas declined between 2013 and 2019, they increased in rural counties and in small and midsized towns and counties, representing "the highest number of people in jail since midyear 2009."[55] Despite temporary declines in some jail populations in 2020 due to COVID-19, rural increases continue to drive the trend toward increased jail bookings and detentions.[56]

The Vera Jails Report for 2019 is based on estimates of *custodial* rather than *jurisdictional* population. That means counting the total number of people incarcerated in jails. It does not parse populations according to which jurisdiction put them there. Local jails absorb many federal detainees because, apart from federal jails in New York, Chicago, and Los Angeles, there is no federal network of jails. ICE and the US Marshals Service (USMS) contract for space, paying a per diem rate for each person detained, revenue considered essential to county sheriffs and the expansion of their power bases.[57] Geographer Jack Norton and research analyst Jacob Kang-Brown point out that the federal government has played a key role in "fueling a quiet jail boom since the 1980s."[58]

Several factors play key roles in this increase. Even as jail populations have declined in many areas, some jurisdictions expanded existing jails and built new ones. In 2019, almost 20 percent of existing jail capacity was unused. Increasingly, the federal government helps to fill it. To a lesser extent, state and other county governments also rent space in local jails. People from other jurisdictions are imprisoned for a host of reasons: pretrial detention, overcrowding in jails and prisons, serving a prison sentence, and awaiting civil immigration proceedings. Rural regions, hard hit by deindustrialization, job losses, poverty, and the impacts of climate change become increasingly entangled with a carceral economy, one that funnels resources to police forces and county jails while slashing spending for social goods and supports.[59]

Increasing numbers of migrants and immigrants, including many who have been living and working in the United States for years, are detained by the federal government in its own centers, those run by its corporate proxies, and in county jails.[60] Most of those detained within US borders are held in Immigrations and Customs Enforcement (ICE) custody. In an exception to the predominantly public character of most US prisons and jails, this is the detention sector that is most heavily privatized.[61] The growth, fostered by both Republican and Democratic administrations, is driven largely by detention of persons with no criminal records, and is driven by the process of "crimmigration"—the racialized conflation of immigration with criminal dangerousness. These populations include people from Mexico, Central America, the Caribbean, and Africa who are fleeing political persecution, violence, and economic instability—much of which has been supported or enabled by the United States.[62] In 2019, the average daily population of detained immigrants was more than fifty thousand, a dramatic expansion from 2001, when the daily population averaged about nineteen thousand. On a yearly basis, hundreds of thousands of people cycle through what Detention Watch Network describes as "a sprawling and unaccountable system of mass detention."[63]

While it can be notoriously difficult to track accurate data, in 2020, the Marshall Project dug through new data to report on skyrocketing numbers of children detained at the US-Mexico border, including both unaccompanied children and those with their families. Those detentions peaked at over three hundred thousand in 2019. Many of these children were held longer than the seventy-two-hour limit required by law. In 2020, those numbers began to drop as the Trump administration began an aggressive policy of expelling migrant children and families at the border.[64] Conditions of immigrant detention are as brutal as US prisons and those run by the Border Patrol. They have been described as concentration camps, due to the emphasis on racial and ethnic immigrants of color arriving via the southern US border as well as the overall conditions of overcrowding and attendant lack of access to basic hygiene, health care, and legal counsel.[65]

Those who have been convicted of crimes carrying a sentence of more than one year are held in state or federal prisons at various degrees of security ranging from minimum to supermax, with twenty-three-hour-a-day lockdown.[66] While the conditions of incarceration vary by institution and state, they are marked at every level by inadequate rehabilitative, health, and educational services; overcrowded conditions; violence; and frequent, extended use of long-term solitary confinement. Physical, sexual, and psychic violence is the mainstay and serves as a tool for correctional control. Work, for pennies on the dollar, is largely confined to menial labor that serves to keep the prison operational or produce goods and services for governmental agencies.[67] Rarely does this contribute to the development of transferrable skills that would provide employment opportunities upon release. Further, these meager wages are typically garnished to pay for prisoner services, victim funds, or restitution, leaving little left for the high costs of commissary and phone calls.[68]

The structural race, class, and gender inequality that characterizes the entire criminal legal system is magnified further at the point of incarceration. The overwhelming majority of those in prison and jail are poor and/or unemployed at the time of their commitment, and low income is the best predictor of pretrial detention.[69] Despite recent claims that racial disparity has decreased, race matters too, especially for Black Americans, who constitute 13 percent of the US population but 40 percent of all prisoners.[70] These racial gaps widen when considering the incarceration of youth under the age of eighteen. Although they account for 15 percent of the youth population, Black juveniles account for 45 percent of the more than sixty-three thousand youth detained in juvenile facilities, and substantial numbers are locked up for status offenses or technical violations of probation. Indigenous and Latinx youth are also disproportionately detained relative to their white peers.[71] Further, Black youth are more likely than any other demographic to be referred to the adult legal system even as juveniles, where they are most likely to receive lengthy prison sentences rather than community supervision.[72]

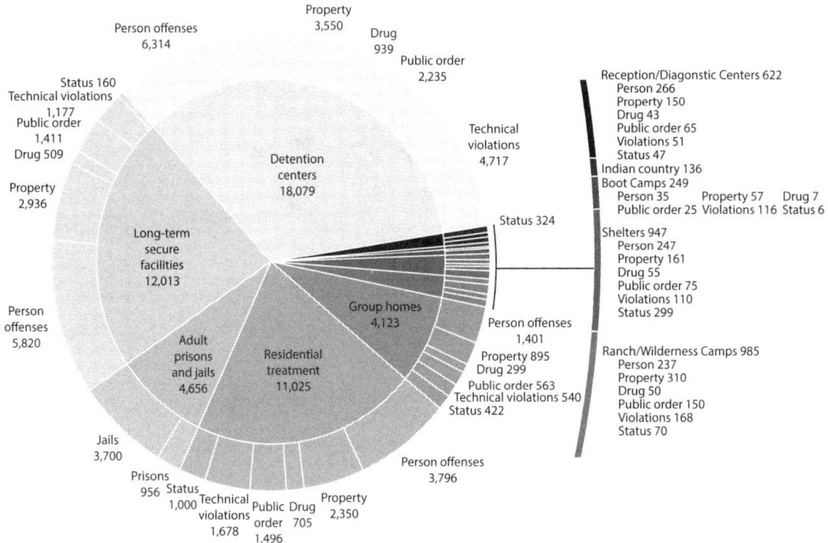

Figure 3: Pie chart of youth confinement in the United States. Wendy Sawyer, "Youth Confinement: The Whole Pie 2019," Prison Policy Initiative, December 19, 2019.

This overrepresentation of youth of color is consistent with the entirety of the juvenile legal system, which is marred by even greater race and gender disproportionality than that found in the adult criminal justice system.[73] Black youth, both male and female, are most at risk for early encounters with systems of policing and punishment. These racial gulfs are not driven by any documented differences in participation in crime but rather by patterns of policing and surveillance that extend from communities into educational settings and shape what scholars and activists describe as a school-to-prison pipeline.[74]

While women represent a numerical minority of those under correctional control, their supervision and incarceration has increased at twice the rate of men. Nearly half of women are held in jails, often prior to conviction (see figure 4).[75] Women under correctional control

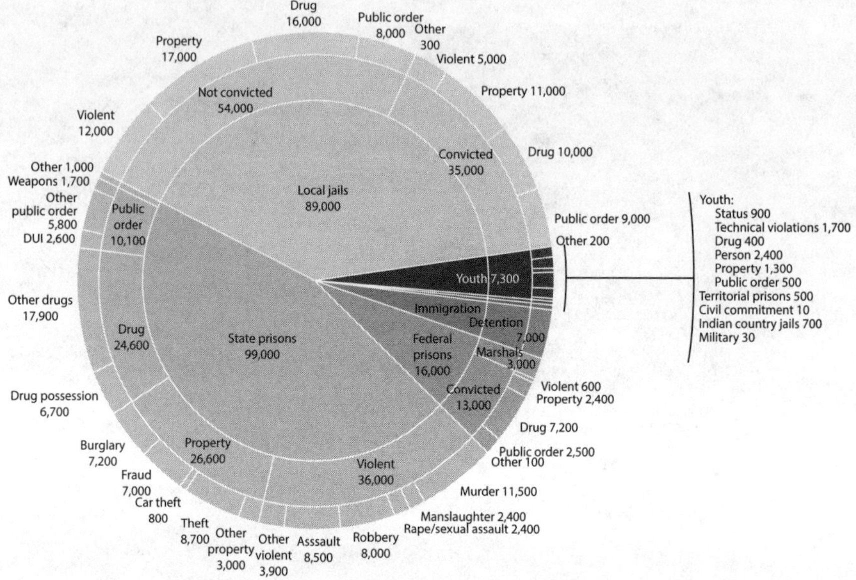

Figure 4: Pie chart of incarceration of women in the United States. Aleks Kajstura, "Women's Mass Incarceration: The Whole Pie 2019," Prison Policy Initiative and ACLU Campaign for Smart Justice, October 29, 2019.

tend to be poorer, people of color, and bisexual or lesbian; moreover, they generally serve longer sentences than men. Black women face a particularly high risk for incarceration. Women's incarceration is complicated by an increased risk of sexual assault by staff, pregnancy risks and reproductive rights, and the criminalization of survivors of domestic assault and sexual violence. Because about 80 percent of women in detention are the primary caregivers of children, their incarceration spirals the impact of the carceral state into family and community in multiple ways.[76]

At the sentencing extreme, twenty-eight states and the federal government retained the death penalty as of early 2021. There were approximately twenty-five hundred prisoners awaiting execution, and they were heavily concentrated in southern states.[77] These numbers have declined in recent years due to growing public opposition to the death penalty, especially as awareness of wrongful convictions and exonerations increase. Still, the federal government resumed the practice in 2020, executing thirteen in what has been described as a "killing spree," and the Supreme Court refuses to bar this penalty entirely, despite an ongoing series of legal challenges related to age; intellectual ability/mental health; method of execution; and, of course, race, class, and gender.[78] Death row prisoners are almost universally poor and represented by public defenders; they are disproportionately Black men. The race of victim and the race of the offender remain the best indicators of prosecutorial decisions to pursue capital punishment.[79] This power dynamic is related in gender as well. Women who transgress gender role norms by killing men or children comprise the bulk of the handful of women who are sentenced to death in the United States. Death penalty cases remain costly to carry out, as legal appeals, court costs, and the maximum-security level of confinement add to expenses that average out to an estimated $2 million per execution.[80]

Prison Industrial Complex

The US correctional apparatus is both costly and lucrative. According to PPI, the estimated total costs were $182 billion in 2017 (see figure 5).[81] Probation, parole, and prison consume the bulk of government expenditures, followed by policing. The figure also accounts for costs to individuals and families, who are overwhelmingly poor, for bail, phone calls and video visits, and commissary costs. Correctional control is funded by public revenue. As correctional expenditures rise, funding for social programs fall, and "corrections" is seen as the one-stop solution for social problems related to unemployment, educational opportunities, physical and mental health care, housing, and poverty.[82] Correctional spending, buttressed by calls for safety and security, continues to be prioritized over any investment in education, health care, or other public goods.

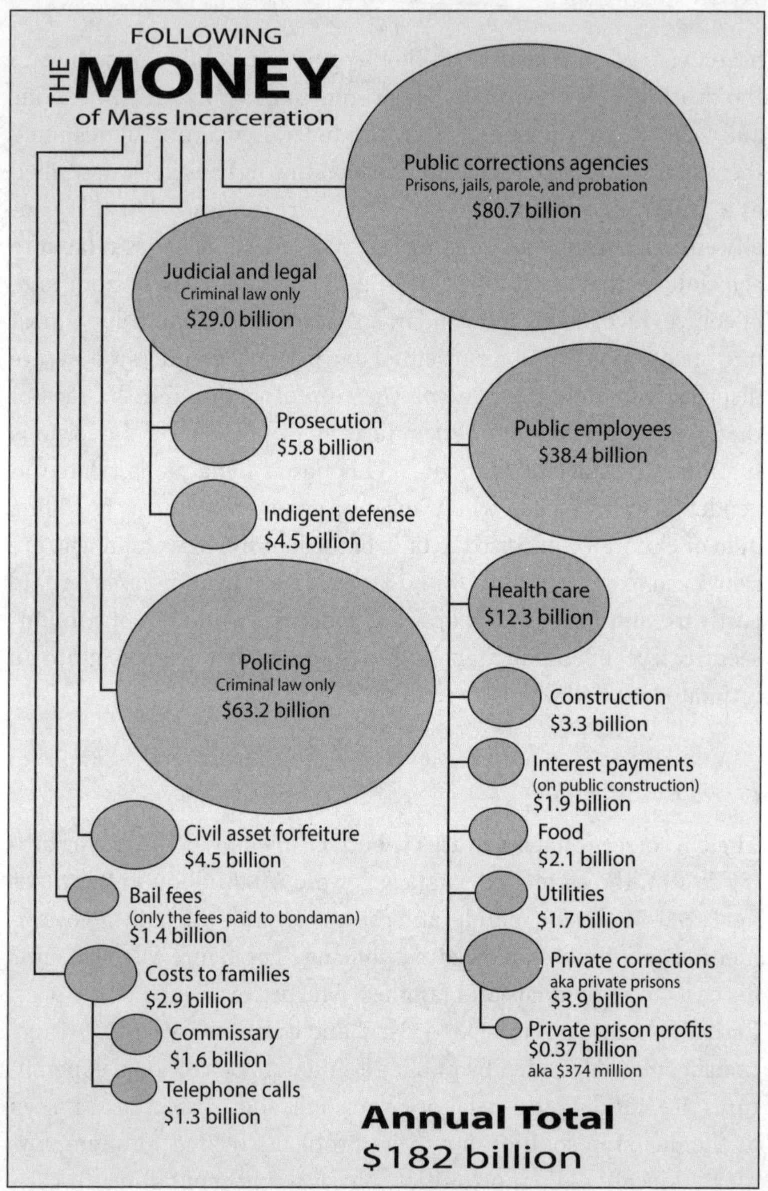

Figure 5: "Following the Money of Mass Incarceration," Peter Wagner and Bernadette Rabuy, "Following the Money of Mass Incarceration," Prison Policy Initiative, January 25, 2017.

Governments contract with many private companies to provide various correctional services. Private prisons hold contracts, to be sure, but they are only one part of a much larger carceral market created by demand for an expanding web of services for publicly owned and operated facilities. These include health care, food services, money transfer, phone services, commissary, and probation services.[83] The governmental sector also realizes some economic benefits by producing revenue via assessments of fees and fines, so-called "offender-funded" initiatives that require those under correctional control to pay the costs of their supervision, and prison labor that produces products for government agencies and supports the operations of the prison. The creation of employment opportunities in corrections, the courts, and law enforcement also produces economic benefits to the public sector.[84]

The overlapping interests of government and industry in the arena of policing and punishment have come to be known as the prison industrial complex (PIC). First referenced in 1974 by the North Carolina Prisoners Labor Union as the "judicial-prison-parole-industrial complex," it is now widely mentioned in the shorthand.[85] According to scholar and activist Angela Davis, the PIC is a contemporary variation on the legacy of US settler colonialism and chattel slavery. It includes racialized criminalization, captivity, control of land and labor, and profiteering related to all of it.[86] The roots of the PIC are in racial capitalism, and the resultant impacts are intersectional. The system feeds off multiple marginalized populations whose statuses are shaped not only by racial and class hierarchies, but also by such factors as place, gender, sexuality, ability, and age.

Like the military industrial complex to which the name alludes, the prison industrial complex represents the structural alignment of economic and political interests that creates a reinforcing feedback loop where the threat of crime must be forever both fought and recreated. As sociologists Rose Brewer and Nancy A. Heitzeg explain: "The prison industrial complex is a self-perpetuating machine where the vast profits . . . and perceived political benefits . . . lead to policies that are additionally designed to insure an endless supply of "clients" for the criminal legal system."[87] This machinery is characterized by the aforementioned collusion of government and private industry in contracts and services, the management of unemployment and employment opportunities, and "tough-on-crime" political rhetoric that materializes through draconian sentencing policies and a plethora of collateral consequences that nearly guarantee continued participation in "crime" and return to the prison industrial complex following initial release.[88] The PIC is additionally supported by mass media through exaggerated crime reporting, crime and punishment presented as profitable entertainment, and the production and reproduction of stereotypes that mark "people of color, poor people, queer people, immigrants, youth, and other oppressed communities as criminal, delinquent, or deviant."[89] The PIC is a closed circle, spinning along, self-reinforcing, uninterrupted.

The "logic" of the prison industrial complex affirms that all social problems can be addressed through criminalization and correctional control, and further, that any attempts at reform of the criminal legal system must be found within the confines of the system itself. The favored bipartisan reforms rarely feature actual institutional alternatives to the criminal legal system; they are most likely to advocate for variations on current practices, technological fixes, or new avenues for supervision/surveillance. The tendency always is the expansion of this apparatus, and so, too, the flow of bodies, money, and social control.

THE LIMITS AND CONTRADICTIONS OF "REFORM"

The complexity of the contemporary correctional juggernaut illustrates the challenges and limits of meaningful reform. If the goal is the reduction of prison populations and related costs, then it is clear that just targeting singular policy shifts is not enough. Changes in federal sentencing policy will barely dent incarceration rates, as the majority of prisoners are held at the state level or in local jails. Decriminalizing drugs, while important, will address only 20 percent of the overall prison population, and less than that if sentencing changes do not apply retroactively. Closing private prisons will only impact 8 percent of the prison population, with the likelihood that these prisoners would be transferred to publicly funded institutions rather than released. Community corrections such as probation and parole theoretically offer an alternative to prison but have ended up as feeders since revocations for technical violations serve as an engine for imprisonment.[90] Jail and prison populations can be significantly reduced by reducing pretrial detention and by considering release for prisoners beyond those who are incarcerated for nonserious, nonviolent and nonsexual offenses, and both require a level of political will that is not immediately available.[91]

Technological fixes such as electronic monitoring and body cameras for police have expanded the scope of surveillance without offering remedies for the underlying problems at hand. Efforts to abolish capital punishment lead to the proliferation of life without parole sentencing. And in the midst of any efforts to reduce mass incarceration, the foundational issues of race, class, and gender discrimination continue to structure the focus of law enforcement and the flow of bodies into the prison industrial complex.

Beyond this, virtually all proposed bipartisan criminal justice reforms leave intact the presumption that the current system of policing and punishment is an essential, permanent feature of the civic landscape. The world of criminal justice reform is self-contained and self-referential. It is a world of tunnel vision and no imagination, providing no possibility of answers outside the confines of criminal justice itself. Rhetorical flourishes that disguise the complexity of the issues often hide this reality from well-intended supporters of reduced mass incarceration. But, as ensuing chapters illustrate, proposed and enacted reforms have largely resulted in an expansion, rather than reduction, of the carceral state. It is fair to ask if many proposed "reforms" aren't meant to end mass incarceration at all, but rather to create opportunities for mass forms of social control, supported by expanded privatizing and profiteering.

Reducing mass incarceration and the expanding web of correctional control requires exploration of abolitionist alternatives. Abolition is a vision of a world where prisons are indeed "obsolete" and where social problems are no longer criminalized but rather addressed by approaches better designed to prevent and redress their structural roots. Abolition is a call for political and economic shifts—for divestment from policing and prisons and for government reinvestment in education, housing, health care, employment opportunities, and environmental protection. It is a call to develop new, more trustworthy and structurally just social, political, economic, and ecological relationships. Abolition is a practice that seeks solutions outside the criminal legal system via everyday engagement with community rather than the carceral state.[92] And it is a perspective that emphasizes accountability, healing, and repair of harm over retribution and punishment. As Ruth Wilson Gilmore notes, "Abolition isn't just absence; . . . abolition is a fleshly and material presence of social life lived differently. . . . Abolition is a theory of change, it's a theory of social life. It's about making things."[93]

In the midst of steady carceral expansion and bipartisan calls for criminal justice reform, the abolition movement has been a clear and steady voice of challenge; the only source of analysis that doesn't begin and end with the prison at its center. Educators, activists, grassroots organizers, and currently and formerly incarcerated people imagine approaches to violence and harm that do not rely on the criminal legal system. While the abolition movement is frequently referred to as a movement to abolish prisons, it is not focused primarily on the prison per se. Carceral expansion is opposed at every level, and encompasses resistance to the whole of the prison industrial complex.[94]

A seminal 1976 work, *Instead of Prisons: A Handbook for Abolitionists,* outlines three key areas of focus for abolition: moratorium, decarceration, and excarceration.[95] Current abolitionist efforts, enhanced by a deep race, class, gender, and disability analysis, continue this multipronged approach. Moratorium campaigns seek to limit the expansion of the prison industrial complex by opposing new prisons, jails, and ICE detention centers. More recently, moratoriums on the expansion of police forces in terms of new hires, deployment to schools, and expanded militarization have also been a focus. Decarceration is centered on the release of those currently incarcerated through changes in sentencing structure and length, limits on the use of parole boards, the immediate release of criminalized survivors of domestic violence, and the elimination of juvenile detention. Decarceration also requires attention to the immediate needs of those presently imprisoned, thus abolitionists support an end to solitary confinement, the expansion of prisoner rights, and educational opportunities for those imprisoned. Excarceration immediately reduces the reliance on prisons and jailing, with the long-range goal of their elimination. Decriminalization; legalization; calls to defund the police; an end to cash bail and pretrial detention; and removal of barriers to employment, voting, and housing for former prisoners are key examples of efforts to excarcerate.

Abolitionist perspectives offer conceptual and practical frameworks for navigating the deceptive terrain of bipartisan criminal justice reform. How should reforms be analyzed and evaluated? As a starting point, consider whether the proposed reforms

- require that more resources be put into the criminal legal system and its public-private proxies;
- rely on contracts with private companies and nonprofit organizations whose work is tied to the prison industrial complex;
- work decisively to increase public revenues and shift more and more public spending away from carceral control to public education, universal health care, affordable housing, jobs programs, and the like;
- require more technological "solutions" and expanded surveillance and control;

- increase economic and social costs for those under correctional control;
- emphasize changing individual behaviors rather than focusing on structural remedies;
- exacerbate existing race, class, gender, and disability disparities in correctional control;
- solidify the dichotomy between "non-serious" and dangerous offenses/offenders and further entrench permanent carceral control for certain populations of prisoners;
- provide "most favored status" for a particular religious faith or faiths in providing services and programs;
- offer retroactive remediation to those already harmed by the criminal legal system and other forms of state violence;
- steadily and permanently reduce the numbers of people who are incarcerated or under other forms of carceral control;
- halt the contracting for and building of new prisons/jails, including those purporting to offer greater safety to youth, transgender people, people with disabilities, and others;
- work to reduce harms for incarcerated people through strategies of decarceration and provision of community-based supports and services entirely free of the criminal legal system;
- openly acknowledge and address the structural (and race/class/gender-based) violence of policing and carceral control as an issue that undermines public safety.

As proposed bipartisan criminal justice reforms proliferate, it is imperative to scrutinize both their stated intent and potential impacts. If, as the abolitionists observe, the system isn't broken, but is functioning as intended, then what is the end goal of "reform"?

2 Follow the Money

People are starving.
The rich gobble taxes,
that's why people are starving.

—Lao Tzu, *Tao Te Ching*, new English version
by Ursula K. Le Guin, 1998

Like the characteristics that combine to create an intricate fingerprint, the trail of money winding through the criminal legal system and shaping its reform follows a convoluted path of arches and loops, coiling and folding and circling back within great, overlapping whorls. There is no single, straightforward path to follow, but many winding and overlapping routes. It is not possible to know exactly how much money is at play in the fields of reform because so much of it flows through wealthy foundations, donor-directed funds, corporate investments, and nonprofit organizations that are not required to publicly identify donors and amounts from each. Glimpses and snapshots help to establish a larger picture.

Carceral Con's admonition to follow the money refers not only to the endless profits that accrue to corporations that build or administer carceral facilities and provide contractual community supervision, treatment, and reentry programs, but also the enormous fixed costs of the existing criminal legal system. It also refers to the production and sale of policing technologies, a new generation of so-called data-driven assessment and surveillance methodologies and "pay for success" (PFS) investments and contracts. It refers to the ways in which the criminal legal system and its reform are so deeply embedded in and shape so many aspects of US social, political, and economic life. And it refers to the relentless, austerity-driven transfer of public revenues and resources to private interests.

One way to start tracing the money is to identify its sources—to the extent possible—and address the role that billionaires, corporate donors, major foundations, large nonprofit organizations, prestigious university research institutes, and some newly minted reform organizations increasingly play in shaping the content, confines, and implementation of reform agendas. Another is to follow the largesse that builds an entire reform-and-surveillance industry, with many public and private actors having a deep stake in its continuation. Still another approach is to follow the path of reform rhetoric and the seductive promises made or implied to sell an expanding regime of carceral control and monitoring.

A FORESHADOWING

In 2011, the ambiguity and misleading dexterity of bipartisan reform rhetoric was foreshadowed at a press conference convened by the NAACP to announce a new report, *Misplaced Priorities: Under Educate, Over Incarcerate.*[1] The report linked state increases in prison costs and populations to decreases in public school and higher education funding. Both disproportionately and adversely affected impoverished Black, Latinx, and other marginalized communities.

The NAACP's timing was perfect. The previous year, in 2010, Michelle Alexander's landmark book, *The New Jim Crow: Mass Incarceration in the Age of Colorblindness*, galvanized readers, hit the bestseller lists, and served to increase already-growing opposition to the US carceral nightmare.[2] Protests against police violence—the routine abuse as well as the killings—were growing. In 2009, the

New Year's Day killing of Oscar Grant, a young Black man at the hands of a Bay Area Rapid Transit (BART) police officer in Oakland, California, sparked ongoing protests against the unwarranted use of (disproportionately anti-Black) deadly force by police.[3] Protests continued into 2011, through the officer's trial, conviction on a lenient charge of manslaughter, and early release from prison.

The NAACP press conference showcased an all-star lineup of unlikely reform allies.[4] In addition to the NAACP's executive director and CEO Ben Jealous, speakers included representatives from the ACLU and the US National Student Association, two noted technological "entrepreneurs and philanthropists," and the then president of the California Correctional Peace Officers Association (who also represented CorrectionsUSA, an advocacy group for public corrections officials). Other speakers were Grover Norquist of Americans for Tax Reform, Pat Nolan of the Christian evangelical Prison Fellowship, and Rod Paige, a former Secretary of Education during President George W. Bush's first term, a uniquely mordant choice for this particular media event. Paige had also served as superintendent of the Houston public school district during Bush's tenure as governor of Texas. With Paige at the helm, the district vastly underreported student dropout rates in order to falsely claim "a Texas miracle" that purportedly transformed once-high dropout rates for poor Black and Latinx students in "underperforming" schools.[5]

Jealous said that particular sentencing reforms for people convicted of low-level crimes could curb "excessive prison spending." The organization framed its report as a call to action that provided "a framework to implement a policy agenda that will financially prioritize investments in education over incarceration, provide equal protection under the law, eliminate sentencing policies responsible for over incarceration, and advance public safety strategies that effectively increase healthy development in communities."[6] Recommendations included the establishment of "blue ribbon" commissions to study the problem further, a suggestion for youth violence reduction programs, some general sentencing and community supervision reforms, and a call to create and support "reinvestment commissions" to identify ways of shifting savings from prison closures to education budgets. As part of the press rollout, PBS Newshour's Judy Woodruff interviewed Jealous and Norquist, posing a key question that was neither asked nor addressed at the press conference: Did Norquist (and by extension his fellow right-wing reformers) support directing at least some of the money spent on prisons to public education? Norquist replied, "Well, that's the NAACP's analysis. . . . I'm in favor of allowing taxpayers to keep the money that's presently being misspent. But that's a separate conversation. . . . We can have that conversation another time."[7]

Almost a decade later, by 2020, no public conversation or shift of accrued public savings from decreased incarceration to public education or any other social need outside of the criminal legal system had materialized. But many conversations and partnerships among reform insiders had. A reinvestment framework and administrative mechanisms already existed by the time of the NAACP press conference. Justice reinvestment processes already existed in a number of states, and more would quickly follow. Did the promise of significant public revenue savings prove true, and if so, what happened to that money? Trying to discern clear answers is akin to watching a shell game.

THE REFORM SHIFT TO "BUDGET CRISIS"

The contemporary bipartisan reform shift from "get-tough" policies that played to white racial animus and fear and fueled the explosive growth of the carceral state is explained away by its architects as a response to "mistaken policies of the past" and soaring prison costs. But that is simply more smoke and mirrors. Often, despite differences on details, conservative and liberal players have moved forward together, hand in hand.

By the mid-1990s, standard-bearers for both Republicans and Democrats competed for "get-tough" primacy. In 1994, Pete Wilson, then the Republican governor of California, seeking reelection, stewarded the nation's most draconian "three-strikes" sentencing law (mandating life imprisonment for those convicted of third felonies, even if the felonies are minor) into enactment.[8] A subsequent 1994 ballot initiative containing essentially the same elements as the law, but also requiring cumbersome and expensive statewide votes to enact any changes to it, passed handily. Wilson, a master of racially coded fearmongering, went on to urge more "get tough" measures, oppose affirmative action, and promote racist anti-immigration proposals.[9] The same year, President Bill Clinton and then US Senator Joe Biden, Democrats, invoked fears of rampant danger to pass a sweeping crime bill known as the Violent Crime Control and Law Enforcement Act of 1994.[10] Among other provisions, the law placed thousands of additional police on the streets, expanded federal authority to seek the death penalty, and offered financial incentives for prison expansion to states that adopted harsher sentencing laws.[11] By the early 2000s, however, the United States was on the cusp of a reform shift away from crude iterations of "get-tough" crime measures.

The new wave of reform bipartisanship, ushered in by a tidal wave of neoliberal rhetoric and system-tinkering, gained firm footing in the United States in a time of manufactured "budget crises." In the United States, perpetual but highly selective claims of "budget crisis" at all levels of government drive austerity politics. They constitute not real crises, but political manipulation and obfuscation of different possible political and economic choices. The 2011 NAACP *Misplaced Priorities* press conference constituted a major national rollout of a bipartisan reform narrative following this general storyline:

> In a time of budget crisis, when state, federal, and local budgets are all tightening their belts, we're spending too much money to incarcerate

> people. The criminal justice system is broken and bloated. Prisons are only for the most dangerous, hardened, and vicious criminals. We will save taxpayer dollars by reducing the amount of money spent locking up too many people who don't need to be in jail. At the same time, our reforms are "smart" and "evidence-based," so we'll spend less money and reduce racial disparities while increasing public safety.

Like all remedies marketed as miracle cures at medicine shows, this one contains equal measures of half-truths, false promise, hope, and projection. The primary themes, elastic in their political and public relations utility, are: (1) containing and isolating danger, (2) ending "overcriminalization," (3) saving taxpayer dollars, (4) reducing incarceration while increasing public safety, (5) creating safer communities through justice reinvestment, and (6) deploying smart, "evidence-based" solutions. These themes possess that special rhetorical adhesive to which all manner of grievances about budgets, bureaucracies, unruly social movements with radical demands, and "hardened criminals" may be attached. In part, these themes serve to illustrate the carnival barker's art of misdirection: look *here*, at bipartisan consensus reforms and not *over there* where it becomes clear that the selective claims of "budget crisis" simply provide cover for an austerity regime. These claims are accompanied by equally selective calls to reduce the national debt by slashing social spending for health care, education, food assistance, environmental protection, and other public resources. Yet budgets for policing, militarization, and national security grow. While austerity politics are coded into bipartisan reform frameworks, liberal and progressive coalition partners are not organized or even willing to challenge them. Absent better frameworks for fighting for radically different social, political, and economic priorities, the public comes to believe there are no possible alternatives to austerity.

The current wave of bipartisan reforms emerged during a period of deepening income and wealth racial inequality, beginning in the 1970s and considered by 2020 to be at its worst since the 1920s. In 2017, the ultrawealthy received $1.5 trillion in tax cuts, but none of the promised "trickle-down" effects transpired.[12] The cuts did not produce new jobs or deliver meaningful boosts for lower- and middle-income households who had to cope with inflation and rising cost-of-living expenses, medical and student debt, housing, and childcare. But the tax cuts did reduce public (government) revenue by tens of billions of dollars, with much greater reductions predicted for the next decade. In 2019, pundits waxed ecstatic about economic growth because the stock market was booming. But that growth almost exclusively benefitted Wall Street. The *Financial Times* reported, "The richest 1 percent of Americans now account for more than half of the value of equities [public stock and ownership stakes in private companies] owned by US households." The bottom 50 percent of US households have negligible stock holdings, and the lowest 8 percent have virtually none.[13] This is the economic context in which philanthropy-driven bipartisan consensus reform agendas are shaped and implemented.

Philanthropy can and sometimes does leverage influence for justice-serving causes. But even at its best, conditional charity, institutionalized as philanthropy, does not constitute justice and cannot create it. It is neither reliable nor consistent; it is always self-serving. Yet it wields enormous power to grant or withhold critical funding to organizations, buy political influence, advance policy agendas, and facilitate the transfer of public authority and resources to private proxies who have little or no public oversight or accountability. Prior to the emergence of a philanthropic reform industry, universities and government agencies did (and still do) help construct and implement criminal legal policy through a feedback loop of grant-funding, targeted research projects, and contracts. More recently, foundations and major donors have spent hundreds of millions of dollars, perhaps more, to create and institutionalize a contemporary criminal legal reform enterprise that dominates public discourse and policy even as it consistently expands its own work *and* the system it seeks to modify.

The use of "social impact bonds"(SBI), "pay for success"(PFS), or "social innovation" schemes, which encourage the making of private profit in the service of reform, illustrates the point.[14] Promoted as a cost-effective model for public-private partnerships, especially in times of "budget crises," the SBI model is used to implement reforms in such arenas as criminal justice, juvenile justice, education, foster care, and homelessness. The justification for the model is that it shifts the financial risks for failed endeavors from the public to private investors. But it is also designed to be largely invisible to the public; to move decision-making about public policy even further from the already meager forms of democratic oversight provided for by law. Government agencies, foundations, service providers, research organizations and evaluators, and investors identify a specific project they want to address in such areas as parole or probation supervision, substance abuse and mental health treatment programs, and more. Agreed-upon metrics for success are established. Governments contract with nonprofit or other organizations to provide necessary services. Those organizations in turn secure funding from private investors—such as Goldman Sachs and Bloomberg Philanthropies—whose degree of profit is derived from the government savings produced by this model and how successfully client populations meet those ("data-driven" and "evidence-based") criteria for success. In this way, public revenues and reforms to public systems are shifted to private control.

EMERGENCE OF A BIPARTISAN REFORM INDUSTRY

Coteries of influential foundations have long attempted to broker partnerships that would address controversial issues of national importance by bridging polarizing political divides. Earlier efforts to create strategic bipartisan alliances on immigration reform and climate change foundered along fault lines too volatile and discordant to overcome. Educational reform—privatizing public schools and transforming education into a market-based commodity—has met with some success, but unions and a great deal of pro-public education popular opinion stand in the way. Criminal justice reform provided a breakthrough. Speaking on condition of anonymity to a writer for Political Research Associates' *Public Eye* magazine, a highly placed foundation official noted that the United States had already been shifting significantly to the Right, as philanthropists, research institutes and foundations, and large advocacy organizations brokered creation of the new bipartisan consensus.[15] The Right came into discussions far more prepared then the centrist-liberal sector to frame the agenda, set its limits, and promote particular talking points. Moreover, centrists, moderates, and liberals had already embraced or tacitly accepted neoliberal imperatives that determined the nature, scope, and implementation of reform agendas.

The Texas Public Policy Foundation (TPPF), established in 1989 as a libertarian-conservative-Right think tank and policy incubator stands at the epicenter of the new generation of bipartisan reforms that began to emerge in the late 1990s and early 2000s. TPPF enjoys close ties to the American Legislative Exchange Council (ALEC), a highly effective corporate-Right policy mill offering model legislation in many different areas to states. It is also closely allied with the right-wing State Policy Network (SPN) which provides services to "state-focused, free market think tanks" in fifty states, and to their national think tank partners.[16] TPPF has been a leading voice in climate change denial, urging President Trump to abandon the Paris Climate Agreement and mocking clean energy proposals. The organization also led a twenty-state effort to mount a second legal challenge to the constitutionality of the Affordable Care Act, popularly known as Obamacare, after the US Supreme Court (SCOTUS) first upheld the Act's constitutionality in 2012.[17]

Until 2012, lists of donors to TPPF, a nonprofit 501(c)(3) organization, were not publicly available, though it was well known that they included Koch Industries and the Lynde and Harry Bradley Foundation, both behemoths of right-wing funding. In 2012, the *Texas Observer* published a 2010 list of TPPF donors provided to the Internal Revenue Service (IRS).[18] This document, meant only for the IRS, was mistakenly posted publicly on the website of GuideStar, one of many organizations that compiles profiles of nonprofits. While the list provides only a partial and time-limited glimpse into TPPF support, additional information can be gleaned from other sources, including information published by some funders themselves. Significant TPPF donors include a host of corporate energy, communications, private prison, and insurance interests aligned with the foundation's passionate commitment to free market policies, including deregulation, unfettered fossil fuel production, regressive taxation policies, privatization of schools and health care, and more. But TPPF also receives funding from sources widely considered to be centrist or liberal. Between 2011 and 2015, for example, The Pew Charitable Trusts gave $4.7 million for "policy work" primarily but not only in criminal justice reform.[19] Between 2010 and 2020, the social justice–focused Public Welfare Foundation gave about $1.3 million to generate support for Texas and national criminal justice reform among conservative audiences.[20]

Prior to 2010, reform momentum was already in motion. The years 2009–2011 are of special interest. In 2009, citing the common reform litany of systemic brokenness, bloat, and cost, US Senator Jim Webb (D-VA) proposed creation of a National Criminal Justice Commission charged with conducting a top-to-bottom review of the US criminal justice system.[21] The Commission would provide Congress with specific but nonbinding recommendations for reform and restructuring. Webb's proposal attracted bipartisan sponsorship and the support of many law enforcement groups, but the US Senate did not take it up. In 2010, the same year *The New Jim Crow* was published, Webb's bill passed the US House of Representatives on a voice vote. By 2011, citing concerns about federal overreach, trampling states' rights, and possible constitutional problems, US Senate Republicans blocked consideration of the proposal, effectively killing it.[22] Webb, a centrist, was hardly calling for radical transformation. But the Right sought to dominate the reform terrain—and to wrench its control from the hands of the federal government.

In the meantime, in 2010, TPPF launched its influential Right on Crime initiative, a one-stop source for conservative-Right views on reform, hailed by the ACLU as the beginning of "the new politics of prison reform."[23] Right on Crime claims that the conservative movement for criminal justice reform was born in Texas in 2007. But political scientist Marie Gottschalk traces the Texas story to an earlier time, a ruling in response to a legal challenge by David Ruiz, then incarcerated, to "cruel and unusual" prison conditions: severe overcrowding, compromised health care, and more. When Ruiz finally won the court case, years-long legal contests ensued. The result was a series of changes that emphasized "maximum control at minimum cost" and "ultimately gutted many of the court-ordered reforms."[24]

Gottschalk picks up the "origin story" in 2007. Deciding against a $2 billion expenditure for new prisons, Texas "enacted some modest changes in probation and substance abuse and mental health treatment." These reforms produced about a 6 percent drop in the total number of people held in state prisons and county jails between 2007 and 2018, although in the same period, the number of women being incarcerated rose. Gottschalk documents the modest successes and glaring failures of the time, emphasizing the need to look beyond the hype: "All the applause that Texas received for the prisons it did not build and the handful of prisons it has closed has overshadowed the fact that . . . [the state] remains exceptional today not only for the sheer number of people under state control, but also for the brutal and inhumane conditions that persist in its prisons and jails."[25] Along with routine violence, costs for the Texas Department of Criminal Justice remained depressingly consistent over the years. Gottschalk reports, about $3.3 billion per year in constant dollars—that is, for costs after adjustment for inflation. Nonetheless, as long as no one looked too deeply, the press and foundation world generally accepted Texas's claims that it had created another "miracle" of reform. TPPF and Right on Crime were well placed to help advance reforms in other states and nationally. At the same time, more socially liberal organizations that had taken stands against law enforcement violence and mass incarceration for many years—ACLU, NAACP, and others—sought openings for greater impact for their work.

It is not possible to determine with certainty when major donors, wealthy foundations, and policy incubators first began to envision the creation of powerful bipartisan criminal justice reform alliances. Those partnerships didn't spring up overnight; different foundations, organizations, and universities were already engaged in various aspects of reform work. In 2005, for example, John Jay College for Criminal Justice launched The Prisoner Reentry Institute (PRI), rebranded as The Institute for Justice and Opportunity in 2020, to focus on "a range of issues, including reentry from jail, entrepreneurialism and reentry, employing formerly incarcerated people, and siting residential facilities in the community."[26] The Council of State Governments Justice Center, a key bipartisan reform actor, launched in 2006. But the strategic national, state, and local consolidation and expansion of effort was new. Scattered pieces of information from various foundations and organizations suggest it was well underway by the mid-2000s. Despite some disagreements among various actors, they nonetheless came together around specific policy, methodological, and messaging frameworks for reform, and the funding to pursue them.

The federal government supported these efforts under both Republican and Democratic administrations, as did an increasing number of state and local governments. Coalition partners included foundations, think tanks and policy incubators, advocacy organizations, research institutes, and universities. Joining together, major funders enlisted the support of many smaller funders and brought pressure to bear on state, local, and national organizations to partner with unlikely allies in order to have a broader strategic impact. Some groups choose to go along, either enthusiastically or reluctantly, while others do not. Along the way, new public-private partnership organizations and initiatives are created to promote, help implement, and evaluate reforms, some of which are identified in this and subsequent chapters. The first national coalition specifically created to advance bipartisan reforms, the Coalition for Public Safety (CPS) launched in 2015 with initial funding from Koch Industries, the Laura and John Arnold Foundation (LJAF, later becoming Arnold Ventures), the John D. and Catherine T. MacArthur Foundation, and the Ford Foundation. Charter members included the ACLU, NAACP, the Center for American Progress (CAP), and the Leadership Conference Education fund, together with libertarian-Right partners Right on Crime, Americans for Tax Reform, Faith & Freedom Coalition, and Freedom Works. By mid-2019, the ACLU left CPS while Prison Fellowship, the American Conservative Union Foundation, Families Against Mandatory Minimums (FAMM) and #cut50 had joined.

In 2019, the Council on Criminal Justice (CCJ), a new national bipartisan membership organization and think tank, was founded with support from Arnold Ventures, the Ford Foundation, the H.F. Guggenheim Foundation, and others. Headed by Adam Gelb, former director of public safety initiatives at Pew Charitable Trusts, CCJ supports various research activities and advocates "for evidence-based public policy." Its officers and task forces are weighted with law enforcement officials, industry elites, former political officials, and bipartisan reform figureheads.

Since the early 2000s, scores of foundations, corporations, major donors, and wealthy investors have provided funding support for various bipartisan reform initiatives, programs, and campaigns, amounting to hundreds of millions of dollars, possibly more. While it is impossible to discuss all of them, it is important to note that those supporting the emergence of the bipartisan consensus onto state and national stages include foundations traditionally considered bastions of liberalism, the Ford Foundation, the MacArthur Foundation, and Open Society Foundations (OSF).

The Ford Foundation's long history of support for criminal justice reform, an outgrowth of its 1960s-era involvement in community-based "War on Poverty" strategies, began early, in 1970. That year, as researcher Sam Collings-Wells notes, the Ford Foundation announced a new $30 million initiative to establish the Police Foundation, "an independent organization . . . for action-oriented research into new policing strategies and technologies."[27] In the following decades, they poured additional tens of millions of dollars into reform efforts aimed at reducing mass incarceration and racial disparities in the system; the Foundation also supports capacity building for reform organizations and alliances. The MacArthur Foundation provided funding to launch the Pretrial Justice Institute in the late 1970s. Between 2013 and 2020 MacArthur has given about $221.6 million to 109 public and private agencies and institutions to support criminal justice reform, with a primary focus on the "over-use" and "misuse" of jails, and the reduction of racial disparities within them. Some of its largest grants are awarded to close reform partners, including the Urban Institute and Vera Institute of Justice.[28] Since the mid-1990s, Open Society Foundations has supported initiatives and work that seek to catalyze change in the criminal justice system, particularly with regard to promoting racial justice and ending the so-called War on Drugs. In 1997, OSF launched a US Soros Justice Fellowship initiative, providing grants to individuals to pursue projects related to spurring debate and affecting systemic change. In 2020, OSF announced major new spending to support selected Black-led racial justice organizations and local work focusing on producing change in policing and criminal justice.[29]

Billionaire reformers include human rights advocates Charles Feeney (Atlantic Philanthropies) and George Soros (OSF), Robert Kraft of the Kraft Group, and B. Wayne Hughes, the self-storage mogul and real estate investor who also donates generously to the right-wing American Crossroads, a super political action committee (super PAC). Music mogul Shawn "Jay-Z" Carter and Michael Novogratz, a former Goldman-Sachs partner turned Bitcoin investor and founder and CEO of Galaxy Digital—among others—are also involved. But from the beginning, Koch Industries, and Arnold Ventures, formerly known as the Laura and John Arnold Foundation

(LJAF), have played outsized roles in driving the formation and implementation of the bipartisan consensus.

The billionaire brothers David (deceased 2019) and Charles Koch have strongly supported various initiatives and scholarship in criminal justice reform through Koch Industries, Charles Koch Foundation, Charles Koch Institute, and the Koch-connected Donors Trust and Donors Capital Fund, two powerful and influential donor-advised "dark money" funds that hide the identities of major contributors to right-wing causes.[30] While some of this work is pursued independently of the major bipartisan consensus coalitions, most of it closely aligns. Journalist Jane Mayer suggests that the embrace of criminal justice reform was originally part of an effort to more favorably overhaul the Koch's harshly libertarian-Right public image, which is partly true.[31] But there is more to it than that. Charles Koch, long an advocate of dismantling social services and programs, has increasingly appropriated social justice organizing concepts and language to champion what he calls "bottom-up" change that purportedly takes policy decisions out of the hands of political elites.[32] The Koch network possesses a genius for fashioning any major issue, ranging from mass transportation to clean water into a political and economic vehicle for a more extensive agenda of deregulation, privatizing, union-busting, and dismantling publicly owned services and infrastructure.[33] In pursuit of this agenda, the brothers have poured hundreds of millions of dollars into strategic interventions to influence curricula, faculty, and research in higher education.[34]

In her book *Dark Money: The Hidden History of the Billionaires behind the Rise of the Radical Right* (2016), Jane Mayer traces the far reach of Koch money—and that of a relative handful of other plutocrats—to influence US political and economic life in distinctly antidemocratic ways. For the 2016 general election, the Koch brothers' donor network planned to spend almost $900 million, independently of the Republican Party.[35] Following David Koch's death in 2019, *Los Angeles Times* business columnist Michael Hiltzik said his greatest creation was "a network of moneyed donors so potent and ubiquitous that the voice of the individual voter has been drowned out."[36] Scholars Theda Skocpol and Alexander Hertel-Fernandez have documented and analyzed the Koch network's influence on ascendance of the extreme right-wing in the Republican Party.[37] But Koch funding has also gone to some stealth projects to advance neoliberal policies among so-called "Third Way" Democrats. In 2019, the network announced intentions to also support Democratic candidates and policies that further Koch Industries goals.[38]

By contrast, billionaires John and Laura Arnold are less well known beyond philanthropic and bipartisan/neoliberal reform circles. In 2008, the Houston-based Laura and John Arnold Foundation—now known as Arnold Ventures—was established with the fortune John Arnold made as a former Enron energy trader after Enron's collapse in 2001 following disclosure of a massive accounting fraud scheme. A few days prior to Enron's bankruptcy filing, Arnold received an $8 million bonus, even as regular employees lost almost all of their Enron 401(k) retirement funds.[39] Arnold was not personally accused of wrongdoing. He went on to establish his own hedge fund before retiring, in his thirties, to enter the world of philanthropy. Laura Arnold is a former mergers and acquisitions attorney for a law firm providing strategic corporate advice and expertise and, later, executive vice president and general counsel for Houston-based Cobalt International Energy. They identify themselves as Democrats. There is scarcely a single area of the bipartisan reform consensus that Arnold Ventures has not played a key role in funding—and, in some instances, creating. Of special note is the role the Arnolds played since 2012 in developing, testing, and distributing data-based tools, including the Public Safety Assessment (PSA) instrument to help prosecutors and judges determine what risks a given defendant poses to public safety. The PSA and similar risk-assessment instruments are discussed more thoroughly in Chapter 4. Beyond criminal justice reform, Arnold Ventures' funding priorities include research to support market-based "retirement policy" (dismantling public pension structures, which it has pursued for years, in partnership with Pew Charitable Trusts), tax policy, education, and health.[40]

In 2019, the LJAF changed its structure, forming Arnold Ventures, a limited-liability company, in order to be able to engage more directly in political and public policy advocacy. The LLC structure encompasses their private foundation, an existing donor-advised fund, and a 501(c)(4) organization that permits greater lobbying activity than a traditional nonprofit. This change follows the lead of Mark Zuckerberg (the Chan Zuckerberg Initiative) and other prominent billionaires who seek greater political impact than traditional grantmaking allows. It is also harder to track who donates and how funds are spent.

THE RHETORIC OF BIPARTISAN REFORM

The rhetorical strategies used to promote bipartisan reform agendas are as important as the policies and implementing mechanisms. Repeated endlessly, bipartisan rhetoric promises the public that justice can be had more cheaply, more humanely and in tidy, managerial ways, all without the brash interventions of prisoner uprisings and unruly social movements insisting on structural change. Some of the major rhetorical anchors of the bipartisan consensus are briefly noted here; these and other catch-phrases are referenced with regard to specific reforms throughout *Carceral Con.*

"Saving Taxpayer Dollars"

Taxes and fees generated for government services (such as the US Postal Service) are public revenues to be allocated by governments for essential services and the public good. When tax revenues shrink, so do revenues that might otherwise be allocated for human needs and community well-being. The reform promise to "save taxpayer dollars" in the administration of justice is a call to steadily shift public responsibility and revenue to private interests. "Calling public money 'taxpayer money,'" say attorney Raúl Carillo and activist Jesse Myerson, "implicitly affirms that taxation is theft: if the money is taxpayers' by right, what business does the government have using if for healthcare, jobs, or clean water?"[41] It's a seductive, anti-tax message, especially for a public already reeling from the effects of prolonged austerity measures. The idea that the public could demand higher taxes from the ultra-wealthy and different political and economic priorities that benefit many more people is buried under a slogan that combines messages of thrift, theft, and aggrieved plaint.

"Danger" and "Public Safety"

Six weeks before Californian voters decided the fate of California's Proposition 47 in 2014, Right on Crime notable Newt Gingrich and conservative billionaire B. Wayne Hughes Jr. urged voters to follow the leadership of Texas, Georgia, Oklahoma, Mississippi, all "red," or conservative-Right, states. "Obviously," the duo wrote in a *Los Angeles Times* op-ed, "we need prisons for people who are dangerous, and there should be harsh punishments for those convicted of violent crimes. . . . Prisons are for people we are afraid of, but we have been filling them with many folks we are just mad at." That "just mad at" group was described as "non-serious, nonviolent offenders."[42]

The invocation of "danger" establishes the management of purported danger from violent criminals as the nexus of bipartisan criminal justice reform, provides the rhetorical backbeat for its campaigns, and anchors its agenda to policing and prisons as the indispensable guarantors of public safety. Mass media thrives on sensational accounts of violence and crime; the old adage "If it bleeds, it leads" still holds true. The result is an endless recycling of a systemic raced, classed, and gendered "dangerousness" feedback loop in which the rhetoric of "violent offenders" and "dangerous criminals," however apparently neutral on the surface, justifies the carceral state.

The rhetoric of “dangerousness” and “non-serious, nonviolent, low-level offenders” makes it easier to ignore what happens to those who are in prison. It is much more difficult to bring any nuance to discussions concerning people convicted of violent crimes when fearmongering images of ruthless monsters spring so effortlessly to mind. It also justifies the endless expansion of community-based correctional control and surveillance. And while the bipartisan agenda rightly expresses concern for the well-being of victims/survivors of violent acts considered criminal, there is no equivalent acknowledgment of violence and harm inflicted on individuals and entire communities by the state or its authorized public or private agents, through policing, imprisonment, immigration enforcement, or other means. Nor is there consideration of ways in which structural racism, gender violence, ableism, and poverty compromise the safety and increase the precarity of so many people in general. Reform promises to “increase public safety” are measured only by dodgy metrics within the narrow framework of the criminal legal system itself. But what kind of safety is being promised? For whom? At what human cost?

“Smart Justice”

“Smart Justice,” purported to be the answer that provides the third way through “tough” and “soft” approaches to crime, is purportedly race neutral and objective because it is an “evidence-based” and “data-driven” methodology. While “evidence-based” has become a mantra of reform, data literacy is also essential to assess its merit. How are the data collected? From what sources? What assumptions drive the collection of particular kinds of data? How are the data used? Who funds the research? So-called smart justice methodologies, discussed in Chapters 3, 4, and 5, are utilized in policing, pretrial reforms, release decisions, and more. Contrary to public relations talking points, they reinforce rather than erase racial bias.

"Justice Reinvestment"

When the Center for NuLeadership on Urban Solutions, the Movement for Black Lives (M4BL), the Funders' Collaborative on Youth Organizing (FCYO), and other justice-seeking organizations, networks, and coalitions embrace the call to *divest* from mass incarceration in order to *invest* in social infrastructure that strengthens communities, they embrace a long tradition of social justice activism.[43] "Divest/Invest" is a compelling frame that communicates the need to shift a society's investments in institutions and services that require, profit from, and reinforce structural inequality to those that foster collective as well as individual health, well-being, and justice. It evokes the struggle for financial divestment from apartheid regimes in South Africa and Israel. It inspires campus campaigns demanding institutional divestment from investment portfolios and contracts with vendors that profit from the exploitation of human beings and ecologies. More than any other implied bipartisan promise, the "Divest/Invest" frame ignites hopes that local and state governments, properly pressured, will begin to permanently shrink systems of state brutality and carceral control and reinvest in the health and wholeness of communities more generally. No such commitment exists, but enticing schemes for "justice reinvestment" are centerpieces of many state bipartisan reform agendas.

THE BIPARTISAN JUSTICE REINVESTMENT FRAMEWORK

In 2003, the Open Society Institute (now Open Society Foundations) published "Justice Reinvestment." The paper identified prison and parole/probation systems as business failures (from an investment perspective) that destabilize communities. They proposed redirecting a significant amount of the billions spent on prisons and jails to support reinvestment—schools, health care, housing, jobs, public parks, and more—in communities most devastated by mass incarceration. Public spaces would expand, not continue to shrink. The notion of public safety, the authors argued, would be redefined by this shift from carceral control to an emphasis on thriving communities.[44] But, as Marie Gottschalk reports, the bipartisan consensus betrayed the original concept of justice reinvestment, even as it staked claim to the rhetoric.[45]

By 2020, two predominant models for reinvestment existed. For ease of differentiation, we refer to them as the JRI (Justice Reinvestment Initiative) and Proposition 47 models. The JRI model came first. Texas is sometimes credited with efforts leading to creation of Justice Reinvestment that predominates today, through its "data-driven" sentencing reform policies that it introduced, starting in 2007.[46] In 2010, Congress appropriated funds for the federal Bureau of Justice Assistance to establish the Justice Reinvestment Initiative; federal JRI funding assistance from 2010 to 2018 was $162.68 million. With major support from Pew Charitable Trusts, JRI worked in conjunction with a network of public-private partnerships, including the Council of State Governments Justice Center, the Crime and Justice Institute, academic research institutes, and others to advance reforms in thirty-five states.[47] The Justice Reinvestment Initiative is "a data-driven" approach to reduce corrections, including recidivism and related criminal justice spending, and reinvest savings in strategies that improve public safety. But as Gottschalk points out, even Pew Charitable Trusts, a pillar of bipartisan reform, has long recognized that utilizing recidivism rates as a success metric can be misleading.[48]

While JRI-assisted reforms may vary, most of them involve sentencing reforms, conditions for release from prison (including supervision of parole and probation), and establishing oversight systems to track reform progress. The content of reforms and the calculation and reporting of results are overseen in each state by an "interbranch, bipartisan working group of policymakers and other professionals both inside and outside the justice system." The working groups typically are top-heavy with an "insiders" group of law enforcement officials, government officials, and private service providers with long histories in work related to the criminal legal system. Some incorporate a small number of cherry-picked "justice-involved" people (victims of crime and/or those who have been incarcerated). Often, community activists are not aware who is on these working groups if they even know such groups exist.

Between 2010 and 2016, JRI reported cost savings exceeding $1.1 billion in savings or averted costs, saying that nearly half that ($450 million) was reinvested in "crime reduction strategies."[49] JRI and its partners predict that savings will mushroom into more billions over time.[50] But calculating savings and reporting on their distribution can be complicated and ambiguous. Most JRI reinvestment, where it can be documented, goes primarily to criminal legal system modification and expansion. A progress report on JRI efforts in seventeen local jurisdictions, released by the Urban Institute in mid-2016, was generally upbeat, pointing out the advancement of reforms in sentencing, expansion of community corrections, and the use of data-based, evidence-driven tools and procedures. But the Institute also noted that local sites "faced significant challenges in identifying cost savings and reinvesting those funds." According to the report, "Most sites have not been able to identify real savings and reinvest those in the system. Nevertheless, many documented success in other forms that will live on well beyond participation in the initiative." Among the challenges: clearly identifying JRI reform savings, documenting those savings, publicly releasing that information, and actually reinvesting any savings in reform-advancing strategies. In some instances, stakeholders in a particular site could not agree on actual costs and actual dollars saved. Even when some jurisdictions "captured real savings," they felt political pressure to not publish those savings for fear of future budget cuts or reallocation to other agencies.[51]

Those sites that reported difficulties in investing savings as planned to further JRI priorities were encouraged to document success in other ways. Despite these difficulties, the Urban Institute reported later that year that fifteen of twenty-eight JRI states had either modestly decreased prison populations or kept them at below previously projected levels. Savings from decreased or averted costs were significant, even if jurisdictions were not able to calculate or report them with accuracy; in some instances, there was "a disincentive to identify savings that could result in budget reductions."[52] Summary JRI state reports do not address how much of the community-based reinvestment money that supported diversion programs, treatment programs within or without prisons, or supervision capacity went to public and to private entities. Nor do they say whether these expansions of services and carceral capacity are fee based or linked to the use of social impact bonds or pay-for-success contracts. Where reinvestment could be documented, it was in such areas as law enforcement grants, training on evidence-based practices, deployment of risk assessment tools, support of drug and other "problem-solving" courts, substance abuse (and other "behavioral health") treatment in custodial corrections or post-release, and victim services. The complete sham of Mississippi's justice reinvestment process is described in Chapter 5.

By contrast, Californians for Safe Neighborhoods and Schools, the pro-Proposition 47 umbrella organization, directly embedded general reinvestment mandates in the ballot initiative and subsequent statute amendment. Post–Proposition 47 savings are allocated according to a specific formula. Sixty-five percent of savings go to drug treatment, mental health services and reentry supports, housing-related assistance, and other community-based support services; these are administered through the law enforcement–dominated Board of State Community Corrections (BSCC). Twenty-five percent of savings go to crime prevention efforts in public schools administered through the California Department of Education. The final 10 percent of savings are allocated for victim services, administered through the California Victim Compensation Board. While some of this funding passes through community organizations and trauma centers, the predominant result is an extension of the carceral apparatus. The first distribution of Prop 47 savings, $103 million for distribution over a three-year period, came more than two years after passage of the initiative, following resolution of heated disagreements about the actual amount of money to be distributed and who would make final decisions about grants. In 2019, the BSCC announced a second round of Prop 47 savings, estimated at $96 million, and called for proposals for a grant cycle running from August 2019 through May 2023.[53]

Californians for a Responsible Budget (CURB), a statewide coalition of seventy grassroots organizations, works to permanently reduce the number of people in prison, along with the number of prison and jail beds in California. CURB is unequivocal in its belief that "dollars should not continue to increase the capacity of local corrections to supervise returned citizens, but that resources should be shifted into basic human and health care services for all people to thrive once returned to the community."[54] That is the real reinvestment struggle—not only in California, but in every state. After all, as CURB pointed out, years after California realignment and passage of Proposition 47 and other reforms, Governor Gavin Newsom's revised corrections budget for 2019–2020 increased to $12.8 billion, an all-time high. The following year, it increased to $13.4 billion.[55]

BIG MONEY, OUTSIZE INFLUENCE

Private interests have always influenced public policy. But the big money behind the "bipartisan consensus" has literally built the infrastructure and machinery to write the policy, ensure its enactment into law, and engineer its implementation. Public officials increasingly cede oversight to private interests. Significant foundation funding goes directly to such public institutions as police departments, county sheriffs, associations of prosecuting attorneys, and more for planning grants, supporting participation in pilot projects, and additional technologies and resources. The criminal legal system for the future is being institutionalized; it is one of expanded policing, record keeping, monitoring, supervision, and surveillance.

In 2007, INCITE!, a network of radical feminists of color organizing to end state violence and violence in homes and communities, published the landmark anthology, *The Revolution Will Not Be Funded: Beyond the Non-profit Industrial Complex*. From a variety of perspectives, authors describe ways in which many social justice organizations have internalized the governmental and foundation mandates of the nonprofit world, often blunting their original political goals in order to receive funding. Even as they chart the difficulties of imagining radical movement building and structural transformation outside of the nonprofit/foundation/public-private partnership funding models, they engage the challenge to do so. Among the questions they raise are these:

- How are public monies diverted into private hands through foundations?
- How has reliance on foundation funding impacted the course of social justice movements?

Since that time, many of the same organizers and activists, and many others, continue to challenge us all to think critically about philanthropy itself, and its own role in creating and intensifying structural inequality. Ruth Wilson Gilmore says bluntly, "Philanthropy is the private allocation of stolen social wages."[56] That is to say, the wealth allocated by philanthropists is created in no small measure by tax cuts, tax-sheltered profits, and business practices that continue to favor structural inequality. And it is allocated by an elite, ultra-wealthy few in ways that preserve or even strengthen inequality.

Accordingly, additional questions may also be helpful in breaking through the philanthropy-driven drone of bipartisan rhetoric:

- How would our analysis of danger and understanding of justice change if it centered the ways in which raced, classed, gendered, ableist, and other structural forms of inequality and violence construct processes of criminalization, policing, prosecution, and carceral control?

- How would strategies for ensuring public safety shift if we redefined "public safety" to include social, economic, and environmental stability and well-being for all people and communities?

In short, how might we dislodge the plutocrats at the helm of the bipartisan reform consensus (and so many other arenas of reform) from the center of political influence? How might we organize to advance more profoundly democratic and life-giving political, social, and economic priorities?

3 Criminalization, Policing, and Profiling

> The law, in its majestic equality, forbids the rich as well as the poor to sleep under bridges, to beg in the streets, and to steal bread.
>
> —Anatole France, 1894

> Quis custodiet ipsos custodes?
>
> —Juvenal, late 199 CE

> Who Protects Us from You?
>
> —Boogie Down Productions, 1989

The narrative that public safety rests with the police is a group fiction, moored by the unquestioned assumption that the police constitute that mythic "thin blue line" that separates "law-abiding" people from the violent predations of dangerous criminals: murderers, rapists, and thieves. But as the storyline increasingly breaks apart in public view, law enforcement authorities, politicians, and bipartisan reformers race to repair the damage without acknowledging that US policing doesn't save us from violence. To the contrary, it relies upon the threat of violence, the fear that violence produces, and the ability to do violence to others. Simply put, policing *is* violence, deployed by the state.[1]

From the outset, US policing has been rooted in racial capitalism, with the goal of regulating race, class, and gender to prevent public disorder, protect the property of elites and the well-to-do, enshrine and manage systems of exploitation, and preserve traditional hierarchies of power. Professional policing evolved from carceral strands grounded in settler colonialism, chattel slavery, and industrialization. These include the seventeenth-century appointment/election of colonial sheriffs, informal seventeenth- and eighteenth-century night watch systems, the mid-nineteenth-century institutions of metropolitan police forces, particularly in Northern states, and the evolution of Southern police forces from slave patrols from the eighteenth century through the abolition of slavery. The rapid national expansion of professional police forces in the post–Civil War industrial era meant that newly freed Black people, the "riotous," often immigrant, working classes, poor people, and women thought to be gender nonconforming were subject to special scrutiny.[2] Today, the essential function of police forces remains the same: the control, through systems of legalized violence, of those at the margins who are deemed to be a threat to profit and property.

The engine of that control is an expanding web of criminalization. The explosive growth of the carceral state relies upon the presumptive labeling of certain groups of people as intrinsically dangerous. The Interrupting Criminalization Research in Action initiative points out: "While framed as neutral, decisions about what kinds of conduct to punish, how, and how much, are very much a choice, guided by existing structures of economic and social inequality based on race, gender, sexuality, disability, and poverty, among others."[3] Any real effort to disrupt mass incarceration and its community-based expansion must address processes of criminalization, but the bipartisan consensus largely fails to do so. Further, reforms favored by the bipartisan consensus provide technological and procedural cover for the vast discretionary power of police to selectively interpret and violently enforce the law.

"I CAN'T BREATHE" I: BROKEN WINDOWS AND PUBLIC ORDER POLICING

Before he succumbed to the banned chokehold, Eric Garner gasped, "I can't breathe!" eleven times. Garner had been stopped by undercover NYPD officers who accused him of selling loose cigarettes without a tax stamp. This sort of encounter was not unusual for Garner and his friend Ramsey Orta, whose gentrifying neighborhood on Staten Island was subject to excessive surveillance of so-called public-order policing. But on July 17, 2014, the encounter was fatal, and Orta's video of his friend's death at the hands of Officer Daniel Pantaleo became the centerpiece in an ongoing struggle for police accountability and, eventually, his own survival.[4]

More than five years later, Officer Daniel Pantaleo was finally fired by NYPD for the death of Eric Garner. Garner's surviving family was finally awarded a $5.9 million civil settlement from the City of New York, typical of the only possible recourse available to many survivors.[5] The New York State Assembly belatedly passed the Eric Garner Anti-Chokehold Act, which established strangulation as a felony for any police/peace officer causing death by any sort of neck restraint. And Ramsey Orta—the man who filmed the deadly encounter? He served five years on a firearm charge in an upstate New York state prison, a target, he says, of endless police harassment and legal frame-ups. The videotape he thought would offer some measure of justice for his friend Eric Garner became, instead, the precipitator of injustice against him.[6]

The death of Eric Garner occurs in the context of the decades-old NYPD practice of "broken-windows" policing. Sometimes called public order policing or quality-of-life policing, the practice is based on a popular but unsubstantiated theory of crime control. The theory claims that "disorder" leads to community withdrawal, loss of informal social control, and then to more serious crime. One unattended broken window purportedly leads to more "physical disorder"; then to "social disorder" in the form of public drunkenness, panhandlers, the homeless, and more; and finally in "criminal invasions" of neighborhoods that seem abandoned, unkempt, or out of control. The theory posits, too, that policing can prevent this, that a repressive zero tolerance approach to public order crimes is necessary to curtail serious violent and property crimes. In reality, it is a means of utilizing policing to facilitate gentrification.[7]

Broken-windows policing coincided with the development of predictive policing tools. Authorities sometimes cite the use of such "evidence-based," analytical tools as COMPSTAT and Predictive Policing (PredPol) to justify the policing of race and place. Like other predictive analytics, they are not "objective" or "bias-free"; they rely on inputs produced by the criminal legal system itself, including arrest and crime report data.[8] In *Policing the Planet: Why the Policing Crisis Led to Black Lives Matter*, Jordan T. Camp and Christina Heatherton describe the reality: "As deindustrialized cities have become veritable landscapes of broken windows—replete with abandoned homes, job sites, and factories—policy makers and police departments have utilized the logic of broken windows to locate disorder within individuals, off-loading liability onto the bodies of the blamed."[9]

From the 1990s on, public order policing in New York City utilized so-called data-driven models of crime mapping and policing. In practice, this constituted "harassment" policing, targeting Black and Brown communities, poor people, trans and gender-nonconforming people, and people profiled as sex workers—especially Black sex workers. In particular, public order policing was a key tool in gentrifying areas, resulting in the criminalization of entire neighborhoods. "Disorder" became the new proxy for race, and public order policing maintains the literal and figurative boundaries of whiteness.[10] This certainly became clear via stop/frisk data revealed in *Floyd v. City of New York*: over 85 percent of the stops were of Black or Latinx individuals, and nearly 90 percent of those stopped were released without the officer finding any basis for a summons or arrest.[11] While the 2013 law suit officially ended stop and frisk in name, in reality, the practice persists. NYPD continues to profile in gentrifying neighborhoods, has devoted massive resources to stopping fare skippers and street vendors in the subways, and has disproportionately issued tickets to African Americans and Latinx New Yorkers for social distancing violations during COVID-19.[12]

The killing of Eric Garner was not an anomaly. In New York City, his name was added to a growing list of those lost to police violence: Michael Stewart, Amadou Diallo, Sean Bell, Ramarley Graham, Kimani Gray, and more. Garner's death and that of Michael Brown in Ferguson one month later also occurred in a national context of growing outrage over police killings—estimated at more than one thousand men and women, disproportionately Black, annually.[13] (These estimates come from grassroots activists and journalists, since there is still no national accounting for civilian deaths at the hands of police. The FBI did create a national "use-of-force" database to help compile such data. But the effort was plagued by problems, including the failure of most law enforcement agencies to provide information. By 2020, no reports had been issued.)[14] Demands to #SayHerName brought the lives and deaths of Sandra Bland, Rekia Boyd, Kayla Moore, Miriam Cary, Michelle Cusseaux, and others into public consciousness. Researcher, legal advocate, and organizer Andrea J. Ritchie's *Invisible No More: Police Violence against Black Women and Women of Color* provides a searing examination of the myriad ways in which gender violence plays out in US policing and immigration enforcement.[15] The failure of grand juries to indict either Officers Pantaleo or Darren Wilson for the respective deaths of Garner and Brown intensified already widespread national protests and calls for change spearheaded by the bourgeoning #BlackLivesMatter movement.

While #BlackLivesMatter began as a hashtag following the killing of Trayvon Martin in 2012, the deaths of Garner and Brown galvanized a national movement. Widespread protests against police violence and the disproportionate targeting of communities of color continued as high-profile cases in cities across the nation—Laquan

McDonald, Freddie Gray, Tamir Rice, John Crawford, Sandra Bland, Alton Sterling, Philando Castile, and more—continued to draw scrutiny.[16] Activists voiced a variety of demands: justice for victims, police accountability, calls for reform, and in some cases, abolition. Grassroots community groups and emergent local chapters of #BlackLivesMatter, along with well-known national advocacy organizations, including the ACLU and NAACP, issued demands for a variety of local, state, and federal initiatives intended to curb police violence. Demands for structural racial and economic justice were also raised, most notably by the newly formed national Movement for Black Lives (M4BL).[17] But the reforms that gained the most traction, including those advocated by the NAACP, ACLU, and Campaign Zero (a well-funded, web-based organization new to the anti–police violence terrain), centered on efforts to curb police violence. These included mandatory police use of body cameras to record encounters with civilians, an end to broken-windows policing, and stronger oversight of police forces.[18]

"I CAN'T BREATHE" II: PROCEDURAL JUSTICE AND COMMUNITY POLICING

In 2015, responding to pressure from protests, the Obama administration embraced a federal agenda of police oversight and reform. The Department of Justice (DOJ) conducted a series of twenty-five federal civil rights investigations that resulted in fourteen consent decrees citing unconstitutional police practices in such cities as Ferguson, Baltimore, and Chicago.[19] Consent decrees, which include agreements and timetables for improvements, can go on for years; they produce decidedly mixed results. In 2015, Justice Department metrics were available for ten cities with consent decrees; in half of them, use of force increased during and after the federal monitoring period.[20] In 2017, the Trump administration swept even this limited tool away.[21]

The Obama administration also encouraged a shift away from public order policing toward "community" policing models and expanded use of technology such as body cameras to record police-civilian encounters. This emphasis on community policing and procedural justice was evident in the recommendations of the 2015 Task Force on 21st Century Policing and put in practice via The National Initiative for Building Community Trust and Justice. This began as a three-year, multimillion-dollar project to improve relationships and increase trust between communities and the police.[22] This was coupled with $43 million Department of Justice funding for body cameras, an indication that, as political scientist Naomi Murakawa notes, "'reform the police' means 'reward the police.'"[23]

With pilot programs in six cities, the National Initiative provided funding for local police departments to develop procedural justice models, offer implicit bias training for officers, and create opportunities to repair police-community relations.[24] The Task Force recommendations and National Initiative agenda were developed by a select advisory group of police chiefs and scholars at major universities coordinated by the National Network for Safe Communities at John Jay College of Criminal Justice, with partnership from the Justice Collaboratory at Yale Law School, the Center for Policing Equity at John Jay College and UCLA, the Office of Justice Diagnostic Programs, and the Urban Institute. Early iterations of the advisory board included representatives from the ACLU, Advancement Project, Teach for America, and Equal Justice Initiative.[25]

Community policing and procedural justice models are often presented in juxtaposition to the broken-windows style of policing; police legitimacy, respect, and trust are emphasized as inducements to law-abiding behavior. In reality, the distinctions are often not that clear.[26] Justin Hansford, a legal scholar and activist, testified at a Task Force listening session on community policing and crime reduction. Reflecting on that experience later, he said, "Government officials, police chiefs, academics, and church leaders insisted that if only the police embraced community policing, the crisis between law enforcement and the Black community would, essentially, end." In this conception of community policing, Hansford says, police grant legitimacy "only to community groups who conform to state conceptions of law, order, and propriety." All of this, of course, requires larger police budgets.[27]

The origins of so-called community policing strategies go back to the 1960s, as a response of some police forces to urban uprisings and the growth of social movements.[28] But the concept solidified in Los Angeles after 2002, when former NYPD commissioner William Bratton, the standard-bearer for "broken windows," took over the Los Angeles Police Department (LAPD). This was less a shift away from public order policing than an "evidence-based" facelift, combined with an energetic public relations campaign. Ruth Wilson Gilmore and Craig Gilmore describe Bratton's community policing strategies as a project to build police power at a time when its legitimacy was in question, utilizing "intensive outreach to the old civil rights leadership and the press" and "significantly increasing the size of the police force."[29] The LAPD also utilized two new predictive policing tools, Predictive Policing (PredPol), to forecast crime, and LASER, to gather information on purported repeat offenders. In 2011, concerned about the racist impacts of the programs, a new watchdog organization, Stop LAPD Spying, was founded. The group's research confirmed serious flaws in the tools, and an audit also confirmed that LASER's "chronic offender" bulletins identified many people who had no history of violent crime. LAPD ended the use of LASER, but Bratton's successor at the LAPD announced the department would pursue "precision policing," described by the free-market think tank The Manhattan Institute as "focused-crime-and-disorder enforcement and Neighborhood Policing.[30] As for Bratton, he returned as NYPD Commissioner in 2014, bringing along his arsenal of predictive profiling, surveillance tools, and "evidence-based" methodologies.[31] The death of Eric Garner occurred on his watch.

The limits of community-based policing reforms were dramatically highlighted in the events and aftermath of the murder of George

Floyd on Memorial Day, May 25, 2020, in Minneapolis, one of the six pilot sites for the National Initiative on Building Community Trust and Justice. Minneapolis Police responded to a call from a store owner alleging that George Floyd had used a suspected counterfeit $20 bill to buy cigarettes. Floyd was questioned and removed without incident from his car, still parked outside the store, by the first two officers at the scene. Then Officer Derek Chauvin and Officer Thou Thao, arrived, and the use of force rapidly escalated. Chauvin, a nineteen-year veteran of the Minneapolis Police Department (MPD) with a history of seventeen use-of-force complaints, took charge of the situation and eventually dragged Floyd from the squad car and to the pavement. There, in full view of body cameras, street security cameras, a Minneapolis Park Police squad, and bystanders who videotaped him, pleading with him to stop, Officer Chauvin pressed his knee into the neck of George Floyd for nine minutes and 29 seconds.[32] Two other officers also pressed Floyd down on his back and legs, while Officer Thou kept the increasingly distressed bystanders at bay. George Floyd uttered, "I can't breathe!' at least sixteen times, but was ignored by Chauvin, who kept the pressure on even after emergency services arrived.[33]

In the early hours of May 26, the Minneapolis Police Department issued a press release, "Man Dies after Medical Incident during Police Interaction." It said, "After [Floyd] got out [of his car], he physically resisted officers. Officers were able to get the suspect into handcuffs and noted he appeared to be suffering medical distress."[34] Hours later, that report had to be withdrawn as citizen video of the incident circulated widely. The four officers, initially placed on administrative leave, were fired. Days later, Chauvin was arrested and charged by the Hennepin county prosecutor with third-degree murder and second-degree manslaughter.[35] At the request of Governor Tim Waltz, the state's attorney general took over the case, amending the charges against Chauvin to also include unintentional second-degree murder while committing a felony, under the felony murder doctrine, explained in Chapter 5.[36] Chauvin was the first white officer in Minnesota to be charged with the murder of a civilian. The attorney general charged the three other officers with aiding and abetting second-degree murder. Minnesota's Department of Human Rights also opened an investigation into the Minneapolis Police Department, while the FBI and DOJ launched their own investigations into Floyd's death.[37]

Those familiar with the history of the MPD were not surprised by the brutality. Despite the city's progressive public image and political history, extreme gaps in racial equality—in education, housing, employment, home ownership, wealth, and health—lurk just below the surface. The MPD's long history of subjecting Black and Indigenous communities to intensive surveillance, disproportionate arrests, brutality, and killings is chronicled by the organization MPD 150 in a report, *Enough Is Enough*, published in 2017, on the 150th anniversary of the department's founding.[38] The American Indian Movement (AIM) was founded in Minneapolis, originally as a street patrol to protect community members from police violence, its work informed by strong commitments to the sovereignty and spiritualities of Native tribes and nations.[39] Communities United Against Police Brutality and other grassroots groups had organized against police violence for more than a decade. The Twin Cities area—Minneapolis and St. Paul—mobilized in support of the Ferguson uprising and #BlackLivesMatter, and more recently in response to the 2016 police killing of Philando Castile in a St. Paul suburb and Jamar Clark, whose 2015 death sparked an eighteen-day occupation of the MPD Fourth Precinct.[40] The department's long and troubled history with communities of color persists, despite multiple efforts, over decades, to implement various reforms.

But the scope of the response was surprising this time. People took to the streets the day after the Floyd killing, and crowds that gathered throughout the day marched to the Third Precinct that night. While the MPD initially responded with tear gas and rubber bullets, the crowd size was overwhelming by the third night of protests, and the MPD vacated the area as the precinct headquarters and much of surrounding Lake Street were set afire.[41] The weeks-long protest in Minneapolis quickly spread to hundreds of cities, all fifty states, and thirteen countries around the world. The call was "Justice for George Floyd," but also for Breonna Taylor, killed in a no-knock raid in Louisville, Kentucky, and Ahmaud Arbery, murdered by white vigilantes in a suburban Georgia neighborhood.[42] And it was a reminder of the thousands of Black, Indigenous, and other people of color killed by police over many years.

Unarmed protesters everywhere were met with a warlike police response. Law enforcement units indiscriminately deployed pepper spray, flash-bang grenades, tear gas—banned internationally as a weapon of war—and long-range acoustic devices (LRADS) or sonic cannons that can produce permanent hearing loss. They fired bullets with rubberized plastic wrapped around a metal core, foam bullets, and so-called "bean-bag" projectiles. These weapons are promoted as "less than lethal" force, but they can—and in some cases did—cause serious, permanent harm.[43] Police made thousands of arrests and use of force resulted in multiple serious injuries and several deaths across the nation. At one point, twenty-three states were under curfews.[44] National Guard troops were deployed to a number of cities. In Washington, D.C., thousands of National Guard troops were joined, at the Trump administration's order, by about seventeen hundred active-duty military troops, US Border Patrol police, and units with no visible identification, later said to be US Bureau of Prisons staff. The *New York Times* reported that the US Department of Homeland Security conducted aerial surveillance of protests in fifteen cities utilizing helicopters, airplanes, and drones. Video footage was instantaneously sent to control centers managed by a branch of US Customs and Border Protection, and later into a Homeland Security digital network that can be accessed by federal agencies and local police departments.[45]

The repressive police response solidified public support for the protests and prompted widespread public support for their message. Rather than calls for police reform or prosecution of individual police officers, this time, the demands turned more broadly toward systemic change and abolition. #DefundthePolice became the central rallying cry, a clear rejection of decades of failed reform efforts. In Minneapolis, the University of Minnesota, Minneapolis Parks and Recreations Board, Minneapolis Public Schools and several major arts, business, and sports organizations cut their ties with the MPD, and the Minneapolis City Council, under pressure from organizations such as Reclaim the Block, committed to a process of dismantling the MPD and imagining new opportunities for public safety.[46] Across the nation, activists pressed cities to reexamine their budgets—many of which allocated a third or more of total discretionary spending for police—and explore how the public might be better served by investments in education, housing, jobs, and health services.[47]

Procedural justice, de-escalation of force, training, and community-policing reforms had been on bipartisan and philanthropy-driven reform agendas for years and were resurrected once more. In their haste to weaken #DefundThePolice demands, some reformers considered new police accountability measures. But in the six years between the "I can't breathe!" of Eric Garner and the "I can't breathe!" of George Floyd, the reform terrain had shifted dramatically. This time, building upon decades of patient, persistent analysis, organizing, educational outreach, and scholarly work, abolitionist demands were now a growing force to be reckoned with. Bipartisan consensus reformers would work even harder to appropriate the rhetoric, applying it to efforts that expand systems of carceral surveillance and control.[48]

CRIMINALIZING INEQUALITY

The rise and rapid growth of the carceral state between 1970 and 2020 begins with expanded processes of criminalization. It is compounded, certainly, by sentencing policy changes, including mandatory minimums that keep people in prison longer, too often until they die. The impacts of these changes are noted in Chapters 5 and 6. But much of the growth of populations under carceral control can be attributed to the expansion of criminal law as well as targeted, aggressive forms of law enforcement. Both methods of criminalization disproportionately impact poor people, and communities of color, trans/gender nonconforming people, people with disabilities, and youth. A quick glance at these methods confirms the structural racial and class inequalities that inform them.

Criminalization by Law Making

Civil and administrative legal system have the power to fine, to require specific institutional or corporate changes, to issue or repeal regulations and standards, and more. By contrast, the US criminal legal system is empowered to create and enforce the law with the full arsenal of state violence. The power is an immense matter of life and death, as "criminals" are created; subjected to search, seizure, and endless surveillance; caged; and potentially killed. Under racial capitalism, such power tends to expand; the entirely predictable impacts of ostensibly neutral laws are raced, classed, and gendered.

As criminal law proliferates, bipartisan consensus relies on the rhetoric of "overcriminalization" to frame a problem in need of reform. This is trickster language. It seems to mean one thing to centrist and liberal reform actors: too many people are being incarcerated. But conservative-Right interests use this framing to cast corporate, institutional, and white-collar actors as victims of overzealous government. The "overzealous" government decried here refers to civil, criminal, and administrative regulations that seek to protect the public from financial, physical, and environmental harm. The Right's preferred remedies for corporate/white-collar overcriminalization are deregulation, evisceration of occupational licensing qualifications and safety standards, and getting rid of corporate and institutional criminal liability for even massive harms to individuals, communities, and entire geographies.[49]

One specific criminal legal vehicle for advancing this agenda is *mens rea*—"guilty mind" or "criminal intent"—reform. Federal *mens rea* reform sought by conservative-Right members of the Coalition for Public Safety (but rejected by centrist-liberal members) stalled during the Obama administration.[50] It will likely be reintroduced. This reform would create a default standard that applies universally: in order to obtain a conviction, federal prosecutors must prove that defendants knew they were committing a crime and that they had good reason to believe that their actions were illegal.[51] Defendants would have to leave a traceable paper, oral, or digital trail discussing their intent to engage in criminal activity in order to be found guilty. That standard of proof is all but impossible to meet. By 2020, bipartisan efforts had produced *mens rea* reforms in at least two states, and more are likely to follow.[52]

Despite its endlessly repeated commitment to end "overcriminalization," the bipartisan consensus has little or nothing to say about the escalating criminalization of ordinary activities and behaviors. Gang-related laws illustrate the point. Since the 1980s, forty-six states, the District of Columbia, and scores of cities have enacted criminal laws targeting "gangs." Most of these laws provide for the possibility of bail enhancements upon arrest and enhanced penalties upon conviction. This means that the offense is defined as legally more serious and subject to harsher sentences if it is deemed to be committed for the benefit of a gang.[53] Gang-related offenses include a wide range of felonies and misdemeanors ranging from carjacking to graffiti, from drive-by shootings to wearing gang-related colors and styles of clothing. Legal definitions of what constitutes a gang are almost always vague; people alleged to be "gang members" are identified by lists of possible markers, including scars, tattoos, use of certain hand signals, and even emoji used in social media posts. While it is not illegal to be part of a group, alleged gang membership is viewed as a reliable marker for violence and criminal purpose. The enforcement of gang statutes rests as much or more on the race, class, gender, and age of the person(s) in question as on the law itself.

The interpretation of gang membership is largely left to law enforcement officials who reify preconceived notions of criminality through the compilation of large databases of alleged gang members, intensified surveillance, and racist patterns of arrests.[54] For example, a 2019 report from the Policing and Social Justice Project at Brooklyn College provides an introduction to what is known about NYPD's secretive Criminal Group gang database.[55] Between 2003 and 2018, more than thirty-seven thousand names were added. A substantial number of those were children; more than 90 percent were Black and Latinx. Complaints of gang policing misconduct are widespread. There are no accurate records of how listing is determined, how many arrests result in formal charges and then in convictions. The problems aren't unique to New York City; reports on gang databases in Chicago and California are riddled with inaccuracies, and in Chicago, data were shared with immigration authorities.[56] The call to abolish all police gang databases and gang units has gained momentum among grassroots anti-police/prison violence groups. But it is absent from bipartisan reform agendas.

The relentless criminalization of poverty and homelessness by law provides another example. Since 2010, the mostly local ordinances that target this population have proliferated rapidly. The de facto criminalization of homelessness places people without an established personal residence, who live much of their lives in public spaces, in the position of being selectively policed for involuntary violations such as lurking, loitering, trespassing, disorderly conduct, actions construed as creating a public nuisance, and more. As homelessness increases, so does the enactment of new measures and intensified enforcement. A 2019 report by the National Law Center on Homelessness and Poverty examined laws targeting the homeless in 187 cities.[57] New ordinances prevent activities essential to sustaining life: sleeping/camping, eating, sitting, and/or asking for money/resources in public spaces. A growing number of cities criminalize the offering of food to houseless people in parks and other public settings. These ordinances include criminal penalties for violations of proscribed acts.[58] While a number of courts have struck down some of the laws, the enactment of new ones continues, without reducing the number of homeless people or impacts of structural poverty. Public investment in housing, health care, food assistance, education, and public jobs programs would reduce both. But the civic choice, to date, is facilitating gentrification.

The bipartisan consensus is also silent on the rapidly expanding criminalization of political dissent, protest, and efforts to document the harmful public impacts of private corporate practices. Between 2016 and 2020, sixteen states enacted twenty-two laws and executive orders establishing new or expanding existing criminal offenses, and harsh penalties for same. Laws passed or pending target people who trespass onto property containing "critical infrastructure" (petroleum refineries, oil and gas pipelines, even telephone poles), protest the appearance of public speakers on campuses, block traffic, and more.[59] As always, highly selective enforcement accompanies enactment. Other laws criminalizing protest and labor organizing have been proposed; those initially defeated are likely to reappear over time, including sanctions against "unlawful mass picketing," the right of teachers to strike for better wages and school conditions, expanding the application of gang statutes, eliminating liability for vigilantes who injure or kill protesters in roadways. and expanding Stand Your Ground laws to allow for the targeting of protesters as part of "anti-mob" action.[60]

Blue Lives Matter laws represent a particular version of the criminalization of dissent and began to emerge as a rejoinder to widespread protests against police violence and killings. Blue Lives Matter laws were introduced in fifteen states in 2016; only Louisiana passed the proposed legislation. In early 2017, the number of proposed Blue Lives Matter laws more than doubled, with passage in Kentucky, Mississippi, and Texas.[61] This legislation seeks to include police among the ranks of groups that are protected by hate crime statutes and conflates occupational choice with ascribed statuses such as race, ethnicity, and sexual orientation. It not only increases legal protections for an already heavily protected occupation but also opens the path to broader criminalization of protest against police violence.[62]

Hate crime legislation proliferated rapidly throughout the 1980s and 1990s, with the announced purpose of "sending a message" that vigilante violence against groups historically subject to discrimination would not be tolerated. "Protected" status categories may include some or all of these: race, ethnicity, national origin, religion, sexual identity, gender, gender identity/gender expression. By 2021, forty-seven states and the federal government had enacted some form of legislation that contained some or all of these components: data collection and reporting, enhanced penalties, civil remedies. Supporters generally emphasized the purported deterrent significance of penalty enhancements, which make it possible to add harsher sentences to the underlying offense (assault, vandalism, physical harm) if it can be proven someone was targeted on the basis of a "protected status" category. For the first time, Blue Lives Matter provisions add an occupational category.

Hate crime laws are already fraught with a host of difficulties. They do not provide proactive "protection" or reduce vigilante violence; moreover, they too often lead to abuse of members of so-called protected status groups, especially people of color who are queer/trans and immigrants attempting to report hate violence.[63] Inclusion of the police as a protected status is guaranteed to compound issues of equity in enforcement.[64] In nearly all states, it is already the case that enhanced penalties can be sought when law enforcement are the targets of harm. Activists and legal experts are rightly concerned that Blue Lives Matter legislation will give officers an additional tool to intimidate by potentially charging anyone who resists arrest, protests police violence, or utters anti-police slogans with a hate crime. Since charges of resisting arrest and assaulting an officer are already sometimes used as police cover for use of excessive or deadly force, concerns are justified.[65]

Legislators at every level have the power to create or repeal laws, but the tendency is toward expansion. Some reforms call for selective "decriminalization," which, in bipartisan-speak, usually means the reclassification of a crime from a felony to a misdemeanor. Several states have reclassified simple drug possession and low-level property crimes as misdemeanors as part of reform packages. This has reduced some prison sentences and related state costs. Nonetheless, misdemeanors still carry the possibility of jail time, lingering records, and a range of fines and fees.[66] This sort of "managerial decriminalization" may reduce some jail and prison sentences, but it shifts rather than concedes correctional control, and does not shrink the carceral state.[67]

Efforts to decriminalize sex work ("prostitution") most clearly illustrate the difference between managerial decriminalization (reclassifying offenses or shifting the focus of who is arrested for certain offenses) and full decriminalization (repealing laws that unjustly criminalize particular actions or behaviors). Some reformers have proposed decriminalizing the sellers of sex work while continuing to criminalize people who purchase it. Other reformers, as journalist Melissa Gira Grant notes, wrongly conflate all sex work with coercive, exploitative human trafficking and oppose any form of decriminalization. (In some cases, this has led to further criminalization, as with FOSTA—the Allow States and Victims to Fight Online Sex Trafficking Act—that federally limits online advertising of sex services.)[68] By contrast, DecrimNY, a broad-based coalition works to decriminalize, decarcerate, and destigmatize the sex trades in New York City and throughout the state. A similar campaign, DecrimNow, exists in the DC metro area, organized by a collective of sex workers, organizers, and allies who work to decriminalize sex work and promote the well-being and safety of people in the sex trade. Black Youth Project 100, a member of the coalition, notes that in DC, "The people most likely to be arrested, searched, fined and imprisoned are Black and Latinx, women, girls and/or LGBTQ. These communities are already at heightened risk for incarceration, poverty, and violence. Criminalization does not assist them in escaping any of these situations. Instead, it reinforces the cycles."[69]

The decriminalization and legalization of marijuana and other drugs is an exception to the tendency to expand criminalization. Even though it is still prohibited by federal law, by early 2021, sixteen states and the District of Columbia had legalized marijuana for recreational use, several more have legalized medical marijuana, and others have reduced possession of small amounts of marijuana from a felony to a misdemeanor.[70] Oregon voters passed Measure 110 in Fall of 2020, decriminalizing personal possession of small amounts of heroin, cocaine, oxycodone, methamphetamine, and psilocybin mushrooms. While possession and sale of larger amounts is still a crime, Measure 110 defines personal possession of these drugs as a civil offense subject to a $100 fine, which can be waived via participation in a health assessment.[71] These legal shifts correspond with growing resistance to the War on Drugs and associated long prison sentences for personal drug use. They also reflect recognition of the economic benefits to states via licensing, taxation, and tourism.

But even legalization or decriminalization at the state level does not fully erase the risk of criminalization or the mark of criminal records for past convictions.[72] The lucrative legal cannabis industry is predominately controlled by white men, and barriers to Black and Latinx ownership may be correlated with the drug war's disproportionate targeting of these communities.[73] And while marijuana arrests have dropped dramatically in states where it is legal, arrests for possession under the legal age of twenty-one, unlicensed sales, and public consumption still occur. Racist policing patterns apply here, as well. Black people are arrested at three times the rates of whites despite comparable patterns of use, and some research has found that these arrests actually increased following legalization.[74] Even as the law occasionally contracts, the heavy boot print of racial capitalism remains.

Criminalization by Law Enforcement

The law becomes reality only when it is enforced, and it is police who are most immediately empowered to do so. The decisions of law enforcement—where to patrol and how, which activities and people to target—shape the contours of the criminal legal system and the demographics of mass criminalization and incarceration. But most debates over police reform are largely limited to questions of militarization, policing style, and accountability.

The neoliberal shrinking of social and governmental services means that police have increasingly taken on roles once handled by communities, with the help of social workers, mental health professionals, and teachers and other school personnel.[75] And, historically, it is also true that, in some instances, as in psychiatric hospitals and asylums, the helping professions have functioned in quasi-policing roles. Increasingly, social workers, mental health workers, and others are drafted into formal law enforcement partnerships, and while the National Association of Social Workers and some others embrace the association, their work should be completely separate from it.[76] Further, the increased criminalization of public space and style has resulted in increased arrests for homelessness, the racialized construction of gang databases, the policing of mental health, and the de facto criminalization of daily survival. Every problem produced by racial capitalism becomes a site for policing. The pervasiveness of police in public housing, welfare offices, child protection services, and in the schools further exacerbates unjust patterns of stops, citations, and arrests; and in the case of the schools, it contributes to a school-to-prison pipeline that criminalizes children of color, including those with disabilities, for minor misbehavior at school.[77]

Echoing the neoliberal commitment to permanent war in service of global capital, US law enforcement agencies are equipped for war. While police public relations initiatives emphasize their vigilant and neighborly presence in communities, twenty-first-century policing is fueled by an ethos that casts marginalized civilians and political dissenters as enemy combatants. With federal support, police departments throughout the United States have acquired armored vehicles, assault weapons, and an array of sophisticated technological weaponry. The use of this equipment often coincides with aggressive police tactics, including frequent deployment of SWAT teams, no-knock raids, and such crowd control techniques as "kettling" demonstrators into confined spaces so they cannot leave.[78] In addition to military equipment, twenty-first-century policing also relies on technological tools to increase the capacity for predictive policing and surveillance. These include facial recognition, thermal imaging, artificial intelligence for data analysis and crime mapping, drones, and biometric databases. The latter include fingerprints, DNA, voice recognition, palm prints, wrist veins, iris recognition, gait analysis, and even heartbeats. Inter-agency data sharing is commonplace. ICE, for example, seeks facial recognition data from local law enforcement agencies to conduct border patrol and deportation raids and, in 2020, began collecting its own DNA samples from immigrants under ICE arrest. Proprietary technologies are developed and implemented through public-private partnerships for which there is no effective oversight or accountability. ICE utilizes software developed by Palantir to compile, store, and share information on immigrants prior to deportation raids. Amazon shares Ring doorbell-cam footage with local police departments.[79]

The scope and scale of US policing raises questions of police accountability for violations of civil liberties, privacy, and use of force policy. Police largely act with impunity, and favorable court rulings, state protections, and union contracts permit this. Federal court decisions have created a higher threshold for prosecuting police or seeking financial redress. In *Graham v Connor*, the US Supreme Court (SCOTUS) gives police the benefit of the doubt if they claim to be in fear for their lives and makes prosecution of police killings extremely difficult.[80] Further, the SCOTUS doctrine of qualified immunity protects government officials acting in good faith—including police officers—from financial liability. Police officers are increasingly protected by state Bills of Rights, and police union contracts in most major cities further constrict officer accountability by limiting complaints and interrogations, allowing officers to see evidence not available to the complainants, erasing disciplinary records and limiting firing, resisting use of force restrictions, and requiring cities to pay the costs of complaints, including paid leave and wrongful injury and death claims.[81] These claims cost cities millions in payouts annually, and are typically paid through self-insurance policies funded by public revenues. Some cities, including Chicago and Los Angeles, also rely on what the Action Center on Race and the Economy (ACRE) calls "police brutality bonds." These bonds provide coverage when revenue is short, and additionally "transfer resources and extract wealth from Black and poor communities to Wall St., through the fees banks charge cities for the bonds."[82]

Following the 2020 uprisings and renewed calls for reform, pundits, mass media, and many bipartisan reformers pointed to Camden, New Jersey, as a model.[83] In 2013, amid rising murder rates and "budget crises," the police department was dismantled. Jurisdictional governance was shifted to the County Sheriff's Office. The stranglehold of the police union was broken. All officers were fired and many rehired at lower wages. New use-of-force regulations were put in place. The end result was a significant expansion of the police footprint. Over time, the number of officers has nearly doubled, technological surveillance and military-style intelligence gathering have mushroomed, the new force has become whiter in a majority-Black city, and complaints against police have risen as homicide rates have fallen. The Camden community policing model has also produced an almost 50 percent increase in disorderly conduct citations.[84] Camden is best read as a cautionary tale, especially for bipartisan consensus reforms. Neoliberal reformers increasingly manipulate growing public ire against police violence and the corrupt protection of that violence by police unions as leverage to try to dismantle all public sector unions, including those for teachers and other public sector workers.[85]

Beyond Camden, millions of dollars—from government, university think tanks, and major foundations—have been poured into the National Initiative's community policing model with the support of a wide mix of bipartisan consensus reformers such as the NAACP, ACLU, Equal Justice Initiative, the Urban Institute, Campaign Zero,

#Cut50, Vera Institute, and Arnold Ventures.[86] While there is little evidence that community policing reduces crime, officer violence, or disproportionate arrests of marginalized groups, it consumes additional resources for more officers, trainings, and technology. The use of technologies has raised additional concerns about privacy and enhanced surveillance. The ACLU, for example, revised their position on body cameras to call for stricter guidelines on use, mandatory public release of any footage that captures use of force, and a national ban on the coupling of body cameras and facial recognition technology.[87] But such measures have not proven workable or enforceable in the past. Finally, it is already clear that reformist calls for community policing only provide another justification for the ongoing encroachment of policing into such arenas as public health and education, expanding the carceral state while simultaneously draining resources from public institutions and programs.

Ultimately, police reform is hampered by the lack of meaningful political effort to fundamentally challenge ways in which policing furthers the reproduction of structural inequality. Proposed reforms of the police fail to address the built-in race, class, and gender biases of policing, and more often than not, they expand, rather than constrict, the scope of their powers. In all cases, police reform efforts perpetuate the status quo, or, as historian Charlotte Rosen observes, become an "engine of carceral violence."[88]

BEYOND CRIMINALIZATION, BEYOND POLICING

It is much easier to create law and socially construct "crime" than it is to repeal and decriminalize. It is much easier to expand the scope and range of policing than it is to remove or rein in law enforcement. The national narrative that public safety rests with more law and more order is a difficult spell to break. In part, the rhetoric of danger has impelled an increase in criminalizing legislation and more policing.

More law and more policing are politically and economically profitable. Challenges to criminalization and policing are swiftly met with backlash from law enforcement and most bipartisan reformers. "Powerful political forces benefit from abusive, aggressive, and invasive policing, and they are not going to be won over by technical arguments or heartfelt appeals to do the right thing," says sociologist Alex E. Vitale, author of *The End of Policing*.[89] Political capital and revenue are generated from expanded law and policing: research grants, foundation funding, contracts for predictive policing models and technology to support surveillance, and ever more bloated budgets for training. Even limited efforts at decriminalization and police reform ultimately tend toward criminal legal system expansion and the widening of the carceral net.

For decades, liberatory organizers and abolitionists have called for solutions outside the legal system and the power of the police. Efforts include demands for the elimination of gang databases; full decriminalization of sex work/decriminalization and legalization of drugs; and repeals of quality-of-life ordinances such as vagrancy, loitering, and lurking. Abolitionists and progressive activists also argue that funding allocated for police should be spent to strengthen communities in such areas as health care, housing, education, public transportation, public utility infrastructure, "green economy" measures, and jobs.[90] Writing in *The Chronicle of Social Change*, legal scholar and sociologist Dorothy Roberts endorsed calls to defund police, but cautions about simply transferring resources and authority to other quasi-carceral systems: "Rather than divesting one oppressive system to invest in another, we should work toward abolishing all carceral institutions."[91]

Strategies and tactics for leveraging such shifts will be different in different communities; not all who join the struggle identify as abolitionists. Even so, the goal is to steadily reduce reliance on police through the development of new visions of and approaches to public safety until US society no longer relies on processes of criminalization, policing, and punishment to secure public well-being. Critical

Resistance offers guiding questions to help evaluate proposed police reforms. Do these reforms

- reduce funding to police?
- challenge the notion that police produce safety?
- reduce tools/tactics/technology that police have at their disposal?
- reduce the scale of policing?[92]

This is a long-term struggle for transformation, not a reformist agenda, where new visions of public safety reject the inherent violence of policing and punishment.

4 The Slippery Slope of Pretrial Reform

> If one really wishes to learn how justice is administered in this country, one does not question the policemen, the lawyers, the judges, or the protected members of the middle class. One goes to the unprotected . . . and listens to their testimony.
>
> —James Baldwin, *No Name in the Street*, 1972

Following arrest, people are either released without charges, incarcerated in jail, or released awaiting trial with or without paying money bail, and with or without conditions of supervision. That sounds straightforward, but it is not. The methods that determine pretrial fates are more accurately understood as raced- and classed-based rites and rituals performed to ration—and often deny—basic civil and human rights.

NIGHTMARE

In 2019, twenty-seven-year-old Layleen Cubilette-Polanco, an Afro-Dominican trans woman with epilepsy, was arrested for allegedly biting a taxicab driver. Authorities discovered a warrant open for her arrest on charges dating back to 2017 related to low-level drug possession and sex work, issued when she missed one or more mandatory classes she was required to attend by a city human trafficking court. Because she could not pay $500 bail, she was imprisoned before trial in New York City's Rikers Island jail complex, a site notorious for rampant abuse and neglect of those in custody. Initially placed in a special unit for transgender women, Polanco experienced multiple epilepsy-related seizures. Nonetheless, she was transferred to a restrictive housing unit, a euphemism for solitary confinement, for allegedly fighting with another inmate. Nine days later, Rikers staff found her "unresponsive."[1] The city medical examiner found the cause of death to be a seizure related to epilepsy.[2]

Lavette Mayes, a forty-five-year-old Black mother of two—a five-year-old son with special needs and a fourteen-year-old daughter—was living on the South Side of Chicago. She operated a small school-van transport company and was in the acrimonious process of ending her marriage of twenty-three years. A physical conflict with her mother-in-law sent both women to the hospital. Charged with aggravated battery against a senior, Mayes was taken directly from the hospital to court for a bond hearing without having been able to contact anyone. Three days after the fight, although she had never been arrested before, a Cook County judge took just thirty seconds to set her bail at $250,000. That required a $25,000 bond deposit, which neither she nor her family could afford. For the next fourteen months, she remained in jail, separated from her children. "When you incarcerate a mother," Mayes later said, "you incarcerate the whole family." Her fear that she might lose her children escalated when her husband sought permanent child custody. Her vans were repossessed; personal savings were quickly depleted. A judge finally reduced Mayes's bail, requiring a deposit of $9,500. With help from her family and the Chicago Community Bond Fund, she made bail and was released—with an electronic monitor. The restrictions, delays, and mix-ups associated with the monitoring severely disrupted her ability to care for her children; she was often unable to attend her son's weekend physical and recreational therapy sessions. Her son also missed his first day of school because she was denied permission by the Sheriff's Department to leave the house to take him there. After five months on electronic monitoring, she took a plea deal, an agreement with the prosecutor in which a person pleads guilty or "no contest, in exchange for reduced charges or sentence, rather than go to trial. A felony record meant that she could have trouble finding a job and housing. Three years later, in 2019, Lavette Mayes, her children still with her, was on staff as an advocate and organizer with the Chicago Community Bond Fund.[3]

Whose lives are considered worthy, and whose are treated as disposable? If patterns and methods of policing have not made that clear, then the ways in which members of poor and criminalized communities are funneled into a Kafkaesque nightmare of pretrial triage should clarify the matter. Triage refers to systems of ranking or prioritizing mass injuries usually suffered on battlefields, in natural or human-caused disasters, and by means of other collective tragedies. The purpose is to allocate limited medical resources to those most likely to survive and benefit from immediate treatment. The criminal justice system also functions as a massive system of triage, though not for the purpose of saving lives. Rather, it determines expendability by sifting, sorting, and prioritizing carceral casualties according to degrees—and at the intersections—of raced, classed, gendered, and ableist disposability. Pretrial processes shatter the legal presumption of innocence, ostensibly a bedrock principle of common law and international human rights. The end result is expansion, not contraction, of systems of carceral control and surveillance. This is called "widening the net." The massive injustices embedded in pretrial triage become clearer when its methods and landmines hidden in its reforms are examined in three areas: money bail and pretrial detention; "evidence-based" predictive risk assessments; and e-incarceration or electronic monitoring (EM).

The overwhelming majority of people in jails—about 70 percent—have not been tried and convicted of the crime for which they have been incarcerated.[4] Most are there because they can't afford the money bail the court imposes (purportedly) as a guarantee that the person will show up for all required court appearances and fulfill any additional requirements or pay fees imposed by the court. In 2020, about 631,000 people were incarcerated in more than three thousand local jails on any given day. People in jail are, as Prison Policy Initiative (PPI) notes, "drastically poorer than their non-incarcerated counterparts."[5] PPI's review of multiple studies drawn from a variety of data sources show that nationwide, Black and Latinx defendants are more likely than white defendants to be detained pretrial or to have to pay money bail, and they receive bail amounts twice as high as white defendants. When Indigenous people are represented in data collection and reporting, they are also much more likely to face higher rates of pretrial detention and higher money bail than white defendants.[6]

Some individuals are released before trial on a "personal" or "own" recognizance bond—on the basis of their written promise that they will return for court dates. The court may impose some conditions on that release, such as drug testing, mandatory participation programs, curfews, or in-person reporting to a supervisory agency. Other people, deemed by the court to be "too dangerous" to release or probable "flight risks" who won't show up for their court dates, are detained without money bail. The overarching criteria for such determinations are almost always some version of "ensuring court appearance and public safety," but in different jurisdictions, rates of detention vary widely, reflecting inconsistency and ambiguity in implementation. Most people in jail are awaiting trials, sometimes for years. Some of these trials will never occur because prosecutors lack sufficient evidence and eventually drop the charges.

Even short periods of incarceration can have a devastating impact on peoples' lives: deportation, loss of employment, housing, child custody, government benefits, and increased risk of premature death. In 2014, federal data confirmed that suicide was the leading cause of death in local jails; most of those suicides occurred within days of being booked into jail.[7] Others going through drug withdrawal die from medical neglect or maltreatment.[8] Incarcerated people are less able to mount strong legal defenses, and people who are detained awaiting trial are more likely to be found guilty. Moreover, the consequences of pretrial detention place enormous pressure on people to plead guilty.

The ACLU calls plea bargaining an "impossible, coercive choice" that "has turned our criminal legal system into a cheap backroom shakedown"—one in which Black and Brown people disproportionately receive the worst prosecutorial deals. Whether or not they committed the offenses they are charged with and regardless of the strength of the case against them, more than 95 percent of people in federal and state courts plead guilty.[9] Prosecutors possess almost unlimited power to intimidate people by means of threats to tack on additional or more severe charges if people choose to go to trial. Prosecutors also often promise to recommend shorter sentences or release on conditions of supervision if a person pleads guilty. Coerced guilty pleas boost prosecutorial "success" rates and attach criminal records, with all the harrowing consequences that accrue, to countless lives. They also reveal the lie of "public safety" arguments for pretrial detention. When many people plead to time served or probation, they are immediately released to the community upon the end of their case, demolishing the claim that they were menaces to public safety while awaiting trial.

CONFRONTING THE MONEY BAIL SYSTEM

Money bail is an amount of money set by a judge that must be paid by a person who is arrested, ostensibly to guarantee that the person will show up for trial. This amount may be hundreds or thousands of dollars, or even hundreds of thousands or millions. When money bail is set, a person may be released on an unsecured or secured bond. An unsecured bond does not require that any part of the amount be paid up front, but if the person fails to appear in court as required, the full amount may be ordered paid. If a secured bond is set, some amount of money must be paid up front. Many people charged—and their families—cannot afford to pay bail of even a few hundred dollars. In most states, that means loved ones may turn to the private, for-profit bail bond industry. In that scenario, families pay a percentage (commonly 10 percent) to the bondsman who then secures that individual's release from jail: $1,000 on a $10,000 bond, for example. That 10 percent premium paid to a for-profit bond agency is nonrefundable, even if charges are dropped, if the person is found not guilty in a court of law, or for any other reason. If the premium is paid on installment, those monthly payments, sometimes with interest, must continue, even if charges are dropped. To secure the remainder of required bail, the bond agent may require the arrested person or their family or friends to have a cosigner or secure the bond with sufficient collateral—a home mortgage with sufficient equity, for instance, or other property or possessions. Framing their work as "protecting the Constitutional right to bail," the predatory for-profit bail bond industry pursues a mission of extracting money from vulnerable people who are least able to pay, often plunging them into even deeper economic hardship and debt.[10]

In the shadows of the bail bond industry stand large bail insurance corporations who underwrite most of the approximately $14 billion in bail bonds issued in the United States each year. The national ACLU and Color of Change describe them as "under-the-radar subsidiaries of large global companies" that have "cultivated a more than 20-year relationship with the American Legislative Exchange Council (ALEC), the pro-corporate, pro-privatization lobby group."[11] The political clout of these companies is enormous: they can write and ensure passage of the laws that benefit them the most even as they undermine, repeal, or defeat alternative reform measures.

Five states—Illinois, Kentucky, Massachusetts, Oregon, and Wisconsin—do not have a private bail bond industry. Direct payment of bail to the court can create an economic incentive to retain the money bail system. In Illinois, circuit courts may permanently retain 10 percent of each "bond deposit" they collect to secure the full bail amount. The second decade of the 2000s saw the emergence of a movement to abolish money bail and end virtually all pretrial detention, or at least most of it. Its overarching goal is transference of more power and resources to communities devastated by structural racism and economic violence. The movement directly names and confronts structural inequalities and violence, seeking transformational change rather than procedural tweaks. MB4L, members of the National Bail Fund Network, and National Bail Out/#FreeBlackMamas, and others educate and organize around these concerns, addressing the needs of Black people, Latinx, Muslims, LGBTQ people, Indigenous peoples, immigrants, and protesters.

One significant accomplishment, designed to reduce the immediate harm of a structurally unjust system, is the creation of community and constituency-based revolving bail funds that pay bond premiums or state deposits for individuals charged with crimes.[12] When a person goes to trial, that money goes back into the fund to pay someone else's money bail and, in some cases, provide other supportive services for those who are released. According to a report by the Smart Decarceration Initiative at Washington University in St. Louis, revolving bond funds have had excellent success rates: 88–98 percent of people honor their bail requirements.[13] Thousands of people have been bailed out, which means they are far more likely to successfully defend against charges. Community-based bail funds also work in partnership with others to effect deeper political and economic change. The Brooklyn Community Bail Fund (BCBF) emphasizes "the power of community bail funds to catalyze and effectuate change as long as they are a wrench in the gears, rather than a cog in the machine."[14]

Scores of people throughout the United States and around the world agree. In the wake of the murder of George Floyd in 2020, according to the *New York Times*, bail funds alone received $90 million in donations to pay money bail in order to release protesters and, more generally, support efforts to end structural police violence against Black communities.[15] The Minnesota Freedom Fund, the largest single recipient of donations, received more than $30 million. They are using this money to strengthen their own work to pay bail and immigrant bonds for those who cannot afford to pay, and to pay bail for people arrested during protests against police violence, including very high money bail amounts imposed on some activists. They also are contributing to the work of the National Bail Fund Network and other bail funds throughout the country.

Not surprisingly, serious obstacles to leveraging bail reform to produce transformational change have become apparent. While a host of powerful political, philanthropic, corporate, and institutional actors are working hard to maintain their power to control the nature and limits of reform, broad-based coalitions of community-based, grassroots organizations are challenging them.

THE CONTESTED TERRAIN OF BAIL REFORM

In 2020, directors of four community bail funds (Brett Davidson in Connecticut, Elisabeth Epps in Colorado, Sharlyn Grace in Chicago, and Atara Rich-Shea in Massachusetts) wrote of the limits of reform. "As tempting as it is to believe that ending money bail is the cure to pretrial injustice," they said, "we must recognize it as merely one piece of a much larger system of racialized social control." The elimination of money bail, they emphasized, would not impede the ability of the state to employ other methods—home confinement, surveillance and monitoring, financial penalties, allegations of "violations, and even outright refusal to release people—for punishing individuals awaiting trial. "Safety," they said, "comes from strong, well-resourced communities, not efficient human caging."[16]

Bail reforms have been enacted or contemplated in a growing number of states. Approaches vary, but the public relations talking points of bipartisan reform are usually simple and clear: (1) reduce or end wealth-based incarceration; (2) detain people pretrial only on the basis of "risk"; (3) save "taxpayer dollars"; and (4) reduce racial disparities. The promises are often misleading; the realities far more complicated. Within reform networks and coalitions, partners with competing interests may engage in double dealing. Bipartisan reform rhetoric often co-opts and distorts abolitionist analysis. Reform organizations created by philanthropic largesse sometimes masquerade as grassroots activism. Law enforcement lobbies and their uncritical supporters are escalating efforts to scale down, derail, repeal, or defeat reforms altogether. A glance at four jurisdictions across the United States illuminates the fraught and rapidly changing nature of the money bail reform terrain.

Cook County, Illinois

The pretrial population in Cook County Jail typically topped 90 percent for years. In 2016, the Chicago Community Bond Fund (CCBF) referred two Cook County plaintiffs to legal advocates to mount a class action lawsuit challenging the constitutionality of their pretrial incarceration based only on inability to afford bail. While the lawsuit was later dismissed on procedural grounds, it helped leverage greater change.

In 2017, Timothy C. Evans, chief judge of the Circuit Court of Cook County, issued General Order 18.8A, a rule instructing judges to set monetary bonds in felony cases only as a last resort, and only in amounts people can pay.[17] That same year, in an effort to undercut much stronger proposals from community bail fund and other grassroots groups, Illinois enacted SB 2034. This weak measure made mild recommendations rather than establishing strong, definite limitations on the use of monetary bond. But the law also contained two significant elements. It affirmed the right to counsel at bail hearings in Illinois, and it required judges to use “the least restrictive conditions or combination of conditions necessary.” SB 2034 also strengthened existing state law authorizing the use of algorithmic risk assessment tools (RATS), discussed later in this chapter. Cook County had already put one of them in use in 2015, the Public Safety Assessment (PSA), created by Arnold Ventures.

According to the Coalition to End Money Bond, the number of people jailed in Cook County on any given day dropped by more than two thousand between 2017 and 2019. Money bonds were used less frequently and set at lower amounts that were more likely to be paid. Less than 1 percent of people released pretrial on felony charges between October 2017 and December 2018 were arrested on new charges considered "violent." Between January and June 2018, when General Order 18.8A was in effect, violent crime in Chicago dropped 8 percent, But implementation has been uneven; many judges ignore the order. The number of "no bond" rulings for people who could afford to post bail rose. Racial disparities between nonmonetary release rates for white and Black people decreased somewhat but remain "significant and disturbing." Moreover, in 2019, about two thousand people remained incarcerated in Cook County Jail solely on the basis of inability to pay a money bond.[18]

In 2019, Chicago's mayor, Lori Lightfoot and then police superintendent Eddie Johnson attacked money bail reform, falsely implying that public safety was endangered by releasing "people with extensive criminal histories."[19] In 2020, Cook County Sheriff Tom Dart made similar charges and attacked the Chicago Community Bond Fund in particular.[20] But in late 2020, a study by researchers for Loyola University's Center for Criminal Justice Research, Policy, and Practice examined the impact of General Order 18.8A on felony bond court decisions, pretrial release, and crime. They found that while the order increased the number of people who were released before trial, there was no significant change in new violent or other forms of crime. Nor was 18.8A associated with any change in the overall amount of crime in Chicago after 2017.[21]

In early 2021, following years of relentless community organizing, galvanized by 2020 uprisings responding to the police murders of George Floyd and Breonna Taylor, and with the leadership of the Illinois Legislative Black Caucus and support of more than one hundred organizations, Illinois became the first (and at the time only) state to completely eliminate the role of secured and unsecured money bond.[22] The historic Pretrial Fairness Act, set for full implementation in January 2023, also will dramatically reduce the number of people in pretrial detention by limiting eligibility for pretrial incarceration and mandating pretrial release in most cases. Notably, it places enforceable restrictions on and regulates the use of risk assessment tools (the use of which was authorized by the state in prior years). It also reduces penalties for people who miss court dates, mandates sentencing credit for time spent and movement permissions on electronic monitoring, and more. Organizers and advocates note that while many challenges remain in order to replace reliance on policing and state violence with new visions of community safety that emphasize living-wage jobs, health, education, and well-being, this marks a major step forward.[23]

California

Senate Bill (SB) 10 originally appeared to be a significant step forward in efforts to name and end the predatory money bail system and the structural racism and poverty that infuse it. But influential community advocates condemned a last-minute, backroom rewrite of the bill, using such phrases as "gutted," "highjacked," and "bait-and-switch" to describe the magnitude of the change. A number of supporters, including California ACLU affiliates, NAACP affiliates, Religious Action Center of Reform Judaism (RAC), CURB, California Attorneys for Criminal Justice, Silicon Valley De-Bug, and Essie Justice Group withdrew endorsement and worked actively for its defeat.[24] Rushed efforts failed to convince its sponsor to pull the bill and then governor Jerry Brown to veto it.[25]

Both versions of SB 10 eliminated money bail altogether. But, as the *Harvard Law Review* noted, "This new law merely replaces an unconstitutional money-bail system with an unconstitutional pretrial detainment system."[26] SB 10 established a new Pretrial Assessment Services Department to determine the risk of release by setting in place procedures that rely heavily on algorithmic risk assessment tools to determine pretrial release risk levels of low, medium, and high, but these can vary by locality. The original version of SB 10 permitted but attempted to limit the scope of use of such tools. But, said Essie Justice Group, an organization that works with women who have incarcerated loved ones, the version finally enacted "broadly refers to risk assessment tools at various stages in the pretrial process to facilitate incarceration."[27] Those tools would become an integral, even universal, part of the process. The final SB 10 also granted broad authority to prosecutors to seek (and judges to approve) preventive detention, even for persons with no prior criminal record who are charged with low-level misdemeanors. SB 10's scheduled October 1, 2019, implementation was stayed pending the outcome of a 2020 referendum to repeal the law, a measure backed by the for-profit bail bond industry.

Proposition 25, titled "Replace Cash Bail with Risk Assessments," was placed on the 2020 ballot as a veto referendum. John Arnold of Arnold Ventures, whose foundation so vigorously promotes the use of its own risk assessment instrument as a linchpin of pretrial reform, donated $5 million to retain the law. A "yes" vote upheld SB 10 and its sweeping reliance upon RATs (the backroom bait and switch measure signed into law); a "no" vote repealed SB 10, keeping in place the use of money bail for people detained awaiting trial.[28] The ACLU, the NAACP, the JusticeLA Coalition, the Essie Group, and others opposed it, but for very different reasons than the bail bond industry, which they also oppose. The measure was defeated. It remains to be seen whether the ACLU, the NAACP, and others can successfully regroup for the fight to end money bail without expanding the widespread use of racially biased risk assessments. Those instruments are discussed later in this chapter.

New York State

The New York state pretrial reform legislation passed in 2019 and implemented in January 2020 significantly reduced but did not completely eliminate money bail.[29] By early April, a powerful political backlash by law enforcement produced a rollback of some of its changes. Several provisions of the original legislation removed or limited the discretionary power of police, prosecutors, and judges to make arbitrary and discriminatory decisions, particularly for people charged with misdemeanors and some low-level felonies. Most people charged with such offenses could not be detained before trial. Money bail could be set in certain circumstances, both for cases involving misdemeanors and felonies, but the law required judges to consider the ability of the person to pay. The law permitted the use of risk assessments, endorsed electronic monitoring as an "alternative" to pretrial detention, and expanded the use of non-monetary conditions for pretrial release: travel restrictions, mandatory check-ins, curfews, and more.

Survived & Punished NY (S&PNY), a grassroots prison abolitionist organization dedicated to ending the criminalization of survivors of gender-based violence, did not support the original reforms. While acknowledging that fewer people would likely be detained before trial, the group pointed out that the bail reform package not only failed to challenge the premise of pretrial incarceration but also endorsed greater use of pretrial surveillance and monitoring.[30]

The Brooklyn Community Bail Fund noted that while the reform had the potential to significantly reduce pretrial jail populations, it also "leaves behind thousands of people who will continue to be subject to money bail and pretrial detention." Moreover, because New York is the only state that explicitly regulates nonprofit bail funds, BCBF said the legislation effectively transforms bail funds "into a permanent fixture of the system which we have fought so tirelessly to dismantle."[31] The Charitable Bail Organizations Act, enacted in 2012, permitted nonprofit bail funds to pay bail only on misdemeanor charges where bail set was less than $2,000. But in 2019, legislators expanded the ability of these funds to pay bonds where bail was set up to $10,000 in both misdemeanor and felony cases. This passed major governmental responsibility for mitigating wealth-based discrimination onto private, nonprofit bail funds. Accordingly, the Brooklyn Community Bail Fund announced that on January 21, 2020, it would no longer operate as a revolving bail fund since the funds "became an escape hatch for a political system that lacked the courage to end money bail." The Fund went on to say:

> Dismantling a system requires that we explicitly be in tension with it. The system required money in exchange for freedom and we paid it to free 4,700 people. We repeatedly fought back against every attempt to institutionalize us, rejecting system actor offers to make our job as a bail fund easier as a way of appeasing us. We were insistent that bail funds could not be part of a long-term decarceral strategy, but rather needed to be a temporary intervention. . . . As the largest community bail fund in the country, we feel a duty to reject half-measures and false compromises that would require us to prop up an unjust system."[32]

BCBF simultaneously launched the New York Immigrant Freedom Fund project, which works in partnership with other organizations, helping to pay immigration bonds required by ICE, strengthen the ability of people to fight deportation efforts, and advocate for just immigration policies.

Prior to implementation of bail reform in New York, law enforcement officials launched a series of efforts to delay and derail it. Outgoing New York Police Department (NYPD) commissioner James O'Neill and his successor, Dermot Shea, claimed reforms would interfere with effective policing. In late 2019, through coordinated press conferences across the state and other public events, law enforcement officials—district attorneys, chiefs of police, and sheriffs—demanded that state leadership delay implementation of the legislation, suggesting it would free dangerous people to pursue crime sprees. Community bail funds across New York countered false claims. In early 2020, as the reforms took effect, lowering the number of people jailed pretrial in New York City alone by about 40 percent,[33] law enforcement fearmongering escalated, relying heavily on sensationalized cases and cherry-picked data, challenged by public defenders and criminal law scholars.[34] New York City's mayor Bill De Blasio and Governor Andrew Cuomo both supported changes in the law, including expanding the existing list of bail eligible or qualifying offenses and concessions to prosecutors, including a new $40 million allocation for additional staff and computer technology updates.[35] Police and law enforcement lobbies didn't feel the changes went far enough.

PREDICTIVE RISK ASSESSMENT TOOLS (RATS)

Risk assessments are algorithmic tools that purport to predict future risks of rearrest and missing court dates. Some also claim to predict "dangerousness," which is to say, the likelihood that people already charged with an offense will be arrested for a future crime of violence if they are released pretrial. Since the early 2000s, private companies, state systems, and public-private partnerships have introduced a variety of algorithmic risk assessment instruments, to help officials make decisions about sentencing and conditions of release. One of the best known is the widely utilized COMPAS (Correctional Offender Management Profiling for Alternative Sanctions) developed by Northpointe, Inc., a for-profit company since rebranded as Equivant. In 2018, the company's research division designed and began validation studies on the California Pretrial Assessment (CAPA) for use in conjunction with that state's SB 10 pretrial reforms.

Leading an effort to expand the use of risk assessments, the John and Laura Arnold Foundation (now Arnold Ventures) prioritized development of a new instrument, the Public Safety Assessment, or PSA, designed exclusively for pretrial use. In development and testing in multiple jurisdictions since 2012, the PSA has been offered to jurisdictions free of charge since 2018. Subsidized assistance and support in utilizing the instrument is made available, although jurisdictions must dedicate technological and staff resources to its use. By 2020, the PSA was being used statewide in Arizona, Kentucky, New

Jersey, and Utah, and in a number of major urban areas throughout the United States. Nine risk factors are taken into account including age at current arrest and a series of factors related to arrests, convictions, pending charges, and failure to appear. Points are assigned for different factors on two separate scales: Failure to Appear (FTA) and New Criminal Activity (NCA). Points are also added to a third scale: New Violent Criminal Activity (NVCA), and this produces a yes/no flag for "elevated likelihood of being arrested for a new violent crime." Unlike some other risk assessments, PSA scoring does not require an interview with the defendant. The PSA began as a proprietary instrument, but the scoring system was made publicly available years later, in response to concerted pushback criticizing the initial lack of clarity about it.[36]

The seductive promise for these assessment tools is that "evidence-based" methodologies are objective and that the predictive information they produce is free of the taint of racial bias. But in 2018, more than one hundred civil rights, digital justice, and community-based organizations said, in a joint statement, "We believe that jurisdictions should not use risk assessment instruments in pretrial decision making, and instead move to end secured money bail and decarcerate most accused people pretrial." Signatories included the ACLU, NAACP, Mijente, Prison Policy Initiative, The Center for Media Justice, National Bail Out, and many more. But without endorsing pretrial risk assessment instruments, the signatories went on to make a series of recommendations for mitigating their harms.[37] Recommendations for "best practices" abound in the field of reform, but they are never universally and consistently implemented. Even if they were, there are no good justice-centered reasons for using risk assessments. There are, however, compelling reasons for rejecting their use.

Risk Factors and Bias

The use of predictive risk assessment instruments is touted as a non-discriminatory, even painless, way of starting to unravel the impacts of racism, poverty, and other inequalities in the criminal justice system. But the data driving predictive risk assessment algorithms comes primarily from policing (arrest) and court (appearances and convictions) records. Accordingly, the results uncritically reflect decisions of law enforcement and criminal legal authorities.

Neither the COMPAS nor PSA instruments openly ask for racial identification, but some instruments do score variables that are highly correlated with race and class, including neighborhood, income, employment history, and more. In 2016, ProPublica conducted an extensive examination of thousands of risk scores, established by a COMPAS instrument, assigned to people arrested in a single Florida county in a two-year period. The predictive benchmark was recidivism, specifically being charged with new violent crimes over the next two years. The study's authors described Northpointe scoring as "remarkably unreliable" in forecasting violent crime." They also "turned up significant racial disparities." Black defendants were wrongly flagged as future perpetrators of crime at almost twice the rate of white defendants. White defendants were more often wrongly labeled as "low risk" than Black defendants.[38] In 2018, different researchers demonstrated that in predictive recidivism, "COMPAS is no more accurate or fair than predictions made by people with little or no criminal justice expertise."[39] Worse, the use of recidivism predictions and rates as a metric of reform success or failure is, as Marie Gottschalk emphasizes in a detailed discussion, unreliable and misleading.[40]

In 2019, twenty-seven prominent researchers from Massachusetts Institute of Technology (MIT), Harvard, Princeton, New York University (NYU), University of California–Berkeley, and Columbia University released an open statement of grave concern regarding the use of algorithmic risk assessments in lowering pretrial jail populations. In addition to noting the "deeply flawed and racially biased" data used to build risk assessment instruments, the researchers noted that there are "no technical fixes" for the production of distorted results drawn primarily from criminal justice data.[41] A 2019 report funded by Arnold Ventures, sought to respond to critiques by arguing that risk assessments could be useful "beyond the algorithm" in producing more safety and justice.[42]

Conflating Failure to Appear with Flight Risk

Pretrial risk assessments score defendants' prior "failures to appear" (FTA) for scheduled court dates without inquiring into the reasons for missing those dates. Law enforcement and political critics of reform often equate aggregate information about FTAs with "flight risk," suggesting an inherent element of danger in those who "fail to appear." Yet most people who miss court appearances aren't intentionally trying to evade the law. Most are poor and often faced with circumstances they can't control: they are in ill-health or have transportation or child-care needs that they can't afford. Some people are homeless; they don't receive the notifications. Many have simply forgotten or have honestly been confused by the court system. Writing in *The Appeal*, Ethan Corey and Puck Lo report that "an increasing number of studies show that FTA rates can be drastically reduced simply by redesigning confusing summons notices and sending text message reminders."[43] Others point out that when circumstances beyond a person's control necessitate rescheduling a court appearance, that ought to be as easy as making a telephone call or texting to set up a new date. Beyond that, people need resources for transportation, childcare, and other essential supports.

"Unintended" Use of Risk Assessment Instruments

The Pretrial Justice Institute insists that pretrial risk assessment tools are designed only to help judges identify *conditions* of release (sometimes referred to as "conditions of supervision"), not to make "release or detain" decisions or set bond amounts. The Institute's *Scan of Pretrial Practices 2019* says that 83 percent of counties surveyed reported using pretrial assessment tools or screens between arrest and first court appearance. Of those counties, 73 percent were misusing pretrial risk assessment tools for unintended purposes, and half of all the counties were using them to set money bail.[44] The widespread use of the tools in an increasing number of jurisdictions strongly suggests that predictive risk assessments can and will be used for and to legitimize any purpose the jurisdiction deems useful.

Misleading Predictions/Overestimates of Violence

Chelsea Barabas and Karthick Dinakar, research scientists at MIT, and Colin Doyle, a Harvard University legal scholar, say that pretrial risk assessment tools are fundamentally flawed and "virtually useless for identifying who will commit violence if released pretrial." That is, in part, because "pretrial violence is so rare, it is virtually impossible for any statistical model to identify people who are more likely than not to commit a violent crime." Yet the simple—and misleading—labels attached to risk scores make the likelihood of future violence more predictable than it is, influencing judges to overestimate its incidence. Barabas, Dinakar, and Doyle say that public safety must be addressed through broader social policies and community investment, not through "big data forecasting" that "risks cementing the irrational fears and flawed logic of mass incarceration behind a veneer of scientific objectivity."[45]

E-INCARCERATION: DIGITAL PRISON EXPANSION

Reforms that promise to reduce rates of pretrial incarceration while also reducing or ending money bail often rely on formulas for establishing "conditions of supervision" or "enhanced supervision" for people who are not released solely on their own recognizance. For some, those conditions include the use of electronic monitoring (EM). The increasing use of EM devices, including for many people charged with minor offenses, is marketed as a humane "alternative to detention"—an ATD in industry jargon. EM devices are used in every state, in the District of Columbia, and by the federal government to monitor the movements and control the activities of tens of thousands of people before trial and those who are on probation and parole. Since 2004, electronic monitoring, especially the use of ankle monitoring, has also been increasingly used by ICE to track and control many immigrants classified as "low risk" who are released from detention pending resolution of deportation proceedings.[46]

But *humane* is one of the most overused, malleable, and hypocritical words in the reform lexicon. Its use is largely rhetorical, deployed to reassure the public that the system needs only a few tweaks to ensure that people are safe and treated with dignity. Electronic monitoring is, first and foremost, a surveillance technology adopted with no effective oversight or regulation regarding the use, sharing, or privacy of the data it collects. Its ready availability permits proponents to argue that they are reducing mass incarceration by replacing cement-and-steel cages with a community-based, supportive alternative. James Kilgore, director of the Challenging E-Carceration project, counters that prisons come in many forms. E-carceration is not an alternative *to* but another form *of* incarceration.[47] Albert Fox Cahn of the Surveillance Technology Oversight Project calls the phenomenon "prisons built from data.[48]

These prisons, utilizing ever more sophisticated technologies and extending into homes, workplaces, and communities, are punitive, unnecessary, and harmful. Writing about house arrest in their critique of popular criminal legal system reforms, longtime journalists and anti-prison activists Maya Schenwar and Victoria Law point out that electronic monitoring turns a person's home into a grim site of carceral confinement. "GPS systems enable every movement to be tracked," they say. "EM is a type of prison that rides along *with you*, strapped to your body."[49]

Ankle shackles are common to most systems; some companies also offer wrist devices and/or smartphone systems. Some devices are capable of two-way communication, with listening functions that can be remotely enabled, resulting in complaints of invasion of privacy.[50] More recently, mobile monitoring apps and services that send notifications and track court appearances and other requirements of supervision have been introduced. Some are experimenting with biometric "compliance monitoring"—technologies requiring voiceprint or facial recognition check-in confirmation.[51]

Most pretrial reforms rely on electronic monitoring as one of a number of possible "conditions of supervision" for release from pretrial detention, with or without bail. At least fifty organizations, including the ACLU, several community bail funds, the National Lawyers Guild, and others, have endorsed a set of guidelines, prepared by Challenging E-Carceration, for respecting the rights of individuals on EM.[52] Intended as a harm reduction tool, the guidelines include such elements as credit for time served under electronic custodial detention and use of GPS-enabled monitors only as a last option. But "best practices" guidelines are impossible to implement consistently throughout a decentralized tangle of jurisdictions, each atop its own terrain of competing political, carceral, and corporate imperatives. While it remains in use, many individuals who face a choice between EM and pretrial detention may, understandably, feel it is the most reasonable option for them. But there are no compelling justice-centered arguments for the use of electronic monitoring as a condition of pretrial release. While advocates for EM suggest that use of the technology helps to improve court appearance rates, no research to date backs up this claim.[53] The key factors to reducing failures to appear for court appearances are making sure people know their court dates, are well enough to attend, and have the resources, including transportation, childcare, and employer support to do so.

Restrictions on movement can, however, adversely affect a person's ability to obtain essential services and exercise essential responsibilities. For example, a person may be unable to obtain health care support—including medications and both routine and emergency care—in a timely way if a supervisor's permission is delayed or refused. A person's access to legal resources and due process may be restricted. Curfews and movement restrictions may adversely affect a person's ability to participate in parenting, caregiving, and community life. Restrictions reduce—in some cases destroy—possibilities for employment.[54]

The claim that EM is cost-effective is a sleight of hand: cost effective for whom? It may be cheaper than the per diem cost of being physically incarcerated; jail costs typically run several hundred dollars per person per day. Seventy-one percent of the respondents surveyed in The Pretrial Justice Institute's *Scan of Pretrial Practices 2019* utilized surveillance technologies, including electronic monitoring. More than half of the jurisdictions using these technologies charged "user fees" for them.[55] These sometimes include initial fees for placement of the devices plus fees ranging from around $10 per day in some jurisdictions to more in others. Monthly fees may amount to as much as $300 and no part of them is refundable, even if criminal charges are ultimately dropped or persons being monitored are not found guilty at trial. People who fail to pay their fees in a timely manner may be sent back to jail.[56] Moreover, EM is big business with little, if any, regulation or oversight. That means it is used in the ways corporations and law enforcement want it used, regardless of ethical concerns. And it means that the data collected are a corporate and/or law enforcement commodity that potentially can be mined for any political or economic purpose.

Then there is the matter of possible conflicts of interest, bribes, and kickbacks. From 2012 to 2014, businessman and Mississippi government consultant Robert Simmons received $4,000 per month from Sentinel Offender Services, LLC, a large corporation providing electronic monitoring services nationwide. Beginning in 2012, Sentinel contracted with the Mississippi Department of Corrections (MDOC) to monitor people on probation or parole. At the time, Christopher Epps was the MDOC commissioner. According to the *Clarion Ledger*, "Simmons paid a kickback of $1,400 a month from his consulting fee to Epps." For both, this was part of a much broader corruption case involving additional MDOC contracts, "consulting fees," bribes, and kickbacks.[57] And in 2019, the

New Orleans watchdog organization CourtWatch NOLA (CWN) reported on a larger pattern in which Parish Criminal District Court Judge Paul Bonin accepted a campaign loan from ETOH Monitoring, LLC executives, along with a decade's worth of campaign contributions from ETOH executives. The company is owned by two New Orleans attorneys. Unlike some other cities, New Orleans did not have a central contract for electronic monitoring services; accordingly, decisions about what company to use were left to judges or the defendants themselves. CWN found that Bonin also steered a number of defendants to ETOH and used his power to refuse to release people from ankle monitoring until they had paid ETOH its approximately $10-per-day fees.[58]

REPRODUCING STRUCTURAL RACISM AND POVERTY

A society honestly seeking to reduce structural forms of inequality and violence cannot ignore race, class, gender, and ableist processes of criminalization, policing, and predictive profiling. And it should never reproduce them. Yet that is precisely what is happening in so much of what passes as pretrial reform. Criminalization is embedded in the very notion of risk assessments and imposition of counterproductive "conditions of supervision." Strategies and procedures for the control, and containment of criminalized notions of "dangerousness" and risk substitute for commitments to structural social and economic justice. Endless resources flow into these strategies and procedures, and into the creation of new capacity to administer, evaluate, and report on them. Procedural tweaks, predictive analytics, and digital prisons are expanding rather than shrinking systems of carceral control and surveillance. In doing so, they legitimate the deepening structural inequalities and violence that the people coming out of jails and prisons inevitably encounter. The challenge is not to fine-tune injustice, inequality, and violence. The challenge is to develop the imagination and collective political will to insist on a different path forward.

5 Courts, Sentencing, and "Diversion"

Those without the capital get the punishment.

—Sister Helen Prejean, *The Death of Innocents*, 2005

Processes of criminalization and policing provide the race- and class-based flow of bodies into the criminal legal system; they identify and stigmatize "disposable" populations. Prosecutors and judges, together with sentencing reforms and processes of diversion and supervision, also constitute a nexus of carceral control. While there is a tendency to think of mass criminalization primarily in terms of jails, prisons, and detention centers, the reality is more complex. It also includes probation and other so-called community-based options: "problem-solving" specialty courts, "alternatives to incarceration," and more. In 2020, about 6.7 million people were under some form of carceral surveillance and control.[1]

More and more, these sentencing options blur together as collective failure.[2] The increasingly onerous requirements of specialty courts, probation, and other diversion programs, combined with schedules of fines and fees, often function as pathways to jail or prison. Those who complete requirements without being incarcerated experience all the harms of being monitored, surveilled, and often thrown into debt or deeper debt. While sentencing reforms provide much-needed relief for some people, they rarely make major permanent dents in rates of incarceration. At the same time, they "widen the net" by placing many more people who should never have been arrested in the first place in some form of fee-generating, "offender-funded" community corrections. The Mississippi experience helps to illustrate the point.

MISSISSIPPI AND THE RUSE OF REFORM

Mississippi House Bill 585, was signed into law in 2014, a time when there was little progressive scrutiny of bipartisan reform agendas. The bill was heralded as "a comprehensive criminal justice reform package that protects public safety, reins in corrections costs and restores clarity to Mississippi's criminal sentencing guidelines."[3] The Mississippi legislation was developed in consultation with the PEW Charitable Trusts' Public Safety Performance Project with support from the Justice Reinvestment Initiative described in Chapter 2. The legislation also had the support of the Mississippi Bar Association, the Southern Poverty Law Center of Mississippi, the Mississippi Economic Council, the Christian Action Coalition, the American Civil Liberties Union of Mississippi, and the Mississippi Center for Public Safety.[4]

At the time, Mississippi was second only to Louisiana in incarceration rates, with more than twenty thousand prisoners in the state, housed in three state prisons, and at that time, six private correctional facilities.[5] This number included more than twenty-five hundred held at the Adams County Correctional Center, a Corrections Corporation of America (since rebranded as CoreCivic) facility that contracts with the Federal Bureau of Prisons to hold immigration detainees. The state was spending $389 million annually on corrections, with public revenue flowing mostly to private corporations that managed the majority of Mississippi's prisons and community corrections.[6]

The promise of cost savings and increasing public safety provided the rationale for Mississippi reform. HB 585 was designed to save costs by limiting expensive prison beds to those classified as violent and "habitual" offenders. In Mississippi, nonviolent offenses are included in "habitual" classifications. For the first time, Mississippi legislation defined "crime of violence" and required people convicted of violent crimes to serve at least 50 percent of the sentence imposed by the court. In addition, HB 585 clarified the difference between drug possession and drug trafficking and increased the monetary limits on what could be considered felony theft. Those convicted of violent offenses would supposedly go to prison while others could be supervised in a community context.[7]

HB 585 promised that savings accrued from prison reduction—Pew suggested that could amount to some $266 million by 2024—would be reinvested in community corrections and in reentry programs. These alternatives and supports included specialty courts for veterans and drug courts for treatment rather than imprisonment; identification (ID) cards for those leaving prison to help them secure housing and jobs; training for incarcerated people who were eligible for parole; and the prevention of return to prison for those guilty of technical probation/parole violations. These justice reinvestment efforts would be data-driven, evaluated with evidence-based assessments, and monitored by an oversight council.

Despite widespread support at the time of passage, HB 585 was met with some suspicion and criticism. The Mississippi Chapter of the NAACP harbored reservations and publicly voiced concern that House Bill 585 might actually increase incarceration costs and rates.[8] That is because the reform legislation also stiffened drug penalties, expanded definitions of "violent crime" to now include burglary (long classified under the federal Uniform Crime Reports as a property offense), and shifted costs of implementation from the state to cities and counties. In addition, the new legislation widened the pool of people—some reformers now refer to them as "clients"—subject to Mississippi's already privatized probation system. Private probation services are, in fact, a system of extortion for poor defendants who face jail time for the most minor infractions, including failure to pay fees. Mississippi is one of the states indicted in a 2014 Human Rights Watch Report, *Profiting from Probation: America's Offender Funded Probation Program.*[9]

Like other bipartisan reform legislation on which it was modeled, Mississippi's HB 585 was designed to make modest adjustments in rates of incarceration with an eye toward future growth and cost savings. The legislation does not address the race and class disparities in the Mississippi system; as of 2019, Mississippi incarcerated Black people at 3.5 times the rate of whites; they accounted for 37 percent of the state's population, but 61.4 percent of its prisoners.[10] Nor was this about stopping the flow of mostly Black youth into the criminal legal system via school-to-prison pipelines. The Meridian School District, for example, was subject to federal intervention.[11] HB 585 also failed to address the egregious conditions in Mississippi youth and adult prisons, which have spurred multiple investigations and federal lawsuits. The notorious Mississippi State Prison, also known as Parchman Farm, is the centerpiece of a state prison system founded as a postbellum-era network of convict lease and prison farms benefitting the prison system and private businesses.[12]

Five years later, as President Trump touted Mississippi as a national model of criminal justice reform, earlier cautionary warnings were confirmed. According to a ProPublica investigation, Mississippi's prison population did fall briefly by two thousand prisoners via early parole, but in 2019, the numbers began to creep back up. The increases—despite promises to the contrary—were primarily due to probation and parole revocations, such as denial of release, due to often minor infractions that constitute the conditions of probation or parole.[13] Reentry programs and other "justice reinvestment" initiatives—drug courts, in-prison programs, and more—were not funded by the state as originally promised. Instead, savings realized by the initial reductions in state prison populations were spent for tax cuts and school voucher programs.[14] This is not to suggest that funding the justice reinvestment initiatives would have done more than widen the net of criminal legal control. But the failure to even comply with the minimal promises illustrates an all too common theme of such bipartisan reform measures—they are sold and resold on the promise of cost savings and reinvestment which rarely materialize for the benefit of communities bearing the brunt of police and prison violence in the long run.

Mississippi reforms did not improve life for the vast majority of people who are arrested and placed under some form of carceral control. Conditions in the state's prisons, always horrific, continued to deteriorate. Bipartisan reformers are quick to attribute the problems to crumbling infrastructure, poor working conditions for staff, and staff shortages—all of which require an even greater influx of money and resources to address. To the contrary: no amount of funding can address the inhumane conditions foundational to the carceral system itself, a subject we explore in more detail in Chapter 6. But Mississippi, a state purportedly committed to a model template of contemporary sentencing reform, continues to regard the people in its custody as disposable. In such circumstances, especially in prisons where staff encourage conflicts among different groups of prisoners as a means of order maintenance, violence invariably erupts.

Between late December 2019 and mid-March 2020, twenty-seven prisoners were killed or died in Mississippi prisons, the result of in-prison uprising and some combination of suicide, medical neglect, and "unknown" causes.[15] Ten of these deaths occurred at Parchman. The uprising led to a state-wide lockdown and the reopening of prison units that had been closed and/or condemned. While state officials blamed the violence on prison gangs and contraband cell phones, prisoner advocates, family members, and a federal lawsuit filed on behalf of twenty-nine prisoners claimed the state was at fault. The situation resulted, they said, from a deadly mix of corrupt guards, lack of supervision, disgusting living conditions, and prisons dilapidated through underfunding and neglect.[16]

Newly-elected governor Tate Reeves announced he would immediately implement a series of reforms to address the issues, and he appointed the controversial former warden of Louisiana State Penitentiary at Angola, Burl Cain, to take charge.[17] The so-called "reforms" were actually calls for more prisoner repression—crackdowns on cell phones and other contraband, additional correctional officers, and the reopening of more secure facilities.[18] This approach blames the incarcerated for the situation while failing to acknowledge that prisons themselves are sites of state violence. Certainly, these new "reforms" have not dented the death toll, and in fact, have ignored and perhaps exacerbated a mounting crisis.

Between March and December of 2020, another sixty-six prisoners died in Mississippi prisons, again, via multiple means: homicide, suicide, illness, and a wave of unchecked COVID-19 cases.[19] The Mississippi Department of Corrections has done little to respond to the COVID-19 pandemic and offers no routine testing, no early releases of prisoners at increased risk, and inadequate sanitation measures. This neglect led to another class action lawsuit, filed on behalf of vulnerable prisoners by the Mississippi Justice Center and the ACLU of Mississippi. The lawsuit was brought under the American's with Disabilities Act, the Rehabilitation Act, and the Eighth Amendment to the Constitution.[20] By the end of 2020, the case was still pending, but the litigation exposes the lie that Mississippi is a model of criminal justice reform.

A look at Mississippi's "sweeping" reforms is instructive. Criminal justice reform rhetoric rolls out easily, but the public relations blitz that accompanies a reform campaign always obscures reality. Few people pay close attention to impacts of implementation over time. In this instance, the justice reinvestment savings were not used as promised. But even the original promise only meant that "saved" money was supposed to be used to increase investment in systems of carceral control and the public/private partnerships that sustain them. The fundamental challenge is decarceration, but the Mississippi reforms did not go deep, and while various offenses were reclassified, some of those reclassifications meant longer sentences. The question of lengthy prison sentences for "habitual offenders" convicted of non-violent offenses was not addressed. The net-widening and fee-based impacts of private probation services and specialty courts on poor Black people and other marginalized populations presumably were acceptable to reformers; at least they were not strenuously challenged. Reentry supports and ID and job readiness services could and should just as easily be located in communities—with no ties, formal or informal, to the criminal legal system—where they would be available to all who need them. But that would require a fundamentally different approach to unraveling carceral harms while simultaneously investing in community well-being.

DETENTION, DIVERSION, AND DISCRETION

At every stage of the criminal legal system, different actors wield different kinds of discretionary authority to determine the fates of people who are stopped, arrested, and adjudicated for alleged wrongdoing. Legislators define what is crime and appropriate punishment—and what is not. Police decide to watch, stop, question, cite, frisk, and arrest—or not. Prosecutors decide to charge and seek bail—or not. Judges and juries find guilt—or not; they determine sentences according to various schemes and distribution of authority: death sentences, detention in prisons or jails, parole or other diversion to community corrections. And at every stage, this decision-making power is tainted by preconceptions of crime and criminality based on race, class, gender, age, disability, and place. While decisions may be tempered or shifted to other agents in the process, and while various predictive risk assessment tools may be used in final determinations, discretionary power is never rendered inoperative.

Current efforts at sentencing reform are marketed as necessary in order to undo the harms of the previous cycle of "tough-on-crime" bipartisan reforms of the 1970s and 1980s.[21] At that time, indeterminate sentencing came under growing liberal and conservative critique. The trend toward indeterminate sentencing was ostensibly rooted in a rehabilitative ideal. This model placed great discretionary power in the hands of judges, who were free to sentence based on their views of rehabilitative potential, with the result that sentence lengths could offer wide latitude—fifteen years to life, for example. Parole boards were similarly empowered to release or deny release based on their assessment of a person's rehabilitative progress.[22]

From the perspective of liberals, judicial discretion often translated into discrimination, with Black people and other defendants of color receiving longer sentences for similar legal offenses. Parole boards were widely perceived to be susceptible to political influence and corruption. For the conservative-Right, indeterminate sentencing meant there was no certainty regarding the real extent to which individual defendants would be punished. Agreement on the issue of determinate sentencing came during one of those calls for retribution and incapacitation as correctional goals that periodically crop up in the United States. Although there were differences regarding the importance of rehabilitation, the debate was ultimately won by growing agreement among both liberals and conservatives that punishment, especially for those with prior records, should take precedence over rehabilitation.[23]

The result was a shift—both federally and on the state level—to more determinate sentencing models that mandated fixed, often lengthy, prison sentences for a range of offenses. Some of these schemes relied on sentencing guidelines that also factored in a defendant's criminal history score and often prescribed mandatory minimums for specific crimes, including mandatory life for "habitual offenders."[24] In addition to criminal history scores, various other penalty enhancements—harsher penalties—were attached for purported gang affiliation, hate crimes, and crimes involving use of firearms. These enhancements often mean the difference between probation and prison; they can add years to sentences.[25]

An assumption that criminal records are an unerring and accurate reflection of criminality pervades these decision-making processes when in fact those records reflect the race-, class-, gender-, and place-based nature of policing. Sentencing guidelines effectively removed a great deal of discretion from judges and shifted it toward legislators, sentencing commissions, police, and prosecutors. To take note of that is not to argue that judges are unbiased; they are not.[26] Judicial discretion can result in severe miscarriages of justice. Yet fixed sentencing models, especially those that factor in "criminal history," create opportunities for both police and prosecutors to opt for—or at least threaten—serious charges. The purpose is to exert immense pressure on defendants to plea-bargain and/or provide authorities with "substantial assistance" by informing on others, truthfully or not.[27]

While the publicly stated goal of fixed sentencing schemes was to ensure detention of serious and repeat offenders, it had profound implications for those who were to be "diverted" from prison by means of probation and other community alternatives. In the truest sense, diversion means removal from the reach of the system altogether. In reform templates, diversion most often means shifting management to a different venue of control; the line between diversion and detention is increasingly moot.

Originally designed as less complicated alternatives to incarceration, probation and other community correctional options increasingly entangle defendants with burdensome expectations and escalating schedules of fines and fees that increase the likelihood of eventual detention. The rise of prosecutorial power in conjunction with broken-windows policing produced a massive increase in the number of misdemeanors, public order offenses, and lower-level drug cases that flow through the system. These cases, while often initially subject to fines, frequently become jailable if conditions of supervision are not met. Since the 1980s, sentencing reforms meant to restrain unaccountable wielding of discretionary authority, now face scrutiny of their own.

Detention: Determinate Sentencing and Criminal History

The bipartisan sentencing reforms agenda is publicly promoted as a way to reduce "overcriminalization" and reduce correctional costs. Moreover, the rise of lengthy fixed sentences is an obvious driver of high incarceration rates. Reform templates typically seek to address this by reducing sentence length, including mandatory minimums, for nonviolent offenses.[28] These efforts cannot produce permanent reductions sufficient to dismantle mass incarceration.

The shift toward mandatory minimum sentences in the 1980s plays a significant role in the expansion of prison sentences and correctional control. The federal 1984 Sentencing Reform Act and the Anti-Drug Abuse Act of 1986 initially embraced this shift. States followed suit, and legislation mandating a definite, often harsh, period of imprisonment proliferated.[29] The most notorious mandatory minimum sentences are for drug-related offenses—for example, the initial 100:1 sentencing disparity for crack and powder cocaine possession. But the mandatory minimum template spread more widely to a range of other legal violations, both violent and nonviolent, and usually mandates lengthy sentences. Over time, at least forty states adopted "truth in sentencing" laws, which require people to serve at least 85 percent of their sentences behind bars.[30]

A particular version of mandatory minimums, "three-strikes," was also adopted by the federal government and twenty-eight states. Popularized in the early 1990s, three-strikes laws mandate life in prison for a third felony conviction. These laws do not always distinguish between violent and nonviolent felonies and are further complicated when the third felony is a "wobbler," or an offense that could be categorized as either a misdemeanor or a felony.[31] Three-strikes laws are ostensibly designed to control "habitual offenders"—those who have prior felony convictions. The flawed notion that criminal convictions are an accurate predictor of future criminality drives these laws.[32]

In addition to three-strikes laws, forty-nine states permit a sentence of life without parole (LWOP) for some violent crimes and, occasionally, for certain drug-related offenses. As states increasingly repeal capital punishment, LWOP has become the preferred alternative to the death penalty.[33] But LWOP is a death sentence in slow motion. Until US Supreme Court rulings prohibited the practice in a series of decisions rendered in 2010, 2012, and 2016, juveniles who were charged as adults could also receive LWOP sentences.[34] A 2017 study from the Sentencing Project found that there were more people serving life sentences (two hundred six thousand) nationally than the entire prison population in 1970 (one hundred ninety-six thousand).[35]

The felony murder doctrine also permits mandatory sentences in most states. This holds that anyone involved in a felony where a death occurs, is liable for that death in the first degree. Felony murder does not require proof of intent to kill. All who are involved in the felony may be charged with felony murder if someone dies, whether or not they participated in causing the death—and sometimes even if they weren't physically present when the death occurred. Due to the unjust application of the harshest penalties for non-premeditated murders, this doctrine has been abolished in a handful of states and its abolition is under consideration in several more.[36]

Mandatory minimum sentences are sometimes attached to sentencing guidelines, which, as of 2020, are in operation in twenty-seven states and at the federal level.[37] First adopted in Minnesota in 1979, this model for calculating determinate sentences quickly spread. Sentencing guidelines are developed and reviewed by sentencing commissions established by legislatures. Members are often appointed by the executive branch. The role of the commission is to set and review sentencing guidelines based on "data-driven" decisions.[38] The implied promise is that sentencing commissions will be more "objective" and less prone to political pressure, though little evidence suggests that this is the case.

Sentencing guidelines calculate a presumptive range of time (either in prison or on probation) that allows judges some latitude in making the final decision. Sentence recommendations are based on a formula that combines Offense and Offender Characteristics.[39] Offense characteristics rank the seriousness of offenses; violent crimes are ranked highest. The ranking of some other offenses may be enhanced by alleged gang affiliation, bias motivation, or the presence of a gun. Offender characteristics include the number and type of prior offenses (felonies, misdemeanors, juvenile adjudications) and custody status (incarcerated or probation) at the time. Typically, sentencing guidelines use grids for calculating the presumptive sentence based on seriousness of the offense and criminal history score. Violent offenses and a lengthy criminal history score both lead to presumptive prison time.

A key feature of all current determinate sentencing models is the substantial weight given to prior criminal legal system records, whether factored into sentencing guidelines or habitual offender laws. "Criminal history"—that is, a record of prior arrests and/or convictions, is believed to have predictive power. This indicator strongly influences the determination of lengthy sentences for nonviolent offenses and is the foundation for risk-assessment measurements.[40]

Reliance on criminal history scores for sentencing assumes that past convictions are predictive of criminal activity both past and future. This approach ignores the role of race, class, gender, age, disability, and place in the likelihood of police encounters/arrests; it fails to consider lack of adequate legal counsel and pressures to plea bargain. Recent research raises questions about the efficacy of criminal history scores in deterring or reducing violent and nonviolent offenses. Worse, reliance on this metric produces increased prison populations and increases in numbers of older and elderly incarcerated people.[41]

Reformers have addressed reliance on criminal history scores in a number of ways, all of which are inadequate. Several states have offered post hoc remediation in the form of criminal record relief.

These plans vary. Some provide for automatic expungement of minor criminal records, while others require going through an application process. Criminal record databases are often fraught with error, and expungement is no guarantee that records are actually sealed. In Chapter 6, we take note of ways some states have eased some restrictions brought about by felony records, including voting, licensing, and employment.[42] While this relief is welcome, such measures mitigate harms without simultaneously addressing the larger social and economic conditions that produce structural inequality. Within some bipartisan coalitions, there is growing difference of opinion concerning the use of any predictive methodologies or instruments to assess criminality or "dangerousness: this is noted in Chapters 4 and 6.

Diversion: Probation and Specialty Courts

While much discussion of sentencing reform focuses on incarceration rates, the reach of community correctional control is much greater. In 2020, more than 3.6 million were on probation in the United States, with approximately 900,000 released from prison under parole or other models of community supervision.[43] While the national numbers are compelling, state-level data reveal that states with low incarceration rates may be more punitive than otherwise noted due to their high rates of probation.[44] While community corrections are preferable to imprisonment for many, these "alternatives" do not free people from many of the same legal, economic, and political barriers their incarcerated peers with felony records face upon release. Increasingly, these restrictions, especially in combination with rising fees and fines, create more pathways to prison.

Since its emergence as a sentencing option in the mid-1880s, probation, which is supervised correctional control in the community, has been the primary sentencing alternative to incarceration. Probation is rooted in the assumption that some people, amenable to rehabilitation, can successfully be diverted from prison so long as they conform to specific supervisory requirements.[45] Court officials have the ability to revoke probation and mandate imprisonment if these conditions are not met. As Schenwar and Law note in *Prison by Any Other Name*, probation is not synonymous with freedom, and the conditions imposed constitute a confinement in community.[46]

While probation does divert from prison, that sentence comes with its own long list of expectations and costs. According to the Prison Policy Initiative, probationers may need to meet as many as twenty requirements, including such conditions as payment of fees (often without considering individual ability to pay): regular reporting to a designated public or private officer; submitting to mandated drug and alcohol tests, often fee-based, even if the individual's offense was not related to same; and attending mandated programs on such topics as anger management. Additionally, people may be required to find and maintain full-time employment or education; to abide by strict curfews and electronic monitoring (often fee-based); to not leave a designated location or geographic area without prior permission; to not associate with people with criminal records, including family and friends; and to not change employment or residence without permission.[47]

These conditions of supervision may be imposed for years. There is great variation in sentencing across both states and judicial jurisdictions. Probation sentences can range from one year to decades, since many states allow for probation terms that match the statutory maximum prison sentence for the crime. Probationers may be on an intensive regime of community supervision for twenty years or more, and states that carry large probation caseloads are characterized by lengthy probation terms.[48]

Increasingly, probation is required for misdemeanors and traffic violations as part of "offender-funded" schemes. In several states, for-profit probation companies handle these cases, and probation is required simply to supervise the payment of costs. It's a classic Catch-22: hundreds of thousands of people are subject to excessive fees and surveillance because they were too poor to pay the initial fines and court fees.[49]

The combination of stringent requirements and sentence length makes probation a powerful driver of incarceration. More than three hundred fifty thousand probation revocations annually result in prison time. Black people constitute 30 percent of probationers and are more likely than white people or Latinx to have probation revoked.[50] Women face additional burdens meeting probation requirements, especially as caregivers for children and elders. Since most people caught up in the criminal legal system are poor, they are particularly challenged by the fines and fees associated with probation, whether administered by public agencies or private companies.

Philanthropy-driven reformers call for reductions in revocations using new "data-driven tools," and shortened probationary periods, especially for nonviolent crimes. They often support reduced fees, an end to private probation, the restoration of some voting and other rights, and an overall reduction in the number of probationers.[51] But these are procedural approaches that create new procedural and technological processes for managing probation; they do not permanently and significantly shrink the far reach of the carceral state. Between 2010 and 2020, thirty-seven states reduced probation caseloads.[52] These reductions, however, do not necessarily mean an actual reduction in criminal legal system supervision. Many would-be probationers are diverted instead to the expanding arena of "problem-solving courts.[53]

"Problem-solving" or specialty courts were established as a means of pretrial diversion prior to a formal finding of guilt; they impose conditions and restrictions comparable to probation requirements.[54] The first one, a drug court, was established in Florida in 1989, and the model has proliferated. Drug courts, established with federal funding as part of the War on Drugs, are the most common type of specialty court; there are more than three thousand of them operating in 56 percent of counties nationwide, supervising nearly one hundred ten thousand defendants annually.[55] Originally designed for adults arrested on drug offenses or other crimes linked to substance use, drug courts may now serve juveniles, families, those charged with DUIs, veterans, and college students. Over time, the problem-solving court model expanded to other issues and populations. A growing number of jurisdictions may also have special courts for homelessness, domestic violence, prostitution/sex work, gambling, truancy, and community courts designed to manage public order offenses. While some specialty courts now serve as part of post-prison reentry services, the model generally diverts people prior to sentencing.[56]

Jurisdictional arrangements vary, but specialty courts typically share several general features. The model embraces what sociologist Kerwin Kaye calls "therapeutic jurisprudence": judges overseeing a multidisciplinary team of professionals including attorneys, treatment experts, and law enforcement.[57] People are promised that if they participate, their criminal charges will be suspended during the course of their compliance and that their arrest records may be expunged upon successful completion. In exchange, specialty court participants essentially submit to the conditions of probation in lieu of the requisite conviction. Depending on the type of specialty court, these conditions may include twelve months or more of intensive supervision with requirements for random drug testing, enforced abstinence, and no new arrests. Participants may also need to observe curfews, find/maintain steady employment, pay fines or fees, perform community service, and/or make restitution to victims.[58] There is no clear evidence that specialty courts have reduced costs or incarceration rates, or improved participant outcomes. The bulk of the research has focused on drug courts, which show a success rate of 59 percent, even though participants are often cherry-picked due to their lack of prior convictions or serious involvement in crime.[59] Those who do not successfully complete the regimen are often worse off than when they started. They may well serve more time on probation or in prison than their non–drug court counterparts.

All specialty courts widen the net of carceral control. These courts absorb and manage cases that should never have been prosecuted, involving people who pose no real risk to their communities. Were this option not available, far fewer people would be ensnared by the system. For example, New York City's misdemeanor courts developed in order to manage the explosion of public order cases that resulted from stop-and-frisk policing and to ensure the collection of fines and fees.[60] Similarly, drug court ensnares a number of cases that involve mere possession but also assumes that all participants require treatment for addiction. Other specialty courts, such as those for the chronically unhoused use the criminal legal system to address a set of social problems that would better be served by community-based groups, services, and programs that have no connection with the criminal legal system but are widely available, with no onerous fines and fees, to all who would like to utilize them.

Prosecutorial Discretion, Plea Bargains, and the Limits of Indigent Defense

Once they are in the maw of the criminal legal system, the fates of defendants are largely determined by prosecutorial discretion and the quality and strength of their defense. Prosecutors have the full resources of the state at their disposal while defendants must mount their own defenses with private attorneys or public defenders. The quality of this defense and the resources available to defense attorneys play critical roles in outcomes related to bail, pretrial release or detention, possibilities for dropping or reducing, plea-bargaining, and the likelihood of going to trial.

Prosecutors are law enforcement officials who serve as intermediaries between police and the courts. Prosecutors decide which cases to charge and what charges to bring, when to seek bail and what bail amounts to recommend. They also present the state's case in court. In criminal cases, most prosecutions are carried out at the county level, while federal cases are pursued by US attorneys in ninety-four judicial districts. The number of prosecutors has increased over time; more than thirty thousand prosecutors represent over twenty-three hundred offices nationwide. While federal prosecutors are appointed by the executive branch, the overwhelming majority of state and county attorneys are elected. Over 90 percent of them are white and male.[61]

The power and discretionary authority of prosecutors have steadily increased over time. A growing consensus of scholars and activists argues that the problems with prosecutors include "the power that prosecutors have, the discretion they exercise, the illegality in which they too frequently engage, the punitive ideology that shapes many of their practices, their often-frustrating unaccountability, and the organizational inertia that afflicts prosecutors' offices."[62] Some scholars argue that prosecutorial "over-charging"—even as crime rates fall—is a major driver of mass incarceration. Politically rewarded for "tough-on-crime" and "lock-'em-up" swagger, prosecutors are free to pursue the harshest penalties for the most vulnerable and marginalized people with little oversight or accountability.[63]

In the late twentieth and early twenty-first centuries, determinate sentencing, mandatory minimums, and the use of criminal history scores have become key tools for prosecutors to increase the size and scope of the prison industrial complex. Prosecutorial power rests on the decision to charge and what charges to bring; these decisions are also correlated with prosecutor requests for high bails, pretrial detention, conditions of pretrial release, and referrals to specialty courts. The power to threaten serious and multiple charges is a key tool in creating pressure to plea-bargain—that is, to obtain a guilty plea from the defendant in exchange for reduced or dropped charges.

More than 90 percent of all cases are settled by plea agreements rather than trials, and our court system depends on that rate to avoid a decades-long backlog of cases awaiting trial.[64] Prosecutorial pressure is essential here, and a key element of rendering assembly-line functioning of the criminal legal system. With the legal ability and discretionary authority to threaten and pursue harsh sentences, prosecutors are able to pressure defendants, whether guilty or not, into guilty pleas or participation in problem-solving courts. In some instances—three-strike cases bring the issue into clear focus—prosecutors have wide latitude to charge certain offenses as either felonies or misdemeanors. The threat of a life sentence is more than enough to persuade most defendants into plea agreements.

Prosecutors may target certain defendants based on criminal history scores rather than actual evidence of a particular case or on the basis of race, class, and gender. A large body of research indicates that prosecutorial discretion plays a significant role in shaping both racial disparities in imprisonment and the fact that the overwhelming majority of those incarcerated were poor and/or unemployed at the time they were arrested and charged.[65] Decisions to pursue the death penalty offer the best glimpse into the roles that race, class, and gender—of the accused and those they are accused of harming—play in charging. Growing numbers of exonerations of persons sentenced to death help illustrate ways in which prosecutorial misconduct and limited access to strong defense attorneys helps shape landscapes of punishment.[66]

Lack of adequate systems and resources for public or indigent defense also enhances the inordinate influence of prosecutors. More than 80 percent of defendants charged with felonies and over 90 percent of all defendants in criminal courts cannot afford an attorney and are represented by a court-appointed attorney. These defendants are more likely to be detained prior to trial, and 90 percent of people who have public defenders accept a plea bargain.[67] Since communities of color bear the brunt of structural poverty and racism, both drivers of criminalization, they also are hit the hardest by what are called "indigent defense systems."

Despite the promise of *Gideon v. Wainwright* (1963), the guarantee of counsel if one cannot afford it is not an assurance of a strong, well-resourced defense.[68] Nationally, indigent defense systems are organized and funded in a variety of ways, with varying degrees of effectiveness. The three main forms of indigent defense provision: public defender offices, assigned counsel, and contract counsel.[69] Public defender offices assign full-time attorneys to indigent cases. This is the most effective model and is typically funded with dedicated state or local funds. Assigned and contract models are more common, relying on private attorneys appointed by the courts to handle cases or being contracted out for a flat fee. These systems produce higher caseloads with fewer resources available to attorneys. States that rely on these models often fund indigent defense with fines from other courts or with fees required from defendants themselves. All indigent defense systems are underfunded relative to prosecutorial budgets, leaving attorneys with impossibly large caseloads that cannot receive the dedicated attention and support they deserve. Publicly provided defenders simply do not have the time or sufficient investigative resources to adequately defend their clients. This contributes to high rates of plea-bargaining and funneling lower-level cases into problem-solving courts. It also enhances the already outsized influence of prosecutorial power.[70]

Various sectors of the bipartisan consensus acknowledge some of these problems, but they do little about them. Advocates and organizations periodically offer recommendations: decriminalization, increased standards and funding (sometimes through private philanthropy) for indigent defense, systemic oversight of prosecutors, and election of "progressive" prosecutors. With the exception of full decriminalization, these reforms rely on investing more resources and more trust in the criminal legal system. Still, in the aftermath of the Ferguson uprising, a push toward progressive prosecutors took hold. A growing number of candidates for district attorney run on platforms that include dramatic reform of the cash bail system, decriminalization of drug possession, prosecution of police misconduct and shootings, and an end to mass incarceration and in relevant jurisdictions, the death penalty.[71] These campaigns have won in major cities such as Philadelphia, Boston, Chicago, Dallas, San Francisco, and Los Angeles, and increasing have in smaller jurisdictions as well.[72] Their success in bringing about change has been mixed, in part due to push-back from police and law-and-order politicians.[73] While supporters of this new brand of prosecutors view their approach as harm reduction strategy, even "progressive prosecutors"—perhaps an oxymoron, given the carceral nature of the position—cannot salvage the catastrophe of the criminal legal system, no matter how dedicated they might be to creating change within it.

THE LIMITS OF SENTENCING REFORMS

Shifts in sentencing structure and length and a concomitant rise in the power of prosecutors play key roles in expanding the scope and reach of carceral control. While sentencing reforms seem to make sense as one tool to reduce prison populations, the realities of implementation and impact complicate the public relations promises.

Even "justice reinvestment" at its best is a con game, producing public "savings," only to reinvest them in expansions of the system, within carceral institutions or through often privatized community corrections and public/private partnerships tied to the criminal legal system. This constitutes, in significant measure, a transfer of public revenues to private, unaccountable interests. Exhaustive lists of conditions of supervision and the endless extraction of fines and fees from already-impoverished populations set people up for failure and, in many cases, "failure" means going to prison. "Diversionary" options such as specialty courts come with comparable restrictions and pitfalls; under the guise of carceral humanism, they only widen the net of correctional control. Moreover, the bipartisan consensus has expanded, not reduced, reliance on "criminal history" scores, whether through sentencing guidelines or risk assessment tools used in pretrial processes and for release decisions. This constitutes a failure to confront the structural inequality that undergirds the system at every juncture.

Neoliberal austerity measures propel reliance on fees and fines as a significant source of public revenue. This is another Catch-22. Turning this around means that social movements must work to compel state and local governments to reduce or eliminate most fines and fees while simultaneously defunding carceral systems, reinstating progressive tax policies, and organizing for new social and economic priorities. While the bipartisan consensus rhetorically acknowledges the shortcomings of systems of indigent defense, it fails to address the intersections of structural racism and poverty that set up those systems for failure. Instead, philanthropists contract for research to study the problem and to develop better ways of reforming indigent defense, ignoring the unnecessary criminal processing of many misdemeanor cases while simultaneously entangling the criminal legal system in additional costly "data-driven" research.[74]

The bipartisan consensus also fails to challenge the power of prosecutors; in some cases, pretrial reforms may even expand it. But abolitionists, fighting for a world where social problems are not addressed by policing, prosecution, and punishment, do challenge that power. A group of organizations—Community Justice Exchange, CourtWatch MA, Families for Justice and Healing, Project NIA, and Survived & Punished NY—have created a framework and principles for "prosecutor organizing" utilizing an abolitionist lens. "Our organizing," they say, "focuses on how a prosecuting office's policies and practices result in decriminalization, decarceration, and shrinking the resources of the office of the prosecutor. Elected prosecutors are not co-strugglers, but targets we can push on the path to eliminating prosecution altogether."[75]

Sentencing reform efforts fail to address people convicted of violent offenses. Nearly all sentencing reforms focus on the decarceration of the three "nons": non-violent, non-serious, and non-sexual offenders.[76] Popular narratives and imagery of intrinsically violent murders and rapists run amok, and their innocent but damaged victims drive pursuit of vengeance and retribution in the name of public safety. This forecloses any meaningful discussion of community alternatives for over 50 percent of the current prison population. Common Seed, a Brooklyn-based program that operates the first US "alternative-to-incarceration" and victim service program to focus on people involved with violent felonies seeks to open that conversation. Danielle Sered, Common Seed's founder and director, describes its work in *Until We Reckon: Violence, Mass Incarceration, and a Road to Repair*.[77]

Incite!, Project NIA, Survived & Punished, and other organizations have long challenged these narratives, pointing out that multiple forms of violence—interpersonal, vigilante, community, and structural—inflict harms. Discussion should shift from punishing "crime" to addressing and repairing harms. Victim/survivors are found both within and without prisons, and all of them should receive support—outside of the criminal legal system—for meeting their immediate and long-term needs. And the state itself is the greatest perpetrator of mass violence. *Carceral Con* takes up this discussion in Chapters 6 and 7.

As Prison Policy Initiative reports, those convicted of violent and sexual crimes are less likely to be rearrested than any other group of offenders. Most are held long beyond the point at which they may pose any threat to public safety. Those involved in violent crimes may also have been victims of violence, interpersonal or structural, and survivors themselves with unresolved trauma. Incarceration fails to address this root, and in fact, represents additional structural violence and trauma.

While many law enforcement officials claim the criminal legal system offers crime victims "closure" and "justice," research suggests that many survivors' voices are not heard. This is particularly true of marginalized communities who already have a fraught relationship with the police; many do not report these crimes at all. People who have suffered harm do want a sense of safety, healing, and resources for helping them deal with trauma. And they want those who inflicted harm to help repair it as best they can.[78] Many reformers claim this can happen within the criminal legal system, but that system ignores those who suffer the harms of carceral violence. It is obvious that solutions other than prisons offer better possibilities for justice, healing, and transformation of the social and economic conditions that produce violence. Restorative justice models, which seek to address and repair harm and with their focus primarily on individuals, can be helpful in many circumstances. Yet they also have increasingly been integrated into the criminal legal system as an add-on to carceral punishment. For over two decades, grassroots activists have also explored and begun to develop transformative justice practices that emphasize safety and accountability without relying on policing, incarceration, or any form of state or systemic violence.[79] These explorations and practices have opened new spaces for thinking both individually and structurally about justice.

A bolder vision is required to challenge the notion that the structural violence of the criminal legal system can deter, reduce, or prevent violence. Efforts at sentencing reform have not shrunk the footprint of the prison industrial complex, but rather have expanded its reach—without producing either safety or justice—and reproduced inequality and pain.

6 Imprisonment and Release

> The worst violators of nature and human rights never go to jail. They hold the keys.
>
> —Eduardo Galeano, *Upside Down*, 1998

> The Constitution has always demanded less within the prison walls. Time and again, even when faced with constitutional rights no less "fundamental" than the right to be free from state-sponsored racial discrimination, we have deferred to the reasonable judgments of officials experienced in running this Nation's prisons.
>
> —US Supreme Court Justice Clarence J. Thomas, *Johnson v. California*, 2005

To the extent that reform seeks to rehabilitate and legitimize the prison itself—arguably US society's most oppressive contemporary institution—it expands and strengthens the infrastructure of inequality. And it reproduces violence.

INCARCERATED

The 2007 death by suffocation of seventeen-year-old Isaiah Simmons, a Black youth from Baltimore, was entirely preventable. He was incarcerated in a state-authorized, privately run juvenile detention center reassuringly named Bowling Brook Preparatory School. He died because counselors sat on and restrained him in a variety of positions and locations over a period of three hours. "When Simmons was unresponsive," reported Black studies scholar and poet Jackie Wang in her book *Carceral Capitalism*, "the counselors dumped his body in the snow and did not call for medical assistance for more than forty minutes."[1] The state medical examiner ruled the death a homicide. Reckless endangerment charges against five former staff members were dropped in 2012.[2] The use of "prone restraint," which involves placing a person face-down on the ground, was banned by state juvenile justice authorities. The Bowling Brook juvenile detention center was closed weeks following the death but later reopened with a different name, under new management.

Kelly Savage, a twenty-three-year-old white woman in California was, as journalist Victoria Law reported, "marked by a history of physical and sexual abuse beginning when she was three years old." She gave birth to her son Justin shortly after leaving her abusive first husband. Her second husband, Mark Savage, the father of her second child, a girl, was also physically and sexually abusive. In 1995, following consultation with a domestic violence hotline, Kelly Savage was on the cusp of escaping with her children when her husband discovered her plans. Mark Savage beat his wife and three-and-a-half-year-old stepson. Justin died. Tried and convicted of first-degree murder in 1998, both Kelly and her husband were sentenced to life without parole. Although Kelly Savage did not physically harm her son and attempted to protect him by escaping an abusive partner, California is one of many states with some version of a "failure-to-protect" law that criminalizes a parent's—almost always a woman's—inability to protect their children from abuse by another party. Victoria Law underscored the rapidity with which the abuse borne by Savage marked her as a criminal: "At her trial, the prosecutor argued that Kelly Savage enjoyed the beatings and that, because she had not fled, she was equally at fault for her son's death."[3] The sexual and physical abuse she had suffered most of her life was finally of interest to authorities only when they could fashion it into a criminalizing narrative that sent her to prison for more than two decades. While in prison, she trained to become a domestic violence peer counselor when she realized that most of the others inside had also suffered prior physical and sexual abuse.

Changes in the California penal code in the early 2000s permitted abuse survivors convicted of violent felonies to petition for a review of that conviction. In the review, expert testimony about their abuse could be considered if it was not raised at trial. Savage's petition was opposed by the state's attorney general, but in 2017, after twenty-three years in prison, then governor Jerry Brown commuted her sentence, and she was granted parole. Another nightmare of post-release carceral supervision in a mandatory, year-long assignment to a residential treatment program was just beginning—an oppressive snarl of conditions, restrictions, fees, and requirements that keep many people on a razor's edge of being sent back to prison for technical violations that are often beyond their control.[4]

Thousands of men—virtually all of them poor, most of them Black—are routinely subjected to squalid and brutal conditions in South Carolina's level-3 (high-security) prisons. Most of them are at the mercy of guards who beat people under their custodial authority, arbitrarily restrict visitation, and consign people to solitary confinement for prolonged periods. Many windows are covered with steel plates, blocking access to natural sunlight, and people are confined to small nine-by-twelve-foot cells for twenty or more hours a day. Access to the outdoors is severely restricted. Most of the people incarcerated in unsanitary level-3 prisons eat food of poor quality that is sometimes moldy and rotten and drink water that is sometimes putrid.[5] They and their families describe medical and dental care as grossly inadequate. Protests began in 2016. In 2018, an explosion of despair and fury against abuse and neglect at South Carolina's Lee Correctional Institution resulted in the deaths of seven and injuries to at least two dozen men. As the South Carolina Department of

Corrections cracked down following the riot, incarcerated people and their outside supporters called for a nationwide prison strike. Their demands included access to educational, vocational, and life-skills programs, an end to exploitation of prison labor, and voting rights.[6]

US jails, prisons, and detention centers distill racial capitalism's racism, economic violence, and organized abandonment to its lethal essence. Those who are released from confinement return to a society in which structural inequality is widening and deepening. Most reform agendas ignore this larger context, calling for a greater flow of resources, public and private, into the institutions themselves, often in the name of carceral humanism. In 2020, Shadowproof, an independent press organization, reported that correctional authorities in all fifty states were calling for infusions of more money and staff. As Brian Sonenstein noted, "'[S]taff shortages' are historically used to push for greater investments in prison systems, oftentimes riding reform waves like the one the United States is experiencing currently."[7] Trapped between paradoxical exhortations to "save taxpayer dollars" and increase the flow of public resources into carceral systems, we should focus attention on who is being locked up.

In 2020, Prison Policy Initiative and VOCAL-NY, a grassroots organization that builds power among low-income people affected by HIV/AIDS, the drug war, and mass incarceration, released a first-of-its-kind report on the geography of incarceration in New York State. It provides a grim snapshot of economic and social precarity, confirming that in predominantly Black areas, heavily impacted by incarceration, "high imprisonment rates correlate with other community problems related to poverty, employment, education, and health."[8]

People who want to understand what it is like inside jails and prisons should turn to those who have been identifying the problems, branch and root, especially from the 1960s on.[9] The struggles of women in prison in the 1970s, for example, anticipated clashes in the present. In *All Our Trials: Prisons, Policing, and the Feminist Fight to End Violence*, Emily L. Thuma documents the ways in which women's prison organizing around the country surged in opposition to behavior modification initiatives and the creation of "special" or "alternative" program units. Part of a corrections policy shift toward expanding the use of administrative segregation—solitary confinement—through an emphasis on biomedical methods, the real purpose was to maintain order threatened by radical inside/outside opposition to racist prison and societal conditions. New policies of punishment, isolation, and "treatments"—including administration of drugs and electroshock therapy—primarily targeted Black, Latinx, and Indigenous women who were labeled "violent" and "mentally ill."[10]

Decades later, their fights for racial, gender, and economic justice continued to reverberate as corrections officials sought to expand carceral capacity again, this time under the guise of creating "gender responsive" units and jails purportedly designed to meet the special needs of women. An inside/outside movement of activists, organizations, and coalitions—including California Coalition of Women Prisoners (CCWP), founded by cis and trans women; Justice Now, a leader in the fight against so-called "gender responsive" units; Critical Resistance; the California Prison Moratorium Project; Californians United for a Responsible Budget (CURB); the JusticeLA Coalition; and others—fought for long years against the creation of special prisons, jails, and units. In 2019, they won a major victory by stopping implementation of a long-standing Los Angeles plan to renovate a closed immigration detention center in rural Lancaster and reopen it as the sixteen-hundred-bed Mira Loma Women's Detention Center.[11] This marked only the most recent attempt to resurrect a facility originally opened in 1945 as a vocational school for juveniles in trouble, repurposed to house incarcerated women and repurposed again when county officials rented it to federal immigration authorities.

Historian Heather Ann Thompson, the Pulitzer Prize–winning author of *Blood in the Water: The Attica Prison Uprising of 1971 and Its Aftermath*, says, "Listening carefully to the incarcerated and protecting their right to speak freely to the public is a moral imperative."[12] But philanthropy-driven reform organizations filter both voices and content by censoring and cherry-picking which formerly incarcerated people will be heard, and in what ways. Dissidents inside jails and prisons constantly risk retaliation from correctional staff, and there are powerful legal barriers to legal complaints. In 1996, the federal Prison Litigation Reform Act (PLRA) was enacted with strong bipartisan support, purportedly to limit the number of "frivolous" lawsuits filed by incarcerated people. It remains in effect. Filing fees were increased with no indigent waivers allowed. While claims of physical injury are permitted, those alleging mental or emotional harm are restricted. Other adverse impacts on jail and prison litigation have been substantial.[13]

INSIDE: ORGANIZED VIOLENCE AND ABANDONMENT

A look at just a few of the ordinary conditions within jails and prisons, along with the mainstream reforms put forth to address them, confirms the mutually reinforcing relationship between inside/outside inequality, organized abandonment, and violence.

Solitary Confinement

Eastern Penitentiary in Philadelphia opened in 1829 as the product of liberal reform. Designed as a "first-of-its-kind" humanitarian replacement for harsh corporal punishment, it embraced institution-wide solitary confinement as the best method for encouraging residents to reflect upon and repent their misdeeds. The English novelist Charles Dickens visited the penitentiary. Horrified by what he had witnessed, he likened the conditions to being "buried alive."[14]

Almost 200 years later, tens of thousands of adults and youth are held in solitary confinement in the United States on any given day. Solitary Watch, a watchdog and advocacy organization, defines solitary confinement as "the practice of isolating people in closed cells for 22–24 hours a day, virtually free of human contact, for periods of time ranging from days to decades."[15] Albert Woodfox, a member of the Black Panther Party, was held in isolation for forty-three years.[16] The Florida Department of Juvenile Justice routinely uses solitary confinement for hundreds of youth daily. According to litigants for a class-action lawsuit, in a one-year period between 2017 and 2018, more than four thousand children (70 percent of whom were Black) in twenty-one state juvenile detention centers were isolated, many of them on multiple occasions.[17]

Solitary confinement goes by many names: closed-cell restriction, restricted housing, security housing, administrative segregation, the hole, "room confinement" (in juvenile detention centers), and more. Federal supermax prisons typically have only solitary confinement cells. Often the cells are no larger than a parking space; most have solid metal doors and little or no access to direct sunlight. While many believe that solitary confinement is only used to house those who are exceptionally violent, people are sent there for an almost limitless set of reasons, including having the flu or COVID-19, retaliation for filing grievances, or such minor (and often fabricated) infractions as "talking back" to a guard. Authorities invoke the phrase "involuntary protective custody" to justify solitary confinement for children in adult prisons. The ACLU says, "solitary is often used on the most vulnerable: women who are pregnant, individuals with mental illness, transgender women and other LGBTQ people and—in a particularly disturbing trend—victims of sexual assault by correctional officers." Women as well as men are subjected to solitary confinement; women of color, particularly Black women, the ACLU reports, "are held . . . at rates far exceeding those of white women."[18] According to Stop Solitary for Kids, the same patterns hold true for young people in both adult and juvenile institutions.[19]

Advocates have worked for decades to severely restrict or abolish its use altogether. Yet placing human beings in extended solitary confinement is commonplace. Hundreds of prisoners in Texas prisons have been relegated to solitary for months, a year, a decade, or more.[20] Starting in 2011 and continuing through 2013, thousands of people imprisoned in so-called security housing units (SHUs) at

California's notorious Pelican Bay State Prison fought back against deplorable conditions and policies designed to foster distrust and conflict among prisoners with a series of hunger strikes. State correctional officials claimed that SHU was not solitary confinement, but in response to constant inside/outside organizing and legal challenges, the state began to transfer some prisoners to other facilities or less restrictive units. Practices designed to foster inter-prisoner divisiveness continue, and people can be returned to SHU at any time.[21]

Many who are subjected to solitary confinement experience profound anxiety and terror, cognitive deficits, depression, hallucinations and delusions, self-cutting and mutilation, and suicidal despair. Indeed, studies indicate that rates of prison suicide are highest among those placed in solitary confinement.[22] According to Stop Solitary for Kids, half of all suicides in juvenile facilities occur in solitary confinement.[23] In 2020, a study of more than two hundred thousand individuals incarcerated and released from North Carolina prisons between 2000 and 2015 found that placement in restrictive housing/solitary confinement increased first-year mortality risks by 24 percent. In that first year of release, those who had lived in restricted housing were 78 percent more likely to die of suicide than peers who had no such placement, and they were far more likely to die of an opioid overdose in the first two weeks following release.[24] Even brief stays in solitary may increase post-prison vulnerability to premature death.[25]

As the COVID-19 pandemic surged in 2020, the use of solitary confinement as one means of attempting to contain viral spread in state and federal prisons exploded. According to a report from Unlock the Box, a national campaign to end solitary confinement, by June 2020, the use of solitary confinement increased by 500 percent, from about sixty thousand pre-COVID-19 to three hundred thousand since the pandemic began.[26] This did not include figures for solitary confinement in immigrant detention centers and local jails, but there were COVID-19-related increases in its use there, as well. Some authorities likened the increased use of solitary to medical isolation or quarantine, but the comparison is egregious. In reality, this practice further compromises already horrific health conditions in jails, prisons, and detention centers.

Most reforms in adult jails and prisons focus on reducing the use of solitary confinement, providing for a little more time outside a restricted housing placement, placing clear limits on how long people can be held in solitary, and limiting or banning its use for certain categories of people, such as pregnant women, people with physical and mental disabilities, and younger people.

The First Step Act now prohibits use of solitary confinement as a punishment for youth in federal carceral institutions but permits limited use of the practice, ostensibly only when youth behavior poses an immediate threat of physical harm and cannot be addressed in any other way.[27] While a growing number of states are restricting or prohibiting use of solitary confinement in juvenile detention centers and youth prisons, compliance is difficult, often impossible to track with accuracy and in timely ways.

Increasingly, reforms that produce "alternative" forms of severely restricted confinement tend to quickly expand, morphing into remodeled solitary.[28] Implementation of stricter guidelines reforms is often slow, uneven, and piecemeal. The Massachusetts Criminal Justice Reform Act of 2018 embraced a number of measures intended to drive down the use of solitary confinement. A year later, *Boston Globe* columnist Adrian Walker observed, "The Department of Correction has instituted changes that are widely viewed as an end run around the new law, policies that allow for 21 hours a day of solitary confinement rather than 22. Regulations for reviewing the status of prisoners in solitary have stalled."[29]

Sexual and Gender Violence

Sexual harassment, coercion, and violence, commonplace in custodial institutions, may come at the hands of incarcerated people, but more often, incarcerated people report assault by guards and other staff who wield absolute power over them.[30] As remedy, the bipartisan Prison Rape Elimination Act (PREA) of 2003 was signed into law with the intention of system-wide prevention of the sexual abuse of incarcerated people by staff and fellow prisoners in US custodial facilities operated under the authority of federal, state, or local governments. Standards for implementation and reporting were established by DOJ in 2012. States may elect to comply or not, but the only sanctions for noncompliance are DOJ grant reductions.

Michael Cox, executive director of Black and Pink Massachusetts, a state affiliate of a US abolitionist organization of LGBTQ and HIV-positive prisoners and outside supporters, say that advocates initially hoped for meaningful investigations of, responses to, and public reporting of allegations. When PREA was implemented, said Cox, who at one time served a prison sentence, "most of our hopes were crushed. The application of PREA has been harsh and selective." Even though incarcerated youth and adults have the right to file complaints, deterrents to reporting include fear of not being believed, retaliation by their abusers, and fear of being blamed—the same fears that suppress reporting of sexual harassment and violence outside carceral settings. While PREA-compliant facilities are required to publicly report the final results of investigations, those reports, Cox says, "are silent on the factual basis upon which they were filed. Instead, we receive only the investigatory outcome. A clear pattern emerges that shows almost all allegations against staff are found not to be credible. Allegations between incarcerated people meet a similar fate."[31]

The findings of other advocacy groups and investigative reporters support Cox's concerns. Coleman Federal Correctional Complex near Wildwood, Florida, operated by the Bureau of Prisons, houses about six thousand people, including about five hundred women. In late 2019, fourteen women filed a lawsuit against the United States citing years of systemic abuse, at the facility's women's work camp and naming specific officers, some of whom were subjects of prior complaints. Anyone who complained was, by prison policy, transferred to a more restrictive county jail—purportedly for the person's own safety.[32] In 2020, a US Department of Justice report documented pervasive sexual violence by correctional staff in a New Jersey prison, confirming that such abuse is widespread and systemic.[33] Sexual abuse in youth detention institutions also remains widespread.[34] And also in 2020, Su'ganni Tiuza, a Black bisexual man imprisoned at MCI-Norfolk documented long-standing, widespread abusive behavior toward LGBT people incarcerated in Massachusetts prisons.[35] As his report documents, authorities actively foster a homophobic and transphobic environment that weaponizes PREA against people it purportedly protects.

For many incarcerated people, especially women, transgender people, and LGBTQI people, sexual violence in prison reproduces earlier trauma experienced prior to carceral confinement. Girls, primarily girls of color, in juvenile detention often have prior histories of sexual abuse and are criminalized on the basis of those histories.[36] While much less information is available about men, including trans and gender-nonconforming men, many are known to have prior personal histories of physical and sexual abuse. Many people believe that the solution to sexual violence can be found in intensified policing, but policing itself is part of the violence. Andrea J. Ritchie notes that, "Research on 'police sexual misconduct'—a term used to describe actions from sexual harassment and extortion to forcible rape by officers—overwhelmingly concludes that it is a systemic problem."[37]

Health and Well-Being

Governments have a constitutional responsibility to provide incarcerated people with necessary health care. In *Estelle v. Gamble* (1976), the U.S. Supreme Court ruled that deliberate indifference to serious medical needs of prisoners violates the Eighth Amendment to the US Constitution, which proscribes cruel and unusual punishment; there is an expectation of "reasonably adequate" care, an ambiguous standard.[38] Translated into practice, it permits the continual unfolding of an ever-growing health care catastrophe.

In mid-2020, the rapid spread of COVID-19 through US jails, prisons, and detention centers underscored the essential meaninglessness of this standard and the ways in which incarcerated people are marked as disposable. Earlier that year, incarcerated people, with support from their community advocates, demanded access to sanitizing and cleaning supplies, masks, and other supports. Emphasizing the public health nature of the crisis, health officials, physicians, medical researchers, justice advocates, and criminal legal scholars called repeatedly for mass releases from jails and prisons in order to avoid rapid viral spread into, out of, and through carceral institutions.[39] But the incarcerated people, many of whom were elderly and/or had underlying health conditions were trapped in places where sufficient sanitation and social distancing were impossible—unless people with the novel coronavirus disease were placed in solitary confinement. That was its own special hell. The situation was made worse by ill-considered efforts to transfer people from one prison to another in order to avoid overcrowding. Viral spread increased. There never had been any possibility of confining viral spread to jails, prisons, and detention centers; staff movement in and out guaranteed community spread. But politicians, even those who claim liberal credentials by virtue of their support for LGBTQI equality and the like, lacked the political will to do what was right. There were some releases in various facilities and jurisdictions, but nowhere near enough.

In July 2020, a report from the UCLA School of Law's COVID-19 Behind the Bars Data Project and Johns Hopkins found that the case rate inside prisons was 5.5 times higher and the inside death rate, when adjusted for age and sex differences, was three times higher than in the US population as a whole.[40] Researchers noted that the full range of systemic data they needed was lacking; the real magnitude of the in-prison crisis was, they believed, larger than could be documented. Not long before this report appeared, Prison Policy Initiative and the ACLU issued a report assigning failing grades to all of the states' responses to COVID-19 in jails and prisons.[41] Conditions in ICE detention centers were no better, and through a series of aggressive deportations in a time of pandemic, ICE facilitated COVID-19 spread to other countries.[42]

Carceral institutions don't have health care systems so much as thousands of increasingly privatized patchwork arrangements and contracts intended to provide the minimum amount of care possible for the lowest possible cost. This shambles of a system resembles the frayed, unaffordable, and inadequate system of health care in the United States. Beginning in the 1970s, the direct provision of carceral health care services by public agencies has steadily decreased. The predominant model for jails is contractual arrangement with one or more private carceral health care vendors to provide services, often through a negotiated per diem, per inmate rate—a clear incentive to those private care providers to keep costs down. In some cases, counties may share some measure of financial risk for costly medical care and procedures with vendors. In 2019, ProPublica drew attention to a long-standing law enforcement practice known informally as "medical bond," a tactic some sheriffs use to avoid responsibility for the costs of medical emergencies and expensive procedures. Correctional officials sometimes seek immediate judicial permission to release an incarcerated person on medical bond. If a judge concurs, that person signs a document that states the individual, not the jail, is legally responsible for all medical costs. Some people on medical bond may be required to wear (and pay associated fees for) ankle monitors; when they recover, persons on medical bond may be returned to jail.[43]

State corrections departments use one of four models for providing all or most onsite prison health care: direct care provided by state-employed providers (seventeen states), contracted care, usually per month/per person, through private companies (twenty states), care provided by the state's public medical schools or affiliated organizations (four states), and a hybrid model, utilizing some combination of the other systems (eight states).[44] The Bureau of Prisons provides on-site medical services to those in federal prisons and operates several advanced care medical centers. Privately run immigrant detention centers rely on services provided by the corporations—including CoreCivic and the Geo Group—that own them. All of these models also necessitate obtaining off-site care that cannot be provided in the prisons themselves. In the late 1990s, the DOJ, the US Department of Defense, and the Federal Bureau of Prisons joined with the DOJ's research and development agency, the National Institute of Justice, to evaluate the efficacy of telemedicine to contain transport and related security management costs for incarcerated people.[45] Since that time, the use of remote access diagnostic medicine has increasingly been mainstreamed, in both prisons and society.

Incarceration leads to premature death in multiple ways. The life expectancy of an incarcerated person is reduced by about two years for each year that person remains behind bars.[46] In 2020, chronic illnesses continued to be the leading cause of death in state prisons.[47] Many, perhaps most, people enter jails, prisons, and detention centers with already compromised health, suffering from such chronic conditions as asthma, heart disease, respiratory diseases, diabetes, HIV-positive status, and more. They are at increased risk for hepatitis, tuberculosis, substance abuse, and suicide. This is the result of structural racism and economic inequality, which severely limit access to appropriate health care as well as to housing, education, living-wage jobs, and other life-promoting resources and services.[48]

Increased health vulnerability for incarcerated people is complicated by the well-documented aging of prison populations. On average, more than 10 percent of state prison populations are over fifty-five years of age.[49] Harsh sentencing—life sentences and life without parole—drives the increases. The overrepresentation of people with mental illnesses in US jails and prisons and on probation and parole is also well documented. In 2017, the Justice Advocacy Project at Stanford University reported that over 30 percent of people incarcerated in California state prisons were being treated for severe mental illness.[50]

The incidence of suicide and attempts constitutes a particularly chilling indictment of custodial confinement. An Associated Press investigative report on suicides and suicide attempts in county jails between 2014 and 2019 confirmed suicide as "long the leading cause of death in US jails" and pointed to scores of lawsuits and investigations that, over recent years, indicated institutional neglect.[51] In 2020, the *Philadelphia Inquirer* reported on the rising number of Pennsylvania prison suicides.[52]

Most of the women in US prisons and jails are mothers; a disproportionate number of them are Black. They carry primary responsibility for their children from whom they are separated; some reformers believe that mothers and children should be incarcerated together. Each year thousands of women are pregnant when they enter carceral institutions. Public health researchers suggest that most carceral institutions are not able to safely provide for pre- and postnatal care of pregnant women that is appropriate and adequate according to community standards. Sometimes that care can be overtly cruel.[53] The First Step Act prohibited shackling federal prisoners during childbirth. But in 2020, women in twenty-three states and an unknown number of immigrant detention centers were still being transported to community hospitals or health care centers to give birth where "nonmedical restraints"—shackles—are applied, purportedly for reasons of safety. Yet these practices, maternal care health providers say, "create potentially life-threatening hazards for pregnant women and their fetuses."[54]

Transgender people are often denied access to appropriate medicines and treatments, are frequently taunted by staff, and may intentionally be placed in facilities that do not match their gender identities, a choice that constitutes additional punishment and invites violence. In ICE custody, transgender women are almost always confined with men. The ACLU describes a transgender woman who was gang-raped, threatened with death, and diagnosed with HIV in her home country. She fled to the United States, where she was detained, beaten, given inadequate medical care, and died in solitary confinement.[55]

Environmental Harms

For more than three decades, inside/outside prison and environmental activists in communities from coast to coast—in California, Texas, Michigan, Pennsylvania, Kentucky, and elsewhere—have worked together to make clear the intimate relationships between racial capitalism, the carceral state, and environmental racism. Environmental racism describes the reality that Black, Latinx, and Indigenous people are more likely than white people to live in closer proximity to industries and sites that produce pollution and toxic substances that impair health.

A special report, "America's Toxic Prisons: The Environmental Injustices of Mass Incarceration," details serious environmental problems within particular prisons. "Though some prisons provide particularly egregious examples," the report emphasizes, "mass incarceration in the US impacts the health of prisoners, prison-adjacent communities, and local ecosystems from coast to coast." New prisons and jails are sometimes built on abandoned, polluted industrial sites. Incarcerated people often describe brown, murky water that smells because it contains industrial solvents, chemicals, or toxins. Coal ash and other wastes produce dust that can travel through prison vents. "Valley fever," a virulent fungal infection, has sickened thousands of prisoners in California's Central Valley, killing more than fifty. Prison authorities and knotted tangles of local, state, and federal regulatory agencies have failed to address these harms.[56]

Extraction of Labor and Money

Prison labor is part of an oppressive punishment regime that helps to sustain the prison itself. The use of "convict labor" did not, as many believe, originate with an infamous loophole in the Thirteenth Amendment, ratified after the abolition of slavery. Involuntary labor required of prisoners was already a feature of public prisons in the antebellum period. In the contemporary era, it is unquestionably exploitative. Most of this labor does not provide meaningful job training that will lead to post-release employment; even where it does, profound structural barriers to living-wage employment exist. Reform advocates usually describe initiatives intended to set up formerly incarcerated people for individual success. But exploratory research by Adam D. Reich and Seth J. Prins at Columbia University suggests that exposure to the criminal legal system is "associated with reduced workplace collective action" because employers hold increased power over formerly incarcerated workers. That speaks to a collective structural impact on the low-wage labor market "in ways that further disadvantage those already most marginalized."[57]

Prison Policy Initiative produces the most comprehensive available information on US prison labor.[58] Only a small amount of work done by incarcerated people serves private companies. Most people who work in prison do jobs that maintain the prison itself: clerical, custodial, kitchen-and-laundry-related, grounds maintenance, agricultural, and more. In such prisons as Louisiana's Angola and Mississippi's Parchman Farm, plantation-type agricultural labor evokes days of slavery. While some states do not pay those who do "non-industry" institutional maintenance jobs at all, others pay an average minimum daily—not hourly—wage that decreased from $.93 in 2001 to $.86 in 2017. A state prison's "correctional industries" labor sector, involving less than 10 percent of prison workers, produces goods and services sold to other government departments, agencies, and institutions. On average, workers earn between $.33 and $1.41 per hour. UNICOR, a Federal Bureau of Prisons corporate entity, pays incarcerated workers between $.23 and $1.15 per hour to produce a wide variety of goods sold almost entirely to the Department of Defense and other federal government agencies. Utilizing "free market principles," the Federal Prison Industry Enhancement Certification Program (PIECP) permits private companies to train, supervise, and utilize a small portion of prison labor within correctional facilities. Workers are paid "at a rate not less than that paid for similar work in the same locality's private sector," a nonspecific metric that can legitimize low wages.[59]

These wages are all subject to mandatory deductions that vary by jurisdiction. They may include deductions for crime victims' restitution funds, "costs of imprisonment (room and board)," medical co-pays, child/family support, court-assessed fines and fees, and more. Some workers end up with less than half of the money they earn. People in prison have demanded the right to join unions and more. Some activists call for raising all pay levels to state or federal minimum wage or support unionization. But the structural nature of poverty, economic inequality, and the low-waged job market, argue for strategies of decarceration while fighting for green/sustainable jobs programs, full employment, and living wages for all.

All people confined to prisons and jails are trapped in an insidious system of price-gouging" that is parasitic and feeds off the US carceral system.[60] With few exceptions, they pay inflated fees for the limited ability to communicate with friends, families, and legal advocates, and, in some systems, to read (electronically). Medical co-pays are often required. Incarcerated people also pay inflated costs for commissary items—over-the-counter health products, personal care and hygiene products, writing instruments and supplies, and sodas, snacks, and small food items. These items cannot be brought or sent in but must be purchased through the jail or prison. Such companies as JPay, a subsidiary of Securus Technologies, a behemoth in private corrections technology, and Global Tel Link (GTL) distribute "free" electronic tablets in prison, for example. These are touted as a safe, efficient method of providing people with e-books, audio books, and access to other content and services that comply with strict security requirements. The correctional system pays nothing but receives an institutional kickback for providing access to a captive market while the costs of utilizing the technology are offloaded onto incarcerated people and their families and friends. Costs mount up quickly as companies bundle tablets together with fee-laden services.[61] Relentless activist protest has resulted in some cost reductions in some jurisdictions, but predatory fees predominate. When people are released into the community, they are likely still poor and often in debt, often under fee-based supervision, and faced with basic costs of food, clothing, housing, health care, transportation, and child support.

RELEASE: INEQUALITY AND ORGANIZED ABANDONMENT

In time, the overwhelming majority of incarcerated people are released, but profound challenges face them as they prepare for participation in community life. Eddie Ellis, describing the Center for NuLeadership on Urban Solutions' response to the concept of reentry pointed out that most of the people they work with who were released from prison had never been part of mainstream institutions in the first place. "So for them," Ellis said, it's not a case of reentry but of coming into an entirely new situation."[62]

Millions of people with arrest records and criminal convictions continue to experience punishment in the form of federally or state-mandated legal restrictions and disqualifications long after their cases are closed or sentences are completed. These "collateral consequences" may include disqualifications from voting rights, jury service, and the right to possess firearms. They may restrict access to public housing, government loans and grants, public benefits, job training and employment, driver's and occupational licenses, and more.[63] Some of the specific challenges people face are noted here.

Education

"Throughout their lives," says Prison Policy Initiative, "people who serve time in prison are held back from educational opportunities, making it nearly impossible to earn the credentials they need to succeed after release." They are likely to have fewer educational credentials; more than half of those in prison hold only a high school diploma or General Equivalency Diploma (GED) while about one-quarter do not have any educational credential.[64]

From 1965 to 1994, incarcerated people were eligible for federal Pell grants, noncompetitive, needs-based awards given to low-income people to reduce or eliminate the cost of attending college. While Pell grants to people in prisons constituted a very small percentage of all Pell grants awarded, they provided critical support for thousands of students and hundreds of college programs at prisons throughout the United States. The 1994 Violent Crime Control and Law Enforcement Act banned such grants to incarcerated people. Only eight college programs remained."[65] Some universities and colleges have since secured funding to support programming—New York University's Prison Education Program and the Bard Prison Initiative of Bard College are two examples—but the number of available college programs still remains relatively low. In 2015, the US Department of Education launched a Second Chance Pell pilot program that helps colleges and universities partner with prisons to offer coursework leading toward an associate's or bachelor's degree; the Bard Prison Initiative is part of this effort. The program was expanded in 2020 but remains very limited. In some reform arenas, efforts continue to repeal the 1994 federal ban on Pell Grants for incarcerated people.

It is essential to place the incarceration/education relationship within a larger context, including the falling-domino phenomenon of US public school closures throughout the country which have rapidly accelerated. Between 2000 and 2010, about two hundred elementary and high schools were closed in six cities alone: Chicago, Detroit, Kansas City (MO), Milwaukee, Pittsburgh, and Washington, D.C. In 2013, Philadelphia closed twenty-three schools while Chicago closed another forty-nine schools, the largest mass closure in a single city in US history. Most of those schools served predominantly Black and Latinx students in low-income neighborhoods.[66] The adverse impact on youth is profound.

Jobs and "Ban the Box"

Most prisons do not equip incarcerated people with skills needed to secure living wage jobs with benefits following release. Indeed, the structure of the labor market under late racial capitalism makes that challenge particularly difficult. Some institutions offer focused skill-building programs in such areas as computer technologies and coding, but the vast majority of people do not have access to such training. In some locales, initiatives exist to secure commitments from businesses and other employers to hire people with criminal records, and some reentry programs provide certain limited forms of skill building. By 2020, thirty states had amended occupational licensing laws to modify provisions related to the state's authority to refuse to issue or renew licenses based solely on an applicant's criminal history. But obstacles remain.

California law, for example, still makes it extremely difficult for the roughly twenty-six hundred incarcerated women and men who are qualified to serve on crews battling wildfires to get licensed as emergency medical technicians—a requirement for permanent, often unionized jobs in municipal fire departments. They can apply for entry-level positions with the state's Department of Forestry and Fire Protection, but those are likely to be seasonal, temporary jobs without benefits in rural areas lacking necessary post-release supports and services.[67] In 2020, Governor Gavin Newsome signed a bill that permits formerly incarcerated firefighters to "petition to withdraw their plea of guilty or plea of nolo contendere and enter a plea of not guilty." There are exclusions for people convicted of arson or particular violent or sex offenses. If a petitioner's record is expunged, it may be easier to seek further training and employment.[68]

Realities for young people incarcerated in youth prisons and their purportedly "more humane and smaller" residential detention centers are dismal. Writing about the current political economy and its effects on youth in detention in the juvenile justice system, sociologist Alexandra Cox points out that while systemic focus is often on addressing purported criminogenic characteristics and producing behavioral changes, young people emerging from detention often face a brutal economic landscape. It is one in which they have been and will be impoverished, with few robust educational opportunities. This is essentially the same economy that criminalized them and delivered them into confinement: youth are disproportionately employed in unstable, low-wage, service sector, gig economy work. But even those with somewhat more education face declining opportunities for living-wage work with benefits. Reforms in recent years have reduced the number of young people who are actually imprisoned in juvenile justice detention centers. But those who remain, Cox says, represent an even more intense concentration of structural racism, poverty, and social marginalization.[69]

"Ban-the-box" reforms seek to enact laws that prevent employers from requiring job applicants to disclose any criminal record until later in the hiring process so that qualified candidates with criminal records are not stigmatized and banished from consideration early on. In 2015, President Barack Obama banned the box with regard to federal employment, calling on Congress to pass legislation requiring federal contractors to do the same. The Fair Chance Act, passed in 2019, scheduled for implementation in late 2021, prohibits federal agencies and contractors from requesting criminal background information prior to making an employment offer, albeit with some exceptions. By 2020, at least thirty-five states, the District of Columbia, and more than 150 local jurisdictions had adopted "ban-the-box" laws. While these laws can be helpful, employers who learn about an applicant's criminal record later in the hiring process retain the right to withdraw or not extend a job offer. Since 2016, new controversies have arisen. Some studies suggest that "ban the box" reforms may be backfiring, making young Black men, even those with no criminal records, less likely to get called back or hired once "ban-the-box" policies are in place. The argument is that employers, denied access to concrete information about applicants' criminal records, make assumptions about which candidates have them. But this argument, says economics scholar Terry-Ann Craigie, designates "ban the box" as "a scapegoat for discriminatory hiring practices that have been going on for decades."[70]

Some reformers promote neoliberal alternatives to "ban the box." A Pew Charitable Trusts article speaks favorably about "certificates of employability."[71] State authorities vouch in writing for the rehabilitative integrity of formerly incarcerated people. The certificates also provide employers protection from negligent hiring practices. Arguably, such an approach not only sidesteps the structural reality of racism under racial capitalism but reinforces it. This is the reality the bipartisan consensus refuses to address.

Voting Rights/Voter Suppression

People who are eligible to vote and in jail on misdemeanor charges, and in some cases those under civil commitment confinement, retain their right to vote. But countless votes are functionally suppressed because there are no consistent procedures for protecting and ensuring access to the franchise for eligible incarcerated voters.[72]

The voting rights of people in prison are determined by state, not federal, laws. In 2018, according to The Sentencing Project, about 6 million people were ineligible to vote in midterm elections because of felony convictions. Most of them, nearly 4.7 million, were not imprisoned but were subject to state prohibitions or other restrictions on voting by people who were released from prisons under conditions of probation or parole or had completed their sentences.[73] In 2020, Maine and Vermont, demographically the two whitest states in the nation, were the only two states that did not disenfranchise people with felony convictions, including people who are incarcerated. Iowa permanently disenfranchises all persons with felony convictions unless the government approves individual petitions for restoration of voting rights. The laws in remaining states vary widely. *Can't Pay, Can't Vote*, a national survey and report released by Georgetown Law's Civil Rights Clinic and Campaign

Legal Center, documents myriad ways in which restoration of voting rights on release from prison in about thirty states is contingent upon the individual's ability to pay sometimes onerous fines, fees, court costs, and restitution. The report emphasizes, "As they currently exist, anemic, limited, and confusing waiver processes do not provide an effective avenue for indigent voters to regain their right to vote."[74]

Historically, the United States has employed various stratagems for restricting the right to vote: to property owners, to white people, to men. Each time a restriction falls, new approaches to limit the franchise appear. Most new state restrictions are enacted under the criminalizing rubric of "eliminating voter fraud"—a phrase used to describe an extremely rare occurrence.[75] They take many forms: ID requirements that disadvantage certain segments of voters, extensive and largely unaccountable purges of voter rolls, highly selective closure of polling places, restrictions on voting by mail, and more. Since 2013, following a decision by the US Supreme Court to strike down a key provision of the Voting Rights Act of 1965, voter suppression measures have accelerated. According to the Brennan Center for Justice, "half the states in the nation have placed new, direct burdens on people's right to vote." While the language in these measures is race neutral, in practice the restrictions disproportionately disenfranchise Black, Indigenous, and Latinx people.[76]

Early and Conditional Release

In 2020, about 840,000 people were on parole in the United States. Theoretically, parole is a period of conditional, supervised release before a full prison sentence is completed behind bars. Sixteen states have abolished or severely restricted discretionary parole. That means opportunities for conditional release at the discretion of a parole board—usually gubernatorial appointees—based on its periodic assessment of a person's eligibility and preparedness have decreased. "The remaining states," PPI reports, " range from having a system of presumptive parole—where when certain conditions are met, release on parole is guaranteed—to having policies and practices that make earning release almost impossible." Most of those systems, the research organization says, get below average and failing grades when assessed on the basis of fairness, equity, and transparency.[77] Conditions of parole often involve the same burdensome, often fee-based, regimens of electronic monitoring, mandatory treatment for substance abuse, drug testing, and other requirements described in Chapters 4 and 5. Countless people are reincarcerated for technical parole violations, such as missing a mandated appointment.

Since 1987, people in federal prisons have been ineligible for parole. The First Step Act shortens some federal sentences, provides federal judges with somewhat more discretion to skirt mandatory minimum sentences for certain categories of prisoners, and permits some people to earn credits toward early supervised release by completing in-prison rehabilitative programs geared toward reducing recidivism. First Step also mandated the development of instruments to assess recidivism and "dangerousness" risk, as well as the "criminogenic" needs of every person confined within the federal prison system. PATTERN (Prisoner Assessment Tool Targeting Estimated Risks and Needs) is the algorithmic, gender-specific instrument now in use. In 2019, following release of the first PATTERN report, seven prominent advocacy organizations, including The Leadership Conference on Civil and Human Rights; the ACLU; and the Center on Race, Inequality and the Law at NYU Law, refuted claims that PATTERN is "unbiased across racial and ethnic classifications." They challenged tool design, lack of transparency associated with its design and development, accuracy, and gendered modeling.[78] Additional discussion of the problems with risk assessment tools can be found in Chapter 4.

Reform proposals in different states include elimination or reductions of parole revocation for technical violations. They also include increased use of compassionate release for incarcerated people who are seriously ill and facing imminent death, and greater use of federal and state executive clemency powers—commutation of sentences and pardons. "Second-look sentencing" is a legal mechanism permitting judges to review and modify individual sentences. "Second Chance" reforms at federal and state levels promise to provide funding to support a host of services and supports: supervised transitional housing and treatment programs for people, job training and readiness programs, and efforts to create more employment opportunities for people who are released. Where funding is available, it is often channeled to private entities and nonprofit organizations who, in effect, serve as extensions and proxies of the criminal legal system. Little or no attention is paid to the additional obstacles facing people emerging from prisons, including the steady whittling away at the social safety net, a health care system in shambles, and the structure of the labor market with increasing reliance on low-waged jobs without benefits.

TENSIONS AND CHALLENGES

It is not possible to accurately diagnose cause and remedy for the violent, degrading, and unhealthy conditions of confinement and release without reference to the social and economic conditions from which they arise and which they reproduce.

The tensions and challenges facing all who are working to accelerate decarceration and create a more just society are profound. How is it possible to reduce immediate harms to incarcerated people and their families without allocating more resources to and supporting the expansion of the carceral state? In what ways is it possible to organize to build the power and capacity of social movements so that they are better able to leverage fundamental shifts in financial priorities, policies, and resources? What strategies and tactics help activists and movements traverse the deceptive reform terrain with integrity while amassing strength?

A bad cop/good cop dynamic is at play in the fields of reform. Even as images of containing danger help drive reform, so do philanthropy-driven promises to redeem and set individuals up for success. But in the United States, social, economic, and ecological precarity is collective and increasing. “Success” in this context is a distorting dream proffered by an austerity regime that ties itself to the machinery of expanding carceral management. Underpinning the dream is the promise that innovative approaches to prison and jail environments and design will solve the old problems and the recurring harms and violence of incarceration.

7 Threshold

> What if abolition isn't a shattering thing, not
> a crashing thing, not a wrecking ball event? . . .
> What if abolition is something that grows? What
> if abolishing the prison industrial complex is the fruit
> of our diligent gardening, building and deepening
> of a movement to respond to the violence of the state
> and the violence in our communities with
> sustainable, transformative love?
>
> —Alexis Pauline Gumbs, "Freedom Seeds: Growing
> Abolition in Durham, North Carolina," 2008

Considered as a standalone project, apart from a larger historical, social, and economic context, any reform can be packaged to sound significant, humane, and progressive—especially to those who don't encounter and live with the violent impact of carceral systems on a daily basis. It is so tempting to conflate the sincere good intentions of liberal supporters of the bipartisan consensus with what is actually happening in its name. In 2018, the Vera Institute of Justice amplified this hope by asserting that the need for a "truly decisive step away from the past" involves establishing "a new set of normative values on which to ground prison policy and practice." This, in the Institute's view, will somehow equip US society to "recognize, interrogate, and unravel the heretofore persistent connections between racism and this country's system of punishment."[1]

But structural racism and systems of carceral control and surveillance aren't the result of outdated values, an old set of shopworn ideas and beliefs that can be tossed into the national trash can, to be replaced with reassuring talking points, new carceral blueprints, and endless streams of "best practices." They are rooted in material reality and constitute central features of society-wide custom and public consciousness. The social and economic foundation of the bipartisan consensus is racial capitalism. It is not possible through its reforms to structurally change the severe racialized inequality and economic exploitation required by that system or to fully repair the terrible fractures of human-human and human-environmental-ecological relationships it produces.[2]

The reform road starts from and invariably returns to criminalization, policing, and prisons. Along the way, mainstream reform agendas offer the limitless production of managerial schemes, procedural stratagems, and redesign projects that maneuver, Escher-like, in ascending and descending motion, throughout the edifice of the US criminal legal system, without once confronting or altering the foundation upon which it is built. Neither billionaires and their philanthropy-driven dependents nor law enforcement lobbies and their political enablers will transform it, but they will protect it. If we seek a different path forward, one that leads away from prison and a punishment-based society, then it's up to us, in various social, cultural, and political formations, to come together to create the way forward. We don't have to start from scratch. There are so many people, within and without jails and prisons, so many activists, organizers, visionaries, scholars, artists, poets, and more, spanning generations, who have broken and are breaking trail. Leadership has largely come from Black and other women—cis and trans—of color.

This is a liminal moment. We stand on the threshold between "how things are" and possibilities for radical, liberatory transformation. Within racial capitalism, the rise of neoliberalism with its insatiable need to manage the masses of humanity in a disciplined way has brought the United States to an unprecedented brink. The impact is not only economic. It also influences how people understand their relationships to self, to one another, and to the earth and its biosystems. Yet the continuation and evolution of racial capitalism is not inevitable. Repression and austerity are countered by the impulse for liberation, caring community, and generosity. We live in a time of "in-betweenness," an interstice between already-established but increasingly unsteady categories of political and economic meaning and possibilities for profound transformation. The choices of the elites are neither economically nor ecologically sustainable. They attempt to manage the turmoil and upheaval of unsustainability and deepening inequality with global and domestic policing, surveillance, and control. Established structures of supremacy and inequality are challenged by events (accelerating climate emergency, global pandemics, recessions, expanding systems of policing/carceral control, popular uprisings) and conditions (deepening global structural inequality, accelerating environmental and ecological devastation, routine police violence, mass migrations of people due to violence and poverty, and strong social movements).

The legitimacy of these structures is in question, perhaps even endangered. Justice movements are gaining momentum, addressing a variety of issues through a lens of interdependence, ranging from state and corporate violence to labor rights to climate crisis to disability justice, to trans justice, immigration rights and migrant mobility, and more. The tension is growing between profound challenges to the legitimacy of oppressive structures and the push to authoritarianism that accompanies indicators of systemic collapse. As always in such a time, the established structures move swiftly to prevent the possibility of dislocation by consolidating their power and authority, sometimes through brutal power grabs, but often under the mantle of reform. The good cop is no more reliable than the bad cop; they work together. One way in which elites seek to encounter change is to agree with the need for it, co-opt and water down ideas advanced by grassroots groups and abolitionists, then make sure that the resulting "change" expands their own power and influence.

Think back to 2011, when the NAACP and its allies, both likely (ACLU) and unlikely (Right on Crime, Americans for Tax Reform) stood at a press conference calling for vaguely described sentencing reforms. These changes would, they implied, not only "save taxpayer dollars" but also resolve in unspecified ways the dilemma of "over-incarcerating" and "under-educating" young Black people and other youth of color. A decade later, the problems were worse, not better. Even more money has been slashed or diverted from public education budgets, often with the help of politicians who also endorse bipartisan criminal justice reform. In the "education, not incarceration" reform struggle, incarceration is still winning.

THE EMPIRE'S NEW CLOTHES

In 2016, the Vera Institute of Justice announced its new Reimagining Prison project at the Eastern State Penitentiary Historical Site in Philadelphia, and in 2018 it expanded on the project in a document of the same name.[3] It is time, the institute said, to envision and create new carceral milieus and architectures; time to lead delegations of law enforcement and correctional officials, businesspeople, and selected reform advocates to Germany and other Western European countries with the idea of incorporating what they learned into US correctional systems. In 2019, Arnold Ventures gave the Vera Institute $7 million to implement these ideas and announced funding for a five-year, $10 million Prison Research and Innovation Initiative, helmed by the Urban Institute, to "foster prison-researcher partnerships, using data and evidence to guide innovations in prison design, operations, and culture."[4] An emergent linchpin of philanthropy-driven reform is the promise that innovative approaches to prison and jail environments and design, animated by new values centered on human dignity, will "disrupt" racist prison paradigms, reduce recidivism, and solve the old, recurring harms and violence of incarceration. Incarcerated people and staff alike will thrive in healthy carceral environments that offer anti-recidivism and character-enhancing programming. The mantra is always some version of "Smaller, Safer, Fairer" (New York City) or "Small, Safe, Humane" (Arnold Ventures).

But carceral systems cannot be fundamentally transformed without addressing, as Ruth Wilson Gilmore and James Kilgore say, "its context: tax, housing, health care, education, transportation, immigration, and other policies."[5] Equally problematic is the notion that models imported from countries with strong social welfare programs, without the same histories and enduring legacies of settler colonialism, Indigenous genocide, and chattel slavery, are sufficient to dismantle the violence and inequality of US carceral systems. The redesign route still leads to prison—now better resourced—with no significant increase in public revenues and no accompanying public priority shifts away from policing, technological surveillance and monitoring, and militarization toward community well-being. Here's how it works.

In the late 1920s, New York City officials made plans to replace the existing but badly deteriorated complex of jails on Blackwell Island with modern jail facilities on Rikers Island. Construction began in 1932; two years later, corruption scandals came to light regarding the letting of contracts and shoddy workmanship. But construction continued, the jail complex expanded, and so, too, did overcrowding and brutality. Protests, rebellions, and lawsuits seeking accountability for civil rights violations ensued. In the late 1970s, city officials came up with what was characterized as a bold plan to replace Rikers facilities with eight smaller, borough-based jails. Rikers Island itself would be leased to the state. Community residents protested, corrections officers opposed the plan, and a budget review showed that original estimates for new jail construction and associated costs were far too low. The plan to replace and build anew was scrapped.

Fast forward to 2014 when New York City hired McKinsey & Company, a high-powered corporate consulting firm, to help reduce alarming increases (and accompanying lawsuits) in historically pervasive violence at the Rikers Island jail complex. Before the consultancy was completed, the city paid McKinsey $27.5 million. In 2019, a blistering ProPublica investigation revealed the essential con artistry at the center of the project, pointing out that violence by correctional officers continued to grow and, "using the metrics employed by McKinsey, jailhouse violence has risen nearly 50 percent since the firm began its assignment." At the core of McKinsey's strategy was the establishment of so-called "Restart" housing units. An algorithmic instrument, the Housing Unit Balancer (HUB), was created to assess each resident's "dangerousness" and distribute people across housing units to minimize conflict and violence. The first test results, dramatically promising, were later discovered to be false. It turned out that consultants and correctional officials cherry-picked housing unit assignments, excluding people considered more "troublesome" and replacing them with others. When violence inevitably flared, officials, utilizing McKinsey data, initially doubled down on the cherry-picking, finally excluding young adults aged eighteen to twenty-one altogether and failing to address the issue of violent guards.[6] Mayor Bill de Blasio finally abandoned the Rikers reform effort, announcing instead its eventual closure. As part of an ambitious new decarceration plan, the complex would be replaced with a network of four new high-rise jails to be situated in different NYC boroughs at a cost of about $8.7 billion. City officials promised these jails would be smaller and safer, with better living environments. A firestorm of controversy over the proposed new high-rise jails arose. In 2019, even as strong community opposition to new jail construction mounted, the city council approved the plan. In March 2020, the city reopened a shuttered Rikers Island jail, reportedly to help with social distancing, as COVID-19 spread through NYC's carceral facilities.

Much is made of the closure of some juvenile detention centers and youth prisons throughout the United States. And while the closures are to be applauded, there's a shadow reality as well. As Alexandra Cox points out, when New York State passed a reform that raised the age of criminal responsibility for some teens, the law also included a provision for the creation of special youth prisons said to provide developmentally appropriate services, supports, and interventions. Accordingly, more than $50 million was allocated to "repurpose two prisons in the North Country so they can incarcerate just over 250 teenagers in these "youth-friendly" prisons.[7]

"If the facilities are more broadly 'nicer,'" asks Cox, "does this actually mean that young people's lives will change for the better?" Her work, she says, suggests that this is not possible because it is the state itself that criminalizes and pathologizes marginalized children, and administers a society in which few educational, health, housing, employment, and other resources are available to them. This abandonment serves as a pipeline for carceral confinement, at which point the state then focuses on the moral rehabilitation of these young people.[8]

Makeover projects function to placate growing public concerns about the essential violence of the institution itself even as they reinforce its overweening importance to US political and economic life. John Arnold, in particular, seems determined to rehabilitate the prison. In 2020, he briefly roiled the reform waters with a series of Twitter posts—tweets—questioning restoration of Pell grants for incarcerated people (@JohnArnoldFndtn, January 10, 2020).[9] A more important priority for new federal spending, he said, is "making the many dysfunctional prisons in America humane, safe, and have expanded programming for all."

There it was, if obliquely: the suggestion to shift public funds for a social good—presumably not restricted only to Pell funding—to support prisons in the guise of carceral humanism. Acknowledging that most operational funding for state prisons is local, Arnold suggested funding could be more flexible, that "the new fed $ that would go into Pell Grants could also be used for other things within state prisons." The psychological and safety needs of incarcerated people, he argued, constitute a precondition to the need for college. As he set up the case for increased federal spending for state prison facilities he expressed worry that "the Pell grant debate is sucking oxygen out of the room & distracting away from the real crisis, which is that many prisons in America are inhumane, immoral, and criminogenic at the most basic level." And what about strengthening public support for higher education and universal access to it outside the prison system? In another tweet (@JohnArnoldFndtn, February 25, 2020), also posted in that year, Arnold decried government "subsidies"—he refuses to call the allocation of public revenue to help reduce public structural inequality and increase public well-being anything but a subsidy—for "the 3 H's (healthcare, housing, higher-ed)."

NEOLIBERAL WORLD MAKING

Philanthropy-driven prison/criminal legal system reform serves as only one of many interrelated fulcrums for much larger projects in neoliberal, austerity-based world making. Others include health care reform, education reform, deregulation of industries and occupational licensing, privatization of public utilities and lands, and more. That's why it is so necessary to look beyond the specific foci of various reforms in order to grasp their relational nature to the structuring of an entire society. Geographer and documentary filmmaker Brett Story's award-winning film *The Prison in Twelve Landscapes* provides a haunting introduction to the subject. Charting a deeply unsettling journey through a variety of urban and rural geographies, the film reveals countless unseen ways in which civic life is shaped by the prison and the expansive race- and class-based systems of carceral control that serve it. Viewers never see the prison itself until the final frame.[10] Story extends her exploration of US carceral expansion and, with it, the expansion of oppressive social relations in everyday life in her book *Prison Land*.[11]

In *Decarcerating Disability: Deinstitutionalization and Prison Abolition*, scholar Liat Ben-Moshe takes note of the early promises of psychiatric deinstitutionalization, a shift sparked by relentless activism and advocacy.[12] From the 1960s on, the closure of psychiatric hospitals and residential institutions for people with intellectual or developmental disabilities proceeded apace. Originally, deinstitutionalization was to be coupled with expansions of community-based services and supports, including affordable, accessible housing and health care. For the most part, those expansions did not occur. Ben-Moshe rejects the reductionist storyline that deinstitutionalization itself produced subsequent increases in homelessness and incarceration, making jails and prisons into "the new asylums." Rather, she ties the failure of those early promises to a more historically complex, intersectional analysis in which racism and the rise of neoliberalism, with its antagonism to public funding for service/welfare sectors and reliance on logics of discipline and carceral control, produced betrayals and subsequent harms for people with disabilities. These critical insights not only deepen our understanding of deinstitutionalization as an abolitionist project but also bridge past and present in new, enormously important ways. Ben-Moshe's work also provides a contextual backdrop for understanding the fraudulence of implied "justice reinvestment" promises that helped launch the contemporary wave of reform.

For the big money that is driving reform agendas of any sort, it is essential in an uncertain world to try to maintain economic and political stability and continuity across political parties and administrations. According to the Institute for Policy Studies, the wealth of US-based billionaires rose 1,130 percent (in 2020 dollars) between 1990 and 2020, while between 1980 and 2018, their taxes, measured as a percentage of their wealth, decreased by 79 percent. Even after the 2008 financial crisis and subsequent recession, the wealth of billionaires increased 80.6 percent (in 2020 dollars) between 2010 and 2020.[13]

Every real crisis becomes an opportunity for the increased, upward transfer of wealth. As it initially spread in 2020, the COVID-19 pandemic starkly illuminated neoliberal priorities during a time of catastrophic job losses (at least forty-one million by June 2020) and economic hardship for millions of ordinary residents. Having dismantled its pandemic response capacity, the US government was unprepared to act effectively and ideologically unwilling to heed epidemiological warnings or emphasize nationalized public health responses.[14] More than $2.2 trillion in federal stimulus funds were distributed primarily to large financial institutions and companies, but Black-owned businesses were largely left behind.[15] Private and charter schools, with virtually no community accountability, received Paycheck Protection Program loans that need not be paid off if the funds are used for payroll costs, interest on mortgages, rent, and utilities. Such loans, meant only for small businesses to help them avoid layoffs, were not available to public school districts.[16] Hospitals reduced the hours for some staff, furloughed workers, but continued to give financial rewards to their executives, even as they received federal bailout funds.[17] In the end, the combined responses of the US government and its large corporations might best be classified as economically predatory and covertly eugenic, with a casual indifference to the lives of populations it considered expendable. Death counts rose, especially among vulnerable populations: those with preexisting/underlying health conditions and who were disabled and poor. Black, Brown, Indigenous, and elderly people of all races suffered disproportionately. Custodial institutions, including nursing homes, psychiatric institutions, jails, prisons, and detention centers became epicenters of viral transmission; people in them were made even more vulnerable by administrative incompetence and political cowardice. "Essential workers," disproportionately female, Black, and Latinx, most in low-waged jobs, were forced to choose between risking their own health by returning to work—often without access to proper protective supplies or safe working conditions—or losing unemployment and health care benefits, along with their livelihoods and perhaps their housing.[18]

"Public budgets have always been a reflection of the priorities of those in power," Alice Speri wrote in *The Intercept* in the spring of 2020, "and in the United States that priority for decades has been what leaders have called 'public safety,' which in reality has translated into mass criminalization."[19] Federal government officials and executives in some states instantly took advantage of the rolling COVID-19 emergency to double down on austerity measures, slashing expenditures for health care, education, other public services, workforces, and employee salaries and benefits. This was "budget crisis" writ large. New York governor Andrew Cuomo announced massive cuts for Medicaid.[20] As K–12 and higher education went online in attempts to slow down rates of coronavirus transmission, Cuomo announced that he had asked Microsoft billionaire Bill Gates, ranked among the top three billionaires in the world by *Forbes*, to help the state "reimagine education" through the greater use of technology. Perhaps, Cuomo suggested, the state no longer needed bricks-and-mortar schoolhouses.[21]

Police and corrections budgets fared better. According to Alex Vitale, coordinator of The Policing & Social Justice Project (PSJPP) at Brooklyn College, "New York City spends more on policing than it does on the Departments of Health, Homeless Services, Housing Preservation and Development, and Youth and Community Development combined."[22] Mayor Bill de Blasio recommended cutting the education budget by $641.7 million, twenty-seven times the reduction of $23.8 million for the New York Police Department. He also called for draconian cuts of $116 million for youth programs and initiatives, more than four times the amount of the proposed NYPD reduction. And Los Angeles community activists, writing in *The Appeal*, denounced Mayor Eric Garcetti's proposed budget for the 2020–21 fiscal year as "investing in a police state."[23] He called for a 7.1 percent increase in police funding to $3.15 billion, more than half of the city's unrestricted revenues, which support most general services. By contrast, the proposed Housing and Community Investment budget was reduced by 9.4 percent to $163 million. Almost every department providing vital services was cut in the proposed budget, which anticipated the furloughing of sixteen thousand city workers.

In the aftermath of George Floyd's murder and calls to defund the police, furious community organizers pressured governments to make major cuts, and in response, some jurisdictions took action to try to mollify growing opposition. The New York City Council and Mayor de Blasio announced a cut of $1 billion in the police budget, but critics noted that the changes primarily moved rather than reduced expenditures or relied on promises that may not be fulfilled.[24] About $400 million for school police, for example, was shifted to the Department of Education; the number of police in schools was not reduced. The Los Angeles City Council reduced the proposed police budget by $150 million, out of a $3 billion budget.[25] But a different, more substantive, approach, the fiercely contested charter amendment, Measure J, opposed by the county sheriff and several influential law enforcement–related organizations, was ultimately passed by Los Angeles County voters in 2020.[26] Measure J requires allocation of at least 10 percent of locally generated, unrestricted county funds—estimated to be between $360 million and $900 million—in two specific ways. The first focuses on investments in communities most directly harmed by racism: job training, housing assistance, youth development, and small businesses owned by people of color. Funds will also support community-based restorative justice programs, pretrial non-custody services, and non-carceral, health-related services. Measure J is only the beginning of a longer struggle to shift more public revenue to human needs, by no means the end of one.

In the midst of two simultaneously unfolding nightmares—a pandemic and racist police violence—many people began to develop a clearer understanding of the systemic nature of that violence. As that understanding deepens, it is essential, as abolitionists and transformative justice advocates have long argued, to begin to speak of “harm” and “violence” rather than “crime” and “criminals.”

VICTIMS, SURVIVORS, AND HARM

Despite promises of a new and more dignified day for “justice-involved” people ensnarled in the carceral system, mainstream reforms remain centered around the management of a selectively defined caste of criminals and offenders, stigmatized and portrayed as the primary carriers of societal trouble, dangerousness, and violence. Historically resonant currents of anti-Black racism continue to define the concepts of criminality and danger in the public consciousness, and the racially coded meaning of the word "criminal" helps drive public support for expanded systems of control and surveillance. Yet, as this book has shown, this never produces more safety, only more violence. It's an uphill struggle to make that case when sensationalized images of "criminals"—the purportedly guilty, violent ones—are juxtaposed with the concept of "crime victims and survivors." Indeed, the term *crime* itself serves as a distinct, if false, line of harm demarcation in the public consciousness and public policy. It selects the harm done by selectively policed and prosecuted individuals or small groups of individuals as the proper focus for the criminal legal system. This focus disappears violence, even massive violence, visited collectively on populations and communities by various state, corporate, and other civic actors. It separates the victims/survivors society is told to care about from those who can be abandoned with indifference. While this is seldom openly stated, the fine print in laws and reform initiatives, together with the results of their implementation, provides the answers. Survived & Punished NY believes that one of the central questions grassroot groups should ask in deciding how to respond to a proposed reform is whether it creates a division between "deserving" and "undeserving" people."[27] If it does, the reform will only reinforce this dishonest dichotomy.

It is equally important to take note of the imputation of "not crime" for even massively harmful, sometimes lethal, actions inflicted or authorized by people who slot into some mix of white, male, law enforcement, white-collar, corporate/business, or civic/political leadership statuses. This leaves intact the unspoken presumption that any criminalized person or population must have done *something* "to deserve" whatever harm comes their way. Their lives simply don't count for much in the US justice imaginary. But the more massive the violence done by so-called "respectable" actors, the less willing the US justice system is to confront it. The result is the de facto legitimation of inequality and violence, legalized and extra-legal, against anyone marked as "criminal" and "undeserving." Political writer Joshua Leifer calls this "the logic of fracture." He wrote about it in 2019 amid new global eruptions of anti-Semitic harassment and violence that resulted in a deluge of regressive calls for more policing and punishment.

> The logic of fracture appears when the pain of victimhood leads to callousness or blindness to—or worse, pleasure in—the pain of others who are coded as adversaries; their humanity—their victimhood, too—is obscured by fear and suspicion. . . . The logic of fracture breaks society into hostile, frightened, mutually suspicious groups and subgroups. . . . It turns people who share the same spaces—neighborhoods, buildings, buses, trains—as well as the same interests—affordable housing, clean streets, a living wage—into enemies.[28]

Leifer emphasizes that processes of criminalization and policing inevitably result in "a kind of collective punishment of communities of color." He encourages fighting back against violence with radical and compassionate solidarity strategies in which people act not only for their own survival and well-being, but also for all others whose lives and safety are endangered. This requires strategies of practical solidarity, which provide tangible/material forms of assistance and support even as they work to dismantle structural violence, rather than strategies of conditional charity, which do not. And to do that, it is necessary to deconstruct what the sociologist Everett C. Hughes described as "group fictions." Group fictions are embedded in comforting but false storylines that locate intrinsic violence and danger in targeted people or communities even as they attribute inherent virtue to others, including law enforcement authorities and their proxies, who routinely use violence to protect the wealthy and enforce their will. A group fiction, said Everett, is "collective unwillingness to know unpleasant facts."[29]

Group fictions begin to fall apart when individuals and communities ask deeper questions without resorting to rhetorical shorthand: Who actually perpetrates violence? What kinds of violence? Who suffers from its harms? How? How can these harms best be repaired? How can people who suffer harm be safe? How can the harm be addressed in ways that call for accountability without inflicting more violence on anyone? These larger questions open up the personal and social space necessary for caring about the harms done to individuals, communities, and entire populations without subjecting any of them to a worthiness triage.

The US legal system does not recognize this complexity, and the bipartisan consensus frames "victim" narrowly. "When people dismiss abolitionists for not caring about victims or safety," says Derecka Purnell, a human rights lawyer, writer, and organizer, "they tend to forget that we are those victims, those survivors of violence." She writes of growing up in a neighborhood permeated with environmental toxins, low-waged jobs, and joblessness, where the first shooting she witnessed, at age thirteen, was by a uniformed security guard who stormed into a neighborhood recreation center, drew his weapon, and shot a young boy—his own cousin—in the arm. "My sister and I hid in the locker room for hours afterward," Purnell wrote. "The guard was back at work the following week."[30]

For decades, abolitionists educated about, developed, and shared resources, methodologies, cultural work, and ideas regarding justice practices that speak more expansively to "harm" than to "crime." They continue to offer and expand educational and organizing resources on their websites and through social media. An essential part of the struggle, they all emphasize, is transforming the social, political, and economic conditions that give rise to violence, including the structural violence of policing, prosecution, and punishment.

Such organizations as INCITE!, a network of radical feminists of color organizing to end state and home/community violence; Creative Interventions, which is focused on community-based options for interventions to interpersonal violence; Critical Resistance; and

Survived & Punished address the interrelationships of state, interpersonal, and community violence. The Bay Area Transformative Justice Collective, a community group based out of Oakland, California, works to build and support transformative justice responses to child sexual abuse; the anthology *Love WITH Accountability: Digging Up the Roots of Child Sexual Abuse*, edited by Aishah Shahida Simmons, utilizes the moving power of storytelling to do the same.[31] The anthology *Beyond Survival: Strategies and Stories from the Transformative Justice Movement*, edited by Ejeris Dixon and Leah Lakshmi Piepzna-Samarasinha, explores questions of accountability without relying on the criminal legal system.[32] The website TransformHarm.org, a resource hub about ending violence and providing an introduction to transformative justice, provides access to a multitude of perspectives and resources. Honoring and utilizing integrative healing traditions and practices, Kindred Southern Healing Justice Collective works to intervene, interrupt, and transform generational trauma and violence in southern communities and movements. Serious about shifting power, Kindred seeks to create new modalities for whole community safety, care, and well-being as a strategy for change.[33] In *Mutual Aid*, legal scholar and abolitionist Dean Spade explores ways in which community members can help provide survival support and resources within a framework of organizing for transformational change.[34] Online, the Big Door Brigade offers "solidarity not charity" mutual aid resources. An essential component of the struggle, they all emphasize, is transforming the social, political, and economic conditions that give rise to raciscm, poverty and violence, including the structural violence of policing, prosecution, and punishment.

The task of making choices to reduce as much harm as possible without increasing carceral reach can be difficult, especially when every proffered reform is typically couched in the uplifting rhetoric of "smaller, smarter, less expensive, humane, fairer." A first step toward starting to unravel carceral reach is to gain clarity about reforms that may help to reduce harm without pouring more resources into or expanding policing/punishment systems ("non-reform" reforms)—and also about reforms that, even under the promise of shrinking incarceration, actually expand those systems.

In 2014, commenting on police reforms, Mariame Kaba, an organizer, educator, and curator whose work focuses on ending violence, dismantling the PIC, transformative justice, and supporting youth leadership development, summarized some of both kinds.[35] Among the kinds of reforms that should always be opposed, she says, are those that allocate more money, resources, and staffing to law enforcement agencies, and those that under the guise of such euphemisms as "community policing" actually expand police presence. Reforms that promise technologies to make policing more fair and less lethal should also be opposed; those technologies, Kaba said, would likely be turned against the public in repressive ways. Among the "non-reform" reforms that should be supported are measures to offer reparations to victims of police violence and their families, disarm the police, and more. She has written more extensively on abolitionist organizing and transforming justice in *We Do This 'til We Free Us*.[36]

The abolitionist current runs deep; it does not simply seek to shift the power to harshly sentence, incarcerate, and surveil from elites to those who oppose them. It does, however, seek to shift power by dismantling structural inequality and violence. In 2020, as uprisings gained strength across the United States, young organizers created a vibrant, online #8toAbolition campaign that encapsulated essential demands in eight points, provided graphics (in different translations), and resource links so that people can learn more about abolition, mutual aid, and community-led models of building safety and collective care.[37]

One of the most wrenching dilemmas for many people is whether to support jail/prison expansion, new construction, and new design to replace or augment deplorable facilities and conditions of confinement. This is often framed as a dishonest choice that attempts to maneuver us into an austerity framework justified as carceral humanism: Do we want to help people or leave them trapped in squalor? While inside/outside abolitionists have always undertaken the essential work of harm reduction, they do not endorse building new jails and prisons as a stepping-stone to decarceration. No matter how well-meaning the intentions are, new models, new units, new structures always help perpetuate the old carceral logic. Better options to expansion, new designs, and new construction exist. They include decarceration and access to free and appropriate community-based supports and services with no connection to systems of policing and carceral control. More and more communities are insisting on clear shifts in civic and fiscal priorities, for thinking in new ways about community relationships and forms of accountability. The money and civic space for all of this will come from steadily defunding and shrinking the power of police and prosecutors. From refusing to invest in and deploy technologies of assessment, surveillance, and control. From closing tax loopholes and raising taxes on corporations and the wealthy. From building caring, green, economies.

The same year that the Vera Institute published its lengthy vision for reimagining prisons, Kaba and Kelly Hayes, an abolitionist organizer and journalist, called, instead, for "a jailbreak of the imagination."[38] In a liminal moment, the invitation is to go forward, not backward. It is an invitation not merely to "disrupt" with "innovations" but to dismantle the entire prison paradigm. Without intervention, interruption, and replacement of the usual bipartisan and law enforcement reform measures that favor security and market-based "solutions" over social, economic, and ecological well-being; without interrupting the consolidation of wealth and policing, the world itself is remade into a structure of supervision and control. The structural harms identified throughout this book can never be fought effectively on a standalone, issue-by-issue basis. Racial capitalist and neoliberal paradigms must also be rejected and replaced. That's a tall order, and all of the answers for what will replace them do not yet exist. But those answers are coming into being and will grow ever stronger as people come together in communities and through powerful justice movements to create them. Abolition doesn't happen overnight. It has been emerging for centuries, not only a creation of people like Harriet Tubman and Frederick Douglass, whose names we know, but in the hearts, minds, and imaginations of countless ordinary people, whose names we will never know, who took and are still taking great risks to insist with their lives that something better than white supremacy, economic exploitation, and violence lies ahead. Something they are helping to create.

TOWARD INTERDEPENDENCE

To take on structural violence and inequality with radical and compassionate strategies of solidarity is to recognize its interdependence with other forms of violence and forceful domination. Writing about the ways in which activists began to join forces to address the twinned harms of prisons and environmental destruction in California, anti-prison and environmental justice advocates Rose Braz and Craig Gilmore illustrated the importance of not only linking issues, but also building trustworthy relationships in the process, as well as the importance of documenting the work.[39]

In the mid-1980s, an organization known as Madres del Este de Los Angeles, or Mothers of East Los Angeles (MELA), fought then California governor George Deukmejian's plan to build a new prison in their neighborhood. It took painstaking effort to spread the word and mobilize opposition. Their poor community needed many things to increase its health, safety, and well-being, but it did not need a prison. According to Braz and Gilmore, members went door to door, speaking to neighbors and to people gathered in churches, organizational meetings, and community gatherings. Along the way, in conversation with others, their understandings deepened; their vision grew. The women learned that a new hazardous-waste incinerator would be built in their neighborhood, so they also organized to stop that. And they fought a Santa Barbara–Long Beach oil pipeline that would loop inland through East L.A. in order to avoid more affluent, whiter, coastal communities. The proposed pipeline was eventually rerouted, not through East L.A. In 1990, plans for the hazardous waste incinerator were abandoned. Fierce grassroots opposition to the new prison delayed its building. New studies were done, and eventually it was built, but it was relocated. Along the way, they built, strengthened, and deepened neighborhood relationships by respecting the power of ordinary people to effect change, even when up against entrenched political and corporate interests. They recognized the interdependent nature of struggles against racism, poverty, prisons, and environmental harms. Many people and groups contributed information, insight, research assistance, and other forms of support. More people joined the struggles, realizing that their participation mattered, and that together, they could increase community well-being. And even if an organizing effort did not result in an outright win, as with the relocation instead of cancellation of the prison, it still produced knowledge, insight, and commitment that would be useful in subsequent struggles. The work of Madres del Este de Los Angeles also helped inspire more broad-based organizing initiatives to stop additional prison construction in California.

In 2001, Critical Resistance; the California Moratorium Project; the Southwest Network for Environmental and Economic Justice; the Center on Race, Poverty and the Environment; Fresno State MEChA (Movimiento Estudiantil X/Chicanx de Aztlán); and the West County Toxics Coalition sponsored a daylong conference called "Joining Forces: Environmental Justice and the Fight against Prison Expansion." The purpose was "to explore the place of prisons in the environmental justice movement and the ways that anti-prison activists can learn from environmental justice examples." Juana Guitérrez, a cofounder and leader in Madres del Este de Los Angeles gave the opening remarks. This was prelude to a multifaceted campaign of litigation, coalition building, media efforts to shift public opinion and policy, and grassroots organizing to stop the building of a new

$335 million state prison in Delano in the rural and impoverished San Joaquin Valley. The event and subsequent campaign provided an opportunity for diverse organizations and constituencies, ranging from Critical Resistance, NAACP, the Rainforest Action Network, the National Lawyers Guild Prison Law Project, Friends of the Kangaroo Rat, ranchers, farmers and farmworkers, immigrants, and many others to come together in new ways. The new prison was delayed, but finally built. In the meantime, as the state faced an impending budget crisis, the campaign began to shift the terrain of anti-prison organizing in practical, visionary, and boldly assertive ways. Important relationships had been built; new ones would be forged. From that point on, more and more people began to question the necessity of new prisons, and prison populations began to decline as the result of relentless activist pressure. And organizing produced new successes, over time, defeating new jails and jail expansion.

A great deal of similar work is already in motion, in many different arenas; more and more organizers, activists, and groups are embracing the strength embedded in an ethos of interdependence. It is not necessary to be or promise to become an abolitionist to recognize that one of the most important insights of abolition is that it offers new ways to think about what it takes to create, sustain, and strengthen trustworthy social, economic, and cultural relationships.

It is essential that we find new ways to build collective insights and strategies and to share organizing capacity across movements. We need to create new ways to come together collectively to build the vision, strength, will, and staying power necessary to counter the consolidation of wealth, political control, and policing power with life-giving world making of our own. And we must do this without reifying white supremacist, elite structures and leadership. The purpose is not to fashion rigid templates that dictate what should be said and done, how and when. Rather, it is to build strong and dependable relationships across difference, strong enough to stand in the great storms that always accompany profound challenges to power. It is to build trustworthy relationships in a spirit of mutual learning and willingness, not only so that we can build on and share what we know from different perspectives but also so we can begin to organize our way forward and through what we don't yet know.

If this sounds like a utopian project, it isn't. No one knows what the future holds, especially in a volatile and unstable time. Entrenched power fights back ruthlessly when it is challenged. This work is gritty, always unfinished, but also forever in motion, always moving toward life and liberation rather than toward containment, control, and greed.

Sometimes the work is wearying and wrenching, filled with grief and rage. Sometimes it is exhilarating, filled with possibility, joy, and new insight. It is a growing thing, not unlike systems of transformative mutual aid. And it is organic, arising from and responding to people's needs, not unlike trees in forests that utilize mycorrhizal networks under the soil's surface to communicate, support, share resources, and respond with assistance in times of stress and peril. This is work that tends to the health of the collective as well as individuals, not with policing and punishment, but with nourishment and generosity.

Notes

INTRODUCTION

1. See Stuart Schrader, *Badges without Borders: How Global Counterinsurgency Transformed American Policing* (Oakland: University of California Press, 2019). See also Bernard E. Harcourt, *The Counterrevolution: How Our Government Went to War against Its Own Civilians* (New York: Basic Books, 2018).

2. Mariame Kaba, "Yes, We Mean Literally Abolish the Police," *New York Times*, June 12, 2020, https://www.nytimes.com/2020/06/12/opinion/sunday/floyd-abolish-defund-police.html.

3. Elizabeth Hinton, "The Minneapolis Uprising in Context," May 29, 2020, *Boston Review*, http://bostonreview.net/race/elizabeth-hinton-minneapolis-uprising-context.

4. Aaron Blake, "President Trump's State of the Union Transcript, Annotated," *Washington Post*, February 5, 2019, https://www.washingtonpost.com/politics/2019/02/06/president-trumps-state-union-transcript-annotated/.

5. Lawrence Mower, "Ron DeSantis Signs Amendment 4 Bill, Limiting Felon Voting," *Tampa Bay Times*, June 28, 2019, https://www.tampabay

.com/florida-politics/buzz/2019/06/28/ron-desantis-signs-amendment-4-bill-limiting-felon-voting/.

6. Lawrence Mower and Langston Taylor, "Celebrities Spent Millions So Florida Felons Could Vote. Will It Make a Difference?," ProPublica, November 2, 2020, https://www.propublica.org/article/bloomberg-lebron-james-fines-fees-florida-felons. See also Amber Randall, "'I Felt Voiceless': Thousands of Ex-Felons in Florida Are Voting for the First Times in Their Lives," *South Florida Sun Sentinel*, November 2, 2020, https://www.sun-sentinel.com/news/politics/elections/fl-ne-ex-felons-voting-presidential-election-20201102-4jnteivke5fw5cgozylungdqwm-story.html.

7. Dan Berger, "Finding and Defining the Carceral State," *Reviews in American History* 47, no. 2 (June 2019): 279–85. This review notes the need for developing clearer understandings of what we mean when we say "the carceral state."

8. Robin D. G. Kelley, "Scholar Robin D. G. Kelly on How Today's Abolitionist Movement Can Fundamentally Change the Country," interview with Jeremy Scahill, *The Intercept* (podcast), June 27, 2020, https://theintercept.com/2020/06/27/robin-dg-kelley-intercepted/.

9. For a useful analysis of anti-Blackness within a context of chattel slavery, settler colonialism, and Indigenous genocide and land theft, see Nick Estes and Roxanne Dunbar-Ortiz, "Examining the Wreckage," *Monthly Review*, July 1, 2020, https://monthlyreview.org/2020/07/01/examining-the-wreckage/.

10. Ruth Wilson Gilmore, *Golden Gulag: Prisons, Surplus, Crisis, and Opposition in Globalizing California* (Berkeley: University of California Press, 2007), 28.

11. David Harvey, *A Brief History of Neoliberalism* (New York: Oxford University Press, 2007), 2.

12. Anti-prison activists have written and educated about and organized against prison economies, and especially the siting of new prisons and jails in rural areas for many years. See Kevin Pyle and Craig Gilmore, *Prison Town: Paying the Price* (a comic book) (Northampton, MA: The Real Cost of Prisons Project, 2005), accessed June 15, 2020, http://www.realcostofprisons.org/prison_town.pdf. See also Tracy Huling, "Building a Prison Economy in Rural America," In *Invisible Punishment: The Collateral Consequences of Mass Imprisonment*, ed. Mark Mauer and Meda Chesney-Lind (New York: The New Press, 2002), https://www.prisonpolicy.org/scans/huling_chapter.pdf. See also Ryan S. King, Mark

Mauer, and Tracy Huling, *Big Prisons, Small Towns: Prison Economics in Rural America*, The Sentencing Project, February 2003, https://www.sentencingproject.org/wp-content/uploads/2016/01/Big-Prisons-Small-Towns-Prison-Economics-in-Rural-America.pdf.

13. Dan Berger, "Social Movements and Mass Incarceration," *Souls: A Critical Journal of Black Politics, Culture, and Society* 15, nos. 1–2 (July 24, 2013): 5, https://www.tandfonline.com/doi/abs/10.1080/10999949.2013.804781.

14. Institute for Policy Studies, *The Souls of Poor Folk: Auditing America 50 Years after the Poor People's Campaign Challenged Racism, Poverty, the War Economy/Militarism and Our National Morality*, with editorial assistance from the Poor People's Campaign: A National Call for Moral Revival; the Kairos Center for Religions, Rights, and Social Justice; and Repairers of the Breach (Washington, DC: Institute for Policy Studies, April 2018), 3), https://ips-dc.org/wp-content/uploads/2018/04/PPC-Audit-Full-410835a.pdf.

15. David Barsamian, "'The Land Is the Body of the Native People': Talking with Roxanne Dunbar-Ortiz," *The Progressive*, July 4, 2018, https://progressive.org/dispatches/the-land-is-the-body-of-the-native-people-roxanne-dunbar-ortiz-180703/.

16. Keeanga-Yamahtta Taylor, *Race for Profit: How Banks and the Real Estate Industry Undermined Black Home Ownership* (Chapel Hill: University of North Carolina Press, 2019), 261.

17. See, for example, Van R. Newkirk II, "The Great Land Robbery: The Shameful Story of How 1 Million Black Families Have Been Ripped from Their Farms," *Atlantic*, September 29, 2019, https://www.theatlantic.com/magazine/archive/2019/09/this-land-was-our-land/594742/.

18. See, for example, Francisco E. Balderrama and Raymond Rodriguez, *Decade of Betrayal: Mexican Repatriation in the 1930s*, rev. ed. (Albuquerque: University of New Mexico Press, 2006).

19. See, for example, Richard Reeves, *Infamy: The Shocking Story of Japanese American Internment in World War II.* (New York: Picador, 2016).

20. Institute for Policy Studies, The National Community Reinvestment Coalition, and the Kirwan Institute for the Study of Race and Ethnicity at The Ohio State University, *Ten Solutions to Bridge the Racial Wealth Divide*, April 2019, https://ips-dc.org/wp-content/uploads/2019/04/EMBARGOED-Ten-Solutions-to-Bridge-the-Racial-Wealth-Divide-FINAL-April-11.pdf.

21. Center on Budget and Policy Priorities, "Cuts in Federal Assistance Have Exacerbated Families' Struggles to Afford Housing," April 12, 2016, https://www.cbpp.org/research/housing/chart-book-cuts-in-federal-assistance-have-exacerbated-families-struggles-to-afford.

22. US Department of Housing and Urban Development, *The 2019 Annual Homeless Assessment Report (AHAR) to Congress*, January 2020, https://www.huduser.gov/portal/sites/default/files/pdf/2019-AHAR-Part-1.pdf.

23. National Center for Homeless Education, "National Overview, School Years 2015–2016, 2016–2017, and 2017–2018," http://profiles.nche.seiservices.com/ConsolidatedStateProfile.aspx, accessed July 15, 2020.

24. Brookings, Metropolitan Policy Program, *Meet the Low-Waged Workforce*, November 7, 2019, https://www.brookings.edu/research/meet-the-low-wage-workforce/

25. Chad Stone, Claire Zippel, et al., "Weakening Economy, Widespread Hardship Show Urgent Need for Further Relief," Center on Budget and Policy Priorities, November 10, 2020, https://www.cbpp.org/research/economy/weakening-economy-widespread-hardship-show-urgent-need-for-further-relief.

26. For a detailed account, see Elizabeth Hinton, *From the War on Poverty to the War on Crime: The Making of Mass Incarceration in America* (Cambridge, MA: Harvard University Press, 2016).

27. For a riveting account of how purportedly "race-neutral" policies intended to address violence transmuted into practices that intensified anti-Blackness throughout the criminal legal system, see Naomi Murakawa, *The First Civil Right: How Liberals Built Prison America* (New York: Oxford University Press, 2014).

28. James Kilgore, "Repackaging Mass Incarceration," *Counterpunch*, June 6, 2014, https://www.counterpunch.org/2014/06/06/repackaging-mass-incarceration/.

CHAPTER 1. CORRECTIONAL CONTROL AND THE CHALLENGE OF REFORM

1. Brown, Governor of California, et al. v. Plata et al., 563 U.S. 493 (2011), Justice Supreme Court Center https://supreme.justia.com/cases/federal/us/563/493/.

2. Margo Schlanger "Plata v. Brown and Realignment: Jails, Prisons, Courts, and Politics." *Harvard Civil Rights–Civil Liberties Law Review* 48, no. 1 (2013): 165–15.

3. Ibid.

4. Jason Pohl and Ryan Gabrielson, "California's Jails Are in a Deadly Crisis: Here's How Experts Suggest Fixing Them," ProPublica, January 6, 2020, https://www.propublica.org/article/californias-jails-are-in-a-deadly-crisis-heres-how-experts-suggest-fixing-them.

5. Kay J. Whitlock and Nancy A. Heitzeg, "Prison Reform, Proposition 47 and the California Shell Game," *Truthout*, February 2015, https://truthout.org/articles/prison-reform-prop-47-and-the-california-shell-game/.

6. Ruth Wilson Gilmore. *Golden Gulag: Prisons, Surplus, Crisis, and Opposition in Globalizing California* (Berkeley: University of California Press, 2007).

7. Ibid., 5.

8. "California: Gang-Related Legislation by State" National Gang Center, June 2019, https://www.nationalgangcenter.gov/Legislation/California; Gilmore, *Golden Gulag*.

9. "California Profile," Prison Policy Initiative, 2019, https://www.prisonpolicy.org/profiles/CA.html.

10. Terry A. Kupers, "Compliance or Critical Thinking?," Prisoner Hunger Strike Solidarity, May 25, 2020, https://prisonerhungerstrikesolidarity.wordpress.com/.

11. Whitlock and Heitzeg, "Prison Reform, Proposition 47, and the California Shell Game."

12. Joan Petersilia, "California Prison Downsizing and Its Impact on Local Criminal Justice Systems," *Harvard Law & Policy Review* 8, no. 327 (2014); Jeffrey Lin and Joan Petersilia, *Follow* the *Money*: *How California Counties Are Spending Their Public Safety Realignment Funds*, Stanford Criminal Justice Center (January 2014).

13. Proposition 47: The Safe Neighborhoods and Schools Act, California Courts, https://www.courts.ca.gov/prop47.htm.

14. Proposition 57: The Public Safety and Rehabilitation Act of 2016, California Department of Corrections and Rehabilitation, https://www.cdcr.ca.gov/blog/category/proposition-57/.

15. Whitlock and Heitzeg, "Prison Reform, Proposition 47, and the California Shell Game."

16. "California Profile."

17. Ibid.

18. Michael McGough, "200 San Quentin Workers Infected, 10 Inmates Dead as Coronavirus Devastates California Prison." *Sacramento Bee*, July 14, 2020, https://www.sacbee.com/news/politics-government/the-state-worker/article244215127.html.

19. California Department of Rehabilitation and Corrections, "Budget Information: CDRC's Budget for Fiscal 2018–19," https://www.cdcr.ca.gov/budget/.

20. Whitlock and Heitzeg, "Prison Reform, Proposition 47, and the California Shell Game."

21. Pohl and Gabrielson, "California's Jails Are in a Deadly Crisis."

22. "Abolish Jailing," Critical Resistance, n.d., http://criticalresistance.org/abolish-jailing/ accessed September 9, 2020.

23. Angela Y. Davis, *Are Prisons Obsolete?* (New York: Seven Stories Press 2003).

24. Samuel Walker, C. Spohn, and M. DeLone. *The Color of Justice: Race, Ethnicity and Crime in America*, 6th ed. (Belmont, CA: Wadsworth, 2017); Elizabeth Hinton and DeAnza Cook, "The Mass Criminalization of Black Americans: A Historical Overview," *Annual Review of Criminology* 4, no.1 (2021): 261–86. https://www.annualreviews.org/doi/abs/10.1146/annurev-criminol-060520-033306.

25. Wendy Sawyer and Peter Wagner, "Mass Incarceration: The Whole Pie 2020," Prison Policy Initiative, March 24, 2020, https://www.prisonpolicy.org/reports/pie2020.html.

26. Rachel Kushner, "Is Prison Necessary? Ruth Wilson Gilmore Might Change Your Mind," *New York Times Magazine*, April 17, 2019.

27. Joey L. Mogul, Andrea J. Ritchie, and Kay Whitlock. *Queer (In)justice: The Criminalization of LGBT People in the United States* (Boston: Beacon Press, 2011); Nancy A. Heitzeg, "Differentials in Deviance: Race, Class, Gender, and Age," in *The Routledge Handbook of Deviant Behavior*, ed. Clifton D. Bryant (London: Routledge, 2011), Keith Hayward, Jock Young, and Jeff Ferrell, *Cultural Criminology: An Invitation*. 2nd ed. (London: SAGE, 2015).

28. Alex Vitale, *The End of Policing* (New York: Verso, 2017).

29. Ibid.

30. Emily Baxter, ed., *We Are All Criminals* (Minneapolis: We Are All Criminals, 2017).

31. Devah Pager, *Marked: Race, Crime, and Finding Work in an Era of Mass Incarceration* (Chicago: University of Chicago Press, 2007).

32. Joe Watson, "Study: 95 Percent of Elected Prosecutors Are White," *Prison Legal News*, February 2017, 44.

33. Baxter, *We Are All Criminals*.

34. Alexi Jones, "Correctional Control 2018: Incarceration and Supervision by State," Prison Policy Initiative, https://www.prisonpolicy.org/reports/correctionalcontrol2018.html.

35. Ibid.

36. Ibid.

37. Jesse Jannetta, Justin Breaux, and Helen Ho, The Urban Institute, Jeremy Porter, City University of New York, *Examining Racial and Ethnic Disparities in Probation Revocation* (Washington, DC: Urban Institute, 2014), https://www.urban.org/sites/default/files/publication/22746/413174-Examining-Racial-and-Ethnic-Disparities-in-Probation-Revocation.PDF.

38. Ibid.

39. Peter Wagner and Wendy Sawyer, "States of Incarceration: The Global Context 2018," Prison Policy Initiative, June 2018, https://www.prisonpolicy.org/global/2018.html.

40. Sawyer and Wagner, "Mass Incarceration: The Whole Pie 2020."

41. Ibid.

42. Sawyer and Wagner, "States of Incarceration."

43. Ibid.

44. Ibid.

45. Jacob Kang-Brown, Chase Montagnet, Eital Schattner-Elmaleh, and Oliver Hinds, *People in Jail and Prison in 2020* (Brooklyn, NY: Vera Institute of Justice 2020), https://www.vera.org/downloads/publications/people-in-jail-and-prison-in-2020.pdf.

46. Sawyer and Wagner, "Mass Incarceration: The Whole Pie 2020."

47. Ibid.

48. Ibid.

49. Prison Policy Initiative, "Prison Gerrymandering Project," https://www.prisonersofthecensus.org/impact.html.

50. Ibid.

51. Ibid.

52. Sawyer and Wagner, "Mass Incarceration: The Whole Pie 2020."

53. Ibid.

54. Ibid.

55. Jacob Kang-Brown, Montagnet, Schattner-Elmaleh, and Hinds, *People in Jail in 2019* (Brooklyn NY: Vera Institute of Justice, 2019).

56. Ibid.

57. Kang-Brown, et al., *People in Jail and Prison in 2020.*

58. Jack Norton and Jacob Kang-Brown, "If You Build It: How the Federal Government Fuels Rural Jail Expansion," Vera Institute for Justice, January 10, 2020, https://www.vera.org/in-our-backyards-stories/if-you-build-it.

59. Brett Story, *Prisonland: Mapping Carceral Power across Neoliberal Amer*ica (Minneapolis: University of Minnesota Press 2019).

60. For a useful overview of various government agencies by which noncitizens are apprehended at the border of the United States or within its interior, see American Immigration Council, "Immigration Detention in the United States by Agency, January 2020, https://www.americanimmigrationcouncil.org/sites/default/files/research/immigration_detention_in_the_united_states_by_agency.pdf.

61. "'These People Are Profitable': Under Trump, Private Prisons Are Cashing In on ICE Detainees," *USA Today*, December 19, 2019, https://www.usatoday.com/in-depth/news/nation/2019/12/19/ice-detention-private-prisons-expands-under-trump-administration/4393366002/.

62. C. C. García Hernández, "Deconstructing Crimmigration," *UCDL Rev.*, 52 (2018): 197.

63. "Immigration Detention 101," Detention Watch Network, https://www.detentionwatchnetwork.org/issues/detention-101, accessed December 3, 2020.

64. Anna Flagg and Andre R. Calderón, "500,000 Kids, 30 Million Hours: Trump's Vast Expansion of Child Detention," The Marshall Project, October 30, 2020, https://www.themarshallproject.org/2020/10/30/500-000-kids-30-million-hours-trump-s-vast-expansion-of-child-detention.

65. See, for example, Andrea Castillo, "ICE Provides 'Deplorable" Healthcare to Detained Immigrants, Advocates Allege in Massive Lawsuit," August 19, 2019, https://www.latimes.com/california/story/2019-08-19/immigrant-detention-medical-care-lawsuit.

66. Jean Casala, James Ridgeway, and Sarah Shroud eds., *Hell Is a Very Small Place: Voices from Solitary Confinement* (New York: New Press, 2016).

67. Peter Wagner and Bernadette Rabuy, "Following the Money of Mass Incarceration," Prison Policy Initiative, January 25, 2017, https://www.prisonpolicy.org/reports/money.html.

68. Ibid.; Lucius Couloute and Dan Kopf, "Out of Prison and Out of Work: Unemployment among Formerly Incarcerated People," Prison Policy Initiative, July 2018.

69. Sawyer and Wagner, "Mass Incarceration: The Whole Pie 2020."

70. Ibid.

71. Wendy Sawyer, "Youth Confinement: The Whole Pie 2019," Prison Policy Initiative, December 19, 2019, https://www.prisonpolicy.org/reports/youth2019.html.

72. Peter Lehman, Ted Chiricos, and William D. Bales, "Sentencing Transferred Juveniles in the Adult Criminal Courts: The Direct and

Interactive Effects of Race," *Youth Violence and Juvenile Justice* 15, no. 2 (2017): 172–90.

73. Samuel Walker, C. Spohn, and M. DeLone. *The Color of Justice: Race, Ethnicity and Crime in America*, 6th ed. (Belmont, CA: Wadsworth, 2018).

74. Nancy A. Heitzeg, *The School-to-Prison Pipeline: Education, Discipline, and Racialized Double Standards* (Santa Barbara, CA: Praeger Publishing, 2016); Monique Morris, *Pushout: The Criminalization of Black Girls in Schools* (New York: The New Press, 2016).

75. Aleks Kajstura, "Women's Incarceration: The Whole Pie 2019," Prison Policy Initiative, October 29, 2019, https://www.prisonpolicy.org/reports/pie2019women.html.

76. Ibid.

77. "Facts about the Death Penalty," Death Penalty Information Center (updated March 24, 2021), https://documents.deathpenaltyinfo.org/pdf/FactSheet.pdf .

78. Liliana Segura, "After Trump's Execution Spree, Lingering Trauma and a Push for Abolition," The Intercept, February 6, 2021 https://theintercept.com/2021/02/06/execution-trump-death-penalty-abolish/.

79. Facts about the Death Penalty."

80. Ibid.

81. Wagner and Rabuy, "Following the Money of Mass Incarceration."

82. Alexi Jones and Wendy Sawyer, "Arrest, Release, Repeat: How Police and Jails Are Misused to Respond to Social Problems," Prison Policy Initiative, August 2019, https://www.prisonpolicy.org/reports/repeatarrests.html.

83. Ibid.; Stephen Raher, "The Company Store and the Literally Captive Market: Consumer Law in Prisons and Jails," *Hastings Race & Poverty Law Journal* 17, no. 3 (2020), https://repository.uchastings.edu/hastings_race_poverty_law_journal/vol17/iss1/3.

84. Davis, *Are Prisons Obsolete?*

85. North Carolina Prisoners Labor Union, "Goals of the North Carolina Prison Labor Union" (1974), in *Remaking Radicalism: A Grassroots Documentary Reader of the United States, 1973–2001*, ed. Dan Berger and Emily K. Hobson (Athens: University of Georgia Press, 2020).

86. Ibid.; Angela Davis, "Masked Racism: Reflections on the Prison Industrial Complex" *Colorlines*, September 10, 1998, https://www.colorlines.com/articles/masked-racism-reflections-prison-industrial-complex.

87. Rose Brewer and Nancy A. Heitzeg, "The Racialization of Crime and Punishment: Criminal Justice, Color-Blind Racism and the Political Economy of the Prison Industrial Complex," *American Behavioral Scientist*, 51, no. 5 (Winter 2008): 625–44.

88. Ibid.

89. "What Is the PIC?," Critical Resistance, n.d., http://criticalresistance.org/about/not-so-common-language/ accessed September 2, 2020.

90. Sawyer and Wagner, "Mass Incarceration: The Whole Pie 2020."

91. Alexi Jones, "Reforms without Results: Why States Should Stop Excluding Violent Offenses from Criminal Justice Reforms," Prison Policy Initiative, April 2020, https://www.prisonpolicy.org/reports/violence.html.

92. Mariame Kaba, David Stein, Dan Berger, "What Abolitionists Do," *Jacobin*, August 24, 2017, https://www.jacobinmag.com/2017/08/prison-abolition-reform-mass-incarceration.

93. Rachel Kushner, "Is Prison Necessary?

94. "What Is Abolition?," Critical Resistance, n.d. http://criticalresistance.org/about/not-so-common-language/ accessed September 2, 2020.

95. Mark Morris, ed, *Instead of Prisons: A Handbook for Abolitionists* (Syracuse, NY: Prison Research Education Action Project, 1976).

CHAPTER 2. FOLLOW THE MONEY

1. National Association for the Advancement of Colored People (NAACP), *Misplaced Priorities: Over Incarcerate, Under Educate*, April 2011, https://www.prisonpolicy.org/scans/naacp/misplaced_priorities.pdf.

2. Michelle Alexander, *The New Jim Crow: Mass Incarceration in the Age of Colorblindness* (New York: The New Press, 2010).

3. Marshall Greenlaw, "The Oscar Grant (Oakland) Protests, 2009–2011," BlackPast, December 24, 2017, https://www.blackpast.org/african-american-history/oscar-grant-oakland-protests-2009-2011/.

4. "Benjamin Jealous and Grover Norquist Talk Overincarceration," NAACP, April 11, 2011, video of press conference, 43:12, https://www.youtube.com/watch?v=46X8ClRmDvg.

5. See, for example, "The 'Texas Miracle': 60 Minutes Investigates Claims That Houston Schools Falsified Dropout Rates," program transcript, CBS News, January 6, 2004, https://www.cbsnews.com/news/the-texas-miracle/. See also Michael Winerip, "On Education: The 'Zero Dropout' Miracle: Alas! Alack! A Texas Tall Tale," *New York Times*, August 13,

2003, https://www.nytimes.com/2003/08/13/nyregion/on-education-the-zero-dropout-miracle-alas-alack-a-texas-tall-tale.html.

6. NAACP, *Misplaced Priorities*, 1.

7. "NAACP Report Says Shift in Funding Toward Prisons 'Failing Us.'" *PBS NewsHour*, April 7, 2011, host Judy Woodruff interviews guests Benjamin Jealous and Grover Norquist, video, 8:32, and transcript, https://www.pbs.org/newshour/show/naacp-report-calls-shift-in-funding-toward-prisons-alarming#transcript.

8. For a useful discussion of California's three-strikes law, see Office of the Public Defender, San Diego (CA) County, "Three Strikes Law—A General Summary," https://www.sandiegocounty.gov/content/sdc/public_defender/strikes.html, accessed November 11, 2020.

9. For a succinct account of Wilson's political ability to harness white racial fears, see Dale Maharidge, "California Schemer: What You Need to Know about Pete Wilson," *Mother Jones*, November/December 1995, https://www.motherjones.com/politics/1995/11/california-schemer-what-you-need-know-about-pete-wilson/.

10. Peter Wagner, "Tallying the Extent of the Clinton-Era Crime Bills," Prison Policy Initiative, May 25, 2016, https://www.prisonpolicy.org/blog/2016/05/25/seven_clinton_crime_bills/. See also Sheryl Gay Stolberg and Astead W. Herndon, "'Lock the S.O.B.s Up': Joe Biden and the Era of Mass Incarceration," *New York Times*, June 25, 2019, https://www.nytimes.com/2019/06/25/us/joe-biden-crime-laws.html.

11. Lauren-Brooke Eisen, "The 1994 Crime Bill and Beyond: How Federal Funding Shapes the Criminal Justice System," Brennan Center for Justice, September 19, 2019, https://www.brennancenter.org/our-work/analysis-opinion/1994-crime-bill-and-beyond-how-federal-funding-shapes-criminal-justice.

12. Frank Clemente and William Rice, "Opinion: The Trump Tax Cut Has Amounted to Nothing but Broken Promises for the Middle Class," *Los Angeles Times*, January 1, 2020, https://www.latimes.com/opinion/story/2020-01-01/donald-trump-tax-cut-deficit.

13. Robin Wigglesworth, "How America's 1% Came to Dominate Equity Ownership," *Financial Times*, February 10, 2020, https://www.ft.com/content/2501e154-4789-11ea-aeb3-955839e06441.

14. "Social Impact Bonds Gain Momentum in the Criminal Justice Field," Council of State Governments Justice Center, March 31, 2012, https://csgjusticecenter.org/social-impact-bonds-gain-momentum-in-the-criminal-justice-field/.

15. Kay Whitlock, "Endgame: How 'Bipartisan Criminal Justice Reform' Institutionalizes a Right-Wing, Neoliberal Agenda," *The Public Eye*, Spring 2017, 7. This article, posted June 6, 2017, is also online at the Political Research Associates website, https://www.politicalresearch.org/2017/06/06/endgame-how-bipartisan-criminal-justice-reform-institutionalizes-a-right-wing-neoliberal-agenda.

16. "State Policy Network (SPN), *Desmog* (blog), accessed June 3, 2020, https://www.desmogblog.com/state-policy-network.

17. "Supreme Court to Hear TPPF's Challenge to Obamacare," Texas Public Policy Foundation, March 2, 2020, https://www.texaspolicy.com/press/supreme-court-to-hear-tppfs-challenge-to-obamacare.

18. Forrest Wilder, "Revealed: The Corporations and Billionaires That Fund the Texas Public Policy Foundation," *Texas Observer*, August 24, 2012, https://www.texasobserver.org/revealed-the-corporations-and-billionaires-that-fund-the-texas-public-policy-foundation/. See also "Texas Public Policy Foundation," Sourcewatch, The Center for Media and Democracy, November 13, 2018, https://www.sourcewatch.org/index.php/Texas_Public_Policy_Foundation.

19. Graham Readfern, "Why Has One of the World's Biggest Funders of Environmental Conservation Also Given $4 Million to a Climate Denial Group?," *Desmog* (blog), December 14, 2017, https://www.desmogblog.com/2017/12/14/pew-charitable-trusts-funding-climate-denial-texas-public-policy-foundation-hartnett-white.

20. This information is drawn from the Public Welfare Foundation's grants awarded database, between 2013 and 2020. Through other information sources, it is clear that the Public Welfare Foundation funded TPPF in 2010. The authors have chosen to provide a cautious and hedged estimate of the Foundation's support to TPPF.

21. Jim Webb, "Why We Must Reform Our Criminal Justice System," *The Hill*, June 11, 2009, https://thehill.com/blogs/congress-blog/politics/25328-why-we-must-reform-our-criminal-justice-system-sen-jim-webb.

22. "Shaky Arguments Block Federal Commission on Crime," editorial, *Washington Post*, October 29, 2011 https://www.washingtonpost.com/opinions/shaky-arguments-block-federal-commission-on-crime/2011/10/26/gIQAUwSOTM_story.html.

23. Jennifer Bellamy, "The New Politics of Criminal Justice Reform," ACLU, December 22, 2010, https://www.aclu.org/blog/smart-justice/mass-incarceration/new-politics-criminal-justice-reform.

24. Marie Gottschalk, "The Prisoner Dilemma: Texas Fails to Confront Mass Incarceration," *The Baffler*, no. 46, July 2019, accessed July 16, 2020, https://thebaffler.com/salvos/the-prisoner-dilemma-gottschalk.

25. Ibid.

26. "Mission and History," John Jay College Institute for Justice and Opportunity, https://justiceandopportunity.org/about/history-and-mission/, accessed November 23, 2020.

27. Sam Collings-Wells, "From Community Action to Community Policing: The Ford Foundation and the Urban Crisis, 1960–1975," *The Metropole*, the Official Blog of the Urban History Association, https://themetropole.blog/2019/07/16/from-community-action-to-community-policing-the-ford-foundation-and-the-urban-crisis-1960-1975/, accessed November 13, 2020.

28. "Criminal Justice," MacArthur Foundation, https://www.macfound.org/programs/criminal-justice/, accessed November 12, 2020.

29. Astead W. Herndon, "George Soros' Foundation Pours $220 Million into Racial Equity Push," *New York Times*, July 13, 2020, https://www.nytimes.com/2020/07/13/us/politics/george-soros-racial-justice-organizations.html.

30. See Andy Kroll, "Exposed: The Dark-Money ATM of the Conservative Movement," *Mother Jones*, February 5, 2013, https://www.motherjones.com/politics/2013/02/donors-trust-donor-capital-fund-dark-money-koch-bradley-devos/. See also, for a deeper exploration, Jane Mayer, *Dark Money: The Hidden History of the Billionaires behind the Rise of the Radical Right* (New York: Anchor Books, 2017).

31. Jane Mayer, "New Koch," *New Yorker*, January 18, 2016, https://www.newyorker.com/magazine/2016/01/25/new-koch.

32. Charles Koch and Brian Hooks, "Why We Can No Longer Count on Politics to Solve America's Problems," *Washington Post*, August 13, 2019, https://www.washingtonpost.com/opinions/its-not-just-up-to-policy-leaders-must-empower-people-too/2019/08/13/72eba6fa-bdca-11e9-a5c6-1e74f7ec4a93_story.html.

33. See, for example, Will Lennon, "The Koch Network's Integrated Strategy for Social Transformation," OpenSecrets.org, Center for Responsive Politics, October 26, 2018, https://www.opensecrets.org/news/2018/10/the-koch-networks-integrated-strategy-for-social-transformation/.

34. See, for example, Alex Kotch, "Charles Koch Ramps Up Higher Ed Funding to Fuel 'Talent Pipeline,'" *PRWatch*, Center for Media and

Democracy, February 2, 2017, https://www.prwatch.org/news/2017/01/13210/charles-koch-ramps-higher-ed-funding-talent-pipeline. See also UnKoch My Campus, a website dedicated to challenging the undue influence of wealthy, pro-corporate donors on college campuses and on preserving democracy from actors whose expressed intent is to place private interests over the common good, http://www.unkochmycampus.org/.

35. Nicholas Confessore, "Koch Brothers' Budget of $889 Million for 2016 Is on Par with Both Parties' Spending," *New York Times*, January 26, 2015, https://www.nytimes.com/2015/01/27/us/politics/kochs-plan-to-spend-900-million-on-2016-campaign.html?hp&action=click&pgtype=Homepage&module=first-column-region%C2%AEion=top-news&WT.nav=top-news&_r=0.

36. Michael Hiltzik, "David Koch's Real Legacy Is the Dark Money Network of Rich Right-Wingers," *Los Angeles Times*, August 23, 2019, https://www.latimes.com/business/story/2019-08-23/david-kochs-legacy-dark-money-network.

37. Theda Skocpol and Alexander Hertel-Fernandez, *The Koch Effect: The Impact of a Cadre-Led Network on American Politics*, prepared for presentation at the Inequality Mini-Conference, Southern Political Science Association, San Juan, Puerto Rico, January 8, 2016; slightly corrected version, January 27, 2016, https://scholars.org/sites/scholars/files/the_koch_effect_for_spsa_w_apps_skocpol_and_hertel-fernandez-corrected_1-27-16_3.pdf. See also Theda Skocpol, and Alexander Hertel-Fernandez, "The Koch Network and Republican Party Extremism," *Perspectives on Politics* 14, no. 3 (2016): 681–99, doi:10.1017/S1537592716001122.

38. See, for example, Ryan Grim and Andrew Perez, "The Kochs Funded Third Way to Push Free Trade to Democrats, New Book Says," *The Intercept*, August 13, 2019, https://theintercept.com/2019/08/13/koch-brothers-third-way/. See also Jessica Piper, "Koch Brothers Float Possibility of Backing Congressional Democrats in 2020 Primaries," *Open Secrets.org*, Center for Responsive Politics, June 7, 2019, https://www.opensecrets.org/news/2019/06/koch-brothers-float-backing-democrats-in-2020/.

39. David Barboza, "Corporate Conduct: The Trader; Enron Trader Had a Year to Boast of, Even If . . . ," *New York Times*, July 9, 2002, https://www.nytimes.com/2002/07/09/business/corporate-conduct-the-trader-enron-trader-had-a-year-to-boast-of-even-if.html.

40. Matt Taibbi, "Looting the Pension Funds," *Rolling Stone*, September 26, 2013, https://www.rollingstone.com/politics/politics-news/looting-the-pension-funds-172774/.

41. Raúl Carrillo and Jesse Myerson, "The Dangerous Myth of 'Taxpayer Money,'" *Splinter*, October 19, 2017, https://splinternews.com/the-dangerous-myth-of-taxpayer-money-1819658902.

42. Newt Gingrich and B. Wayne Hughes Jr., "What California Can Learn from the Red States on Crime and Punishment," *Los Angeles Times*, September 16, 2014, https://www.latimes.com/opinion/op-ed/la-oe-0917-gingrich-prop--47-criminal-justice-20140917-story.html.

43. See, for example, "Invest/Divest," Movement for Black Lives Policy Platform, accessed June 13, 2020, https://m4bl.org/policy-platforms/invest-divest/.

44. Susan B. Tucker and Eric Cadora, "Justice Reinvestment," *Ideas for an Open Society* 3, no. 3 (November 2003), https://www.opensocietyfoundations.org/publications/ideas-open-society-justice-reinvestment.

45. Marie Gottschalk, *Caught: The Prison State and the Lockdown of American Politics* (Princeton, NJ: Princeton University Press, 2015), 98–111.

46. "Justice Reinvestment," Council of State Governments Justice Center, https://csgjusticecenter.org/projects/justice-reinvestment/.

47. "35 States Reform Criminal Justice Policies through Justice Reinvestment," Pew Charitable Trusts fact sheet, July 2018, https://www.pewtrusts.org/-/media/assets/2018/07/pspp_reform_matrix.pdf.

48. Gottschalk, *Caught*, 105–7.

49. Samantha Harvell et al., *Reforming Sentencing and Corrections Policy: The Experience of Justice Reinvestment Initiative States* (Washington, DC: The Urban Institute, December 2016 [revised March 2017]), https://www.urban.org/research/publication/reforming-sentencing-and-corrections-policy, https://www.urban.org/research/publication/reforming-sentencing-and-corrections-policy/view/full_report.

50. In 2013, for example, the Urban Institute estimated that, based on early experiences with seventeen states, future savings in these states would, over time, amount to about $3.3 billion, with a reinvestment of about $374 million in "public safety initiatives." See "The Justice Reinvestment Initiative: Experiences from the States," Urban Institute, July 2013, 4, https://www.urban.org/sites/default/files/publication/23881/412879-The-Justice-Reinvestment-Initiative-Experiences-from-the-States.PDF.

51. Erika Parks et al., *Local Justice Reinvestment: Strategies, Outcomes, and Keys to Success* (Washington, DC: The Urban Institute, August 2016), 13–15.

52. Harvell, et al., *Reforming Sentencing and Corrections Policy*, vii–ix.

53. "Second Prop 47 RFP Now Available," Board of State and Community Corrections (BSCC), January 22, 2019, http://www.bscc.ca.gov/news/second-prop-47-rfp-now-available/.

54. "Overview of 2019–2020 Revised Corrections Budget," Californians United for a Responsible Budget, n.d., accessed June 16, 2020, http://www.curbprisonspending.o rg/wp-content/uploads/2019/05/CURB-May-Budget-Revise-2019-20-Overview-.pdf.

55. Amber Rose-Howard, "The People's Response to Governor Newsom's Proposed Corrections Budget," Californians United for a Responsible Budget, January 14, 2020, https://www.curbprisonspending.org/2020/01/14/the-peoples-response-to-governor-newsoms-proposed-corrections-budget/.

56. Ruth Wilson Gilmore, Keynote conversation with Mariame Kaba and James Kilgore, Making and Unmaking Mass Incarceration Conference, University of Mississippi, December 5, 2019. Conference organized by Garrett Felber.

CHAPTER 3. CRIMINALIZATION, POLICING, AND PROFILING

1. Charlotte Rosen, "Abolition or Bust: Liberal Police Reform as an Engine of Carceral Violence," *Radical History Review/The Abuseable Past*, June 25, 2020, https://www.radicalhistoryreview.org/abusablepast/abolition-or-bust-liberal-police-reform-as-an-engine-of-carceral-violence/; Micol Segele, *Violence Work: State Violence and the Limits of Police* (Durham, NC: Duke University Press, 2018).

2. Alex Vitale, *The End of Policing* (New York: Verso, 2017), 31–54.

3. Interrupting Criminalization: Research in Action, http://bcrw.barnard.edu/fellows/interrupting-criminalization-research-in-action/.

4. Nancy A. Heitzeg, "Broken Windows, Broken Lives, and the Ruse of Public Order Policing," *Truthout*, July 17, 2015, https://truthout.org/articles/broken-windows-broken-lives-and-the-ruse-of-public-order-policing/.

5. Ibid.; Paul Butler, *Chokehold: Policing Black Men* (New York: New Press, 2018).

6. Jen Chung, "Ramsey Orta, Who Filmed the Police Killing of Eric Garner, Released from Prison." *The Gothamist* June 9, 2020, https://gothamist.com/news/ramsey-orta-who-filmed-police-killing-eric-garner-released-prison.

7. Abdallah Faayd. "The Criminalization of Gentrifying Neighborhoods," *Atlantic*, December 20, 2017, https://www.theatlantic.com/politics/archive/2017/12/the-criminalization-of-gentrifying-neighborhoods/548837/.

8. James Q. Wilson and G. E. Kelling, "Broken Windows: The Police and Neighborhood Safety," *Atlantic*, March 1982, Randall G. Sheldon, "Accessing Broken Windows: A Brief Critique," Center on Juvenile Justice, 2004, http://citeseerx.ist.psu.edu/viewdoc/download?doi=10.1.1.694.7723&rep=rep1&type=pdf, Jeffery Fagan and Garth Davies, Street Stops and Broken Windows: Terry, Race, and Disorder in New York City," *Fordham Urban Law Journal* 457 (2000), https://scholarship.law.columbia.edu/faculty_scholarship/507.

9. Jordan T. Camp and Christina Heatherton, eds., *Policing the Planet: Why the Policing Crisis Led to Black Lives Matter* (New York: Verso, 2016), 3.

10. Jeffrey Fagan and Garth Davies, "Street Stops and Broken Windows: Terry, Race, and Disorder in New York City," *Fordham Urban Law Journal* 28, no. 2 (2000):457–504, https://scholarship.law.columbia.edu/faculty_scholarship/1241.

11. Floyd, et al. v. City of New York, et al. 959 F. Supp. 2d 540 (2013); Center for Constitutional Rights https://ccrjustice.org/home/what-we-do/our-cases/floyd-et-al-v-city-new-york-et-al.

12. Ashley Southall, "Subway Arrests Investigated over Claims People of Color Are Targeted," *New York Times*, January 13, 2020, https://www.nytimes.com/2020/01/13/nyregion/letitia-james-fare-beating-nypd.htm; Ben Chapman, "New York City Police Arrest Over 100 People for Crimes Related to Coronavirus," *Wall Street Journal*, May12, 2020, https://www.wsj.com/articles/new-york-city-police-arrest-over-100-people-for-crimes-related-to-coronavirus-11589321199.

13. Police Shooting Database, "Fatal Force 2015–2020," *Washington Post*, updated July 15, 2020, https://www.washingtonpost.com/graphics/investigations/police-shootings-database/.

14. Kimberly Adams, "FBI Says New Data on Police Use of Force Is Coming This Summer," *Marketplace Morning Report*, June 1, 2020.

15. Andrea J. Ritchie, *Invisible No More: Police Violence against Black Women and Women of Color* (Boston, MA: Beacon Press, 2016).

16. Keeanga-Yamahtta Taylor, *From #BlackLivesMatter to Black Liberation* (Chicago: Haymarket Books 2016), 263–65.

17. Movement for Black Lives Platform, February 20, 2017, https://policy.m4bl.org/platform/.

18. Christina Heatherton, "#BlackLivesMatter and Global Visions of Abolition: An Interview with Patrisse Cullors," in Camp and Heatherton, *Policing the Planet*, 35–40.

19. Jennifer Gonnerman, "The Last Day at the Civil Rights Division," *New Yorker*, January 21, 2017, http://www.newyorker.com/news/news-desk/last-day-at-the-civil-rights-division; Ian Millhiser and Nicole Flatow, "Eric Holder's Historic and Little-Noticed Civil Rights Legacy," *ThinkProgress*, September 25, 2014, https://thinkprogress.org/eric-holders-historic-and-little-noticed-civil-rights-legacy-6a4ea1f6a0c8.

20. Jaweed Kaleem, "Under Obama, the Justice Department Aggressively Pursued Police Reforms. Will It Continue under Trump?" *Los Angeles Times*, February 2, 2017, http://www.latimes.com/nation/la-na-baltimore-chicago-police-2016-story.html.

21. Brandon E. Patterson, "Jeff Sessions Does Not Think Your Local Police Department Is His Problem," *Mother Jones*, April 4, 2017, http://www.motherjones.com/politics/2017/04/jeff-sessions-consent-decree-review.

22. *Final Report of the President's Task Force on 21st Century Policing* (Washington, DC: Office of Community Oriented Policing Services, 2015); The National Initiative for Building Community Trust and Justice, "Mission" U.S. Department of Justice, n.d. https://trustandjustice.org/about/mission accessed March 24, 2021.

23. Naomi Murakawa, "Three Traps of Reform," Abolition for the People Series, *Level*, October 21, 2020, https://level.medium.com/why-police-reform-is-actually-a-bailout-for-cops-ecf2dd7b8833.

24. The National Initiative for Building Community Trust and Justice, "Mission" https://trustandjustice.org/about/mission accessed March 24, 2021.

25. Ibid.

26. Aaron Stagoff-Belfort, "Biden Plans to 'Reinvigorate' a Community Policing Office That Has a Dark History," *Slate*, February 24, 2021, https://slate.com/news-and-politics/2021/02/biden-cops-office-funding-police-history.html.

27. Justin Hansford, "Five Years after Ferguson, We're Losing the Battle against Police Violence,, *New York Times*, August 9, 2019, https://www.nytimes.com/2019/08/09/opinion/ferguson-anniversary-police-race.html.

28. Camp and Heatherton, *Policing the Planet*, 5.

29. Ruth Wilson Gilmore and Craig Gilmore, "Beyond Bratton," in Camp and Heatherton, *Policing the Planet*, 173–200.

30. William J. Bratton and Jon Murad, "Precision Policing: A Strategy for the Challenges of 21st Century Law Enforcement," from *Urban Policy 2018* (New York: Manhattan Institute, October 1, 2018), https://www.manhattan-institute.org/html/urban-policy-2018-precision-policing-strategy-21st-century-law-enforcement-11508.html.

31. Al Baker and J. David Goodman, "Bratton, Who Shaped an Era in Policing, Tries to Navigate His Most Difficult Divide," *New York Times*, July 25, 2016, https://www.nytimes.com/2016/07/26/nyregion/william-bratton-new-york-city-police-commissioner.html.

32. Richard A. Oppel Jr. and Kim Barker, "New Transcripts Detail Last Moments for George Floyd," *New York Times*, July 8, 2020, https://www.nytimes.com/2020/07/08/us/george-floyd-body-camera-transcripts.html.

33. Chao Xiong and Liz Sawyer, "Bodycam Video in George Floyd Killing Shows Officer Pulled Gun, Swore and Touched Floyd Multiple Times without Explanation," *Star Tribune*, July 15, 2020, V https://www.startribune.com/floyd-video-gun-pulled-without-explanation/571778072/?refresh=true.

34. "What We Know about the Death of George Floyd in Minneapolis," *New York Times*, May 27, 2020, https://www.nytimes.com/2020/05/27/us/george-floyd-minneapolis-death.html.

35. Ibid.

36. "Chauvin Amended Criminal Complaint," https://www.documentcloud.org/documents/6935817-Chauvin-Amended-Criminal-Complaint.html.

37. "What We Know about the Death of George Floyd."

38. MPD150, *Enough Is Enough: A 150 Year Performance Review of the Minneapolis Police Department* (Minneapolis MN: MPD150, 2017), https://www.mpd150.com/wp-content/themes/mpd150/assets/mpd150_report.pdf.

39. Ibid.

40. Ibid.

41. AMW, "George Floyd Uprisings: Anatomy of a Counterinsurgency," Abolition Media Worldwide, July 9, 2020, https://www.amwenglish.com/articles/george-floyd-uprisings-anatomy-of-a-counterinsurgency/.

42. Larry Buchanan, Quoctrung Bui, and Jugal K. Patel "Black Lives Matter Largest Protests in U.S. History," *New York Times*, July 3, 2020,

https://www.nytimes.com/interactive/2020/07/03/us/george-floyd-protests-crowd-size.html.

43. David Hambling, "The Deadly Truth about Rubber Bullets," *Forbes*, June 8, 2020, https://www.forbes.com/sites/davidhambling/2020/06/08/the-deadly-truth-behind-rubber-bullets/#5456d9f921f8 ; https://www.startribune.com/injuries-at-protests-draw-scrutiny-to-use-of-police-weaponry/571407242/.

44. Jack Arnholz, Ivan Pereira, and Christina Carrega, "US Protests Map Shows Where Curfews and National Guard Are Active," ABC News, June 4, 2020, https://abcnews.go.com/US/locations-george-floyd-protests-curfews-national-guard-deployments/story?id=70997568.

45. Juan Arredondo, "U.S. Watched George Floyd Protests in 15 Cities Using Aerial Surveillance," *New York Times*, June 19, 2020, https://www.nytimes.com/2020/06/19/us/politics/george-floyd-protests-surveillance.html?action=click&algo=bandit-story&block=more_in_recirc&fellback=false&imp_id=535225546&impression_id=719000677&index=2&pgtype=Article®ion=footer.

46. Alicia Lee, "Minneapolis Schools and Parks Cut Ties with Police over George Floyd's Death" CNN, June 4, 2020, https://www.cnn.com/2020/06/03/us/minneapolis-schools-police-george-floyd-trnd/index.html.

47. Molly Beckhardt, Paul Bolden, and Eric Goodling, "Defund the Police—and Abolish Laws Used to Target Vulnerable People," *The Appeal*, June 26, 2020, https://theappeal.org/defund-the-police-and-abolish-laws-used-to-target-vulnerable-people/.

48. Ted Gist, "Policing Experts Say Reform Possible without 'Defunding,'" *The Crime Report*, November 16, 2020, https://thecrimereport.org/2020/11/16/policing-experts-say-reform-possible-without-defunding/.

49. "Overcriminlization," Right on Crime, n.d., http://rightoncrime.com/issue/overcriminalization/ accessed November 28, 2020; John Villasenor, "Overcriminalization and Mens Rea Reform: A Primer," Brookings Institute, December 22, 2015, https://www.brookings.edu/blog/fixgov/2015/12/22/over-criminalization-and-mens-rea-reform-a-primer/.

50. Reina Steinzor, "Dangerous Bedfellows: The Stalemate on Criminal Justice Reform," *The American Prospect*, May 11, 2016, https://prospect.org/power/dangerous-bedfellows/; Kay J. Whitlock, "Endgame: How Bipartisan Criminal Justice Reform Institutionalizes a Right Wing Neoliberal Agenda," *Political Research Associates*, June 6, 2017, https://www.politicalresearch.org/2017/06/06/endgame-how-bipartisan-criminal-justice-reform-institutionalizes-a-right-wing-neoliberal-agenda.

51. David Simon, *Elite Deviance*, 11th ed. (New York: Routledge, 2018).

52. Matt Ford, "Could a Controversial Bill Sink Criminal Justice Reform in Congress?" *Atlantic*, October 26, 2017, https://www.theatlantic.com/politics/archive/2017/10/will-congress-reform-criminal-intent/544014/.

53. Vitale, *The End of Policing*, 156–75; National Gang Center, "Gang-Related Legislation," National Gang Center, June 2019, https://www.nationalgangcenter.gov/Legislation.

54. Vitale, *The End of Policing*, 156–75.

55. Josmar Truijillo and Alex Vitale, *Gang Take-Downs in the De Blasio Era: The Dangers of Precision Policing* (New York: The Policing and Social Justice Project at Brooklyn College, 2019), https://static1.squarespace.com/static/5de981188ae1bf14a94410f5/t/5df14904887d561d6cc9455e/1576093963895/2019+New+York+City+Gang+Policing+Report+-+FINAL%29.pdf.

56. Vitale, *The End of Policing*, 164–65.

57. National Law Center on Homelessness and Poverty, *Housing Not Handcuffs 2019* (Washington, DC: NLCPH, 2019), http://nlchp.org/wp-content/uploads/2019/12/HOUSING-NOT-HANDCUFFS-2019-FINAL.pdf.

58. Ibid.

59. The International Center for Not-for-Profit Law, "U.S. Protest Law Tracker," 2020, https://www.icnl.org/usprotestlawtracker/.

60. Ibid.; Erik Ortiz, "Stand Your Ground Law in Florida Could Be Expanded under DeSantis' Anti-mob Proposal," NBC News, November 12, 2020, https://www.nbcnews.com/news/us-news/stand-your-ground-florida-could-be-expanded-under-desantis-anti-n1247555.

61. Gail Mason, "Blue Lives Matter and Hate Crime Law," *Race and Justice*, June 16, 2020, https://doi.org/10.1177/2153368720933665.

62. Ibid.

63. Kay J. Whitlock *Reconsidering Hate: Policy and Politics at the Intersections* (Somerville, MA: Political Research Associations, 2012), http://www.politicalresearch.org/wp-content/uploads/downloads/2012/11/HateFrames.pdf.

64. NAACP Legal Defense Fund, "LDF Urges Kentucky Governor Matt Bevin to Veto 'Blue Lives Matter' Bill," https://www.naacpldf.org/press-release/ldf-urges-kentucky-governor-matt-bevin-to-veto-blue-lives-matter-bill/.

65. Mason, "Blue Lives Matter and Hate Crime Law"; Kira Lerner "Republicans Push Anti-protest Laws Bills Targeting Nonviolent Protests

Are Multiplying across the Country," *ThinkProgress*, January 31, 2017, https://thinkprogress.org/anti-protest-legislation-2afe0d59360a,.

66. Bill Keller, "Nine Lessons about Criminal Justice Reform," The Marshall Project, July 7, 2019, https://www.themarshallproject.org/2017/07/19/nine-lessons-about-criminal-justice-reform.

67. Alexandra Natapoff, "Misdemeanor Decriminalization," *Vanderbilt Law Review* 68 (2015): 1055, https://scholarship.law.vanderbilt.edu/cgi/viewcontent.cgi?article=1189&context=vlr.

68. Melissa Gira Grant, "Liberal Feminism Has a Sex Work Problem, *New Republic*, October 24, 2019, https://newrepublic.com/article/155481/liberal-feminism-sex-work-problem

69. "Decriminalize Sex Work in DC" Black Youth Project 100, n.d., fact sheet available at https://static1.squarespace.com/static/5b0e15eb8f5130668364019e/t/5b0f5712352f534e4afa1064/1527732001631/Sex+Decrim.pdf.

70. "Marijuana Legalization and Regulation," Drug Policy Alliance, n.d., https://www.drugpolicy.org/issues/marijuana-legalization-and-regulation accessed April 5, 2021.

71. Cleve R. Wootson Jr. and Jaclyn Peiser, "Oregon Decriminalizes Possession of Hard Drugs, as Four Other States Legalize Recreational Marijuana," *Washington Post*, November 4. 2020.

72. Janell Ross, "Legal Marijuana Made Big Promises on Racial Equity—and Fell Short," NBC News, December 31, 2018, https://www.nbcnews.com/news/nbcblk/legal-marijuana-made-big-promises-racial-equity-fell-short-n952376.

73. Ibid.; "Chart: Percentage of Cannabis Business Owners and Founders by Race. *Marijuana Business Daily*, September 11, 2017, https://mjbizdaily.com/chart-19-cannabis-businesses-owned-founded-racial-minorities/.

74. Wayne A. Logan, "After the Cheering Stopped: Decriminalization and Legalism's Limits." *Cornell Journal of Law & Public Policy* 24 (2014): 319, https://ir.law.fsu.edu/cgi/viewcontent.cgi?article=1346&context=articles.

75. Camp and Heatherton, *Policing the Planet*; Vitale, *The End of Policing*; Maya Schenwar and Victoria Law, *Prison by Any Other Name: The Harmful Consequences of Popular* Reforms (New York: New Press, 2020).

76. Melissa Murphy and Jessica Pryce, "Deeper Self-Reflection Is Needed around the Role of Social Work in Police Reform," *Chronicle*

of Social Change, July 14, 2020, https://chronicleofsocialchange.org/opinion/self-reflection-needed-around-role-social-work-in-police-reform/45186.

77. Camp and Heatherton, *Policing the Planet*; Vitale, *The End of Policing*; Heitzeg, *The School-to-Prison Pipeline.*

78. Radley Balko, *The Rise of the Warrior Cop: The Militarization of America's Police Forces* (New York: Public Affairs, 2013).

79. Ibid.; Stuart Schraeder, *Badges without Borders: How Global Counterinsurgency Transformed American Policing* (Oakland: University of California Press, 2019); Mara Hvistendahl, Alleen Brown, "Law Enforcement Scoured Protester Communications and Exaggerated Threats to Minneapolis Cops, Leaked Documents Show," *The Intercept*, June 26, 2020, https://theintercept.com/2020/06/26/blueleaks-minneapolis-police-protest-fears/.

80. Graham v. Connor, 490 U.S. 386 (1989), Justia Supreme Court Center. https://supreme.justia.com/cases/federal/us/490/386/.

81. Nancy A. Heitzeg, "#Ferguson/#Everywhere" in "On Ferguson," ed. Rose M. Brewer and Nancy A. Heitzeg, special issue, *Proudflesh: New Afrikan Journal of Culture, Politics, and Consciousness*, no. 10 (August 2015); Amir H. Ali and Emily Clark, "Qualified Immunity Explained," *The Appeal*, June 20, 2019, https://theappeal.org/qualified-immunity-explained/; Reade Levinson, "Across the U.S., Police Contracts Shield Officers from Scrutiny and Discipline," Reuters, January 13, 2017, https://www.reuters.com/investigates/special-report/usa-police-unions/.

82. "Police Brutality Bonds: How Wall Street Profits from Police Violence," ACRE, June 2020, https://acrecampaigns.org/wp-content/uploads/2020/06/ACRE_PBB_2020_2.pdf.

83. Taylor, *From #BlackLivesMatter to Black Liberation*, 132–33; Brendan McQuade, "The Demilitarization Ruse," *Jacobin Magazine*, May 24, 2015, https://jacobinmag.com/2015/05/camden-obama-police-brutality-black-lives-matter.

84. Stephen Danley, "Camden Police Reboot Is Being Misused in the Debate over Police Reform," *Washington Post*, June 16, 2020, https://www.washingtonpost.com/outlook/2020/06/16/camden-nj-police-reboot-is-being-misused-debate-over-police-reform/.

85. Taylor, *From #BlackLivesMatter to Black Liberation*, 132–33.

86. National Initiative for Building Community Trust and Justice, https://trustandjustice.org/about/partners accessed March 24, 2021.

87. Chad Marlow and Jay Stanley, "We're Updating Our Police Body Camera Recommendations for Even Better Accountability and Civil Liberties Protections," ACLU Blog, January 25, 2017, https://www.aclu.org/blog/privacy-technology/surveillance-technologies/were-updating-our-police-body-camera.

88. Rosen, "Abolition or Bust."

89. Vitale, *The End of Policing*, 221.

90. Dereka Purnell, "How I Became a Police Abolitionist," *Atlantic*, July 6, 2020, https://www.theatlantic.com/ideas/archive/2020/07/how-i-became-police-abolitionist/613540/; Mariame Kaba, "Yes, We Literally Mean Abolish the Police, Because Reform Won't Happen," *New York Times*, June 12, 2020.

91. Dorothy Roberts, "Abolishing Policing Also Means Abolishing Family Regulation: *Chronicle of Social Change*, June 19, 2020, https://chronicleofsocialchange.org/child-welfare-2/abolishing-policing-also-means-abolishing-family-regulation/44480.

92. "Abolish Policing," Critical Resistance, n.d., http://criticalresistance.org/abolish-policing/ accessed October 25, 2020.

CHAPTER 4. THE SLIPPERY SLOPE OF PRETRIAL REFORM

1. E. J. Dickson, "How the Tragic Death of Layleen Polanco Exposes Horrors of Criminalizing Sex Work," *Rolling Stone*, June 13, 2019, https://www.rollingstone.com/culture/culture-features/layleen-polanco-transgender-decriminalize-sex-work-847437/. See also Sydney Pereira, "Report: 'Confused' Jail Staff Failed to Regularly Check on Layleen Polanco in Solitary Unit Where She Died," *Gothamist*, June 24, 2020, https://gothamist.com/news/report-confused-jail-staff-failed-regularly-check-layleen-polanco-solitary-unit-where-she-died.

2. Rosa Goldensohn and Reuven Blau, "Layleen Polanco Died of Epileptic Seizure in Solitary, Autopsy Reveals," *The City*, July 30, 2019, https://www.thecity.nyc/2019/7/30/21210880/layleen-polanco-died-of-epileptic-seizure-in-solitary-autopsy-reveals.

3. Matthew McLoughlin and Lavette Mayes, "I Spent 14 Months in Jail Because I Couldn't Pay My Way Out," *Truthout*, June 19, 2017, https://truthout.org/articles/i-spent-14-months-in-jail-because-i-couldn-t-pay-my-way-out/. See also ACLU, "Lavette's Choice," February 8, 2018, https://www.aclu.org/blog/smart-justice/lavettes-choice.

4. "Mass Incarceration: The Whole Pie, 2020," Prison Policy Initiative, March 24, 2020, https://www.prisonpolicy.org/reports/pie2020.html.

5. "Detaining the Poor, How Money Bail Perpetuates an Endless Cycle of Poverty and Jail Time," Prison Policy Initiative, May 10, 2016, https://www.prisonpolicy.org/reports/incomejails.html.

6. Wendy Sawyer, "How Race Impacts Who Is Detained Pretrial," Prison Policy Initiative," October 9, 2019, https://www.prisonpolicy.org/blog/2019/10/09/pretrial_race/. See also Roxanne Daniel, "Since You Asked, What Data Exists about Native Americans in the Criminal Justice System?" April 22, 2020, https://www.prisonpolicy.org/blog/2020/04/22/native/.

7. Bernadette Rauby, "The Life-Threatening Reality of Short Jail Stays," Prison Policy Initiative, December 22, 2016 https://www.prisonpolicy.org/blog/2016/12/22/bjs_jail_suicide_2016/.

8. See, for example, Julia Lurie, "Go to Jail. Die from Drug Withdrawal. Welcome to the Criminal Justice System," *Mother Jones*, February 5, 2017 https://www.motherjones.com/politics/2017/02/opioid-withdrawal-jail-deaths/.

9. Somil Trivedi, "Coercive Plea Bargaining Has Poisoned the Criminal Justice System. It's Time to Suck the Venom Out," ACLU, January 13, 2020, https://www.aclu.org/news/criminal-law-reform/coercive-plea-bargaining-has-poisoned-the-criminal-justice-system-its-time-to-suck-the-venom-out/.

10. American Bail Coalition, "Our Story," accessed July 12, 2020, https://ambailcoalition.org/about/.

11. Color of Change and ACLU Campaign for Smart Justice, *Selling Off Our Freedom: How Insurance Corporations Have Taken Over Our Bail System* (Oakland, CA, and New York: Authors, May 2017), 2, https://www.aclu.org/sites/default/files/field_document/059_bail_report_2_1.pdf.

12. National Bail Fund Network, Community Justice Exchange, accessed June 3, 2020, https://www.communityjusticeexchange.org/national-bail-fund-network.

13. Sarah Phillips, "National Survey of Community Bail Funds: Report to the Community," Smart Decarceration Initiative at Washington University–St. Louis April 2017, https://static1.squarespace.com/static/5a973b49ee1759a6e039e0f4/t/5c0666d1575d1fefff9645f2/1543923411576/national+survey.071417.pdf.

14. "Community Bail Funds and the Fight for Freedom," Brooklyn Community Bail Fund, September 27, 2019, https://brooklynbailfund.org

/bcbfs-statement-on-community-bail-funds-the-fight-for-freedom and https://medium.com/@bkbailfund/community-bail-funds-the-fight-for-freedom-17dc40311230.

15. Shane Goldmacher, "Racial Justice Groups Flooded with Millions in Donations in Wake of Floyd Death," *New York Times*, June 14, 2020, https://www.nytimes.com/2020/06/14/us/politics/black-lives-matter-racism-donations.html.

16. Brett Davidson, Elisabeth Epps, Sharlyn Grace, and Atara Rich-Shea, "Moving from Ending Money Bail to Demanding Pretrial Freedom," The Law and Political Economy (LEP) Project, February 12, 2020, https://lpeproject.org/blog/moving-from-ending-money-bail-to-demanding-pretrial-freedom/.

17. "Cook County Chief Judge Announces New Order Limiting Use of Monetary Bond," Coalition to End Money Bond, n.d. accessed May 12, 2020, https://endmoneybond.org/2017/06/17/chief-judge-evans-issues-court-rule-aimed-at-ending-money-bail/. See also State of Illinois, Circuit Court of Cook County, General Order No. 18.8A—Procedures for Bail Hearings and Pretrial Release," July 17, 2017, http://www.cookcountycourt.org/Manage/DivisionOrders/ViewDivisionOrder/tabid/298/ArticleId/2562/GENERAL-ORDER-NO-18-8A-Procedures-for-Bail-Hearings-and-Pretrial-Release.aspx.

18. "Protecting Pretrial Freedom: Two Years of Bond Reform in Cook County, Coalition to End Money Bond," September 2019, https://endmoneybond.org/wp-content/uploads/2019/09/protecting-pretrial-freedom.pdf.

19. "Mayor Lightfoot Continues Attacks on Bond Reform, Further Backtracking on Criminal Justice Reform Campaign Promises," Chicago Community Bond Fund, August 10, 2019, https://chicagobond.org/2019/08/10/mayor-lightfoot-continues-attacks-on-bond-reform-further-backtracking-on-criminal-justice-reform-campaign-promises/.

20. "*Chicago Tribune* Launches Racist Attack on Bail Funds While Thousands Sit in Cook County Jail at Risk of Dying From COVID-19," Chicago Community Bond Fund, April 29, 2020, https://chicagobond.org/2020/04/29/chicago-tribune-launches-racist-attack-on-bail-funds-while-thousands-sit-in-cook-county-jail-at-risk-of-dying-from-covid-19/.

21. Don Stemen and David Olson, "Dollars and Sense in Cook County: Examining the Impact of General Order 18.8A on Felony Bond Court Decisions, Pretrial Release, and Crime," Loyola University and Safety and Justice Challenge Research Consortium, November 19, 2020, http://

www.safetyandjusticechallenge.org/resource/dollars-and-sense-in-cook-county/.

22. "Governor Pritzker to Sign the Pretrial Fairness Act and Officially End Money Bond in Illinois!," Coalition to End Money Bond, accessed February 22, 2021, https://endmoneybond.org/2021/02/22/governor-pritzker-to-sign-the-pretrial-fairness-act-officially-end-money-bond-in-illinois/.

23. Tanya Watkins, Sharlyn Grace, Will Tanzman, and Sharone Mitchell Jr., "Illinois May Be First State to Eliminate Money Bail, but the Fight Isn't Over," *Truthout*, February 2, 2021, https://truthout.org/articles/illinois-may-be-first-state-to-eliminate-money-bail-but-the-fight-isnt-over/.

24. See, for example, "ACLU of California Changes Position to Oppose Bail Reform Legislation," ACLU Nor Cal, August 20, 2018, https://www.aclunc.org/news/aclu-california-changes-position-oppose-bail-reform-legislation. See also "Silicon Valley De-Bug's Letter of Opposition to California's False Bail Reform Bill (SB10)," Silicon Valley De-Bug, August 14, 2018, https://siliconvalleydebug.org/stories/silicon-valley-de-bug-s-letter-of-opposition-to-california-s-false-bail-reform-bill-sb10.

25. See, for example, "Open Letter, Governor Jerry Brown, Veto SB 10," CURB, August 23, 2018, http://www.curbprisonspending.org/2018/08/23/open-letter-to-governor-brown/.

26. "S.B. 10, 2017-2018 Leg., Reg. Sess. (Cal. 2018): California Replaces Money-Bail System with Pretrial Detainment System," *Harvard Law Review*, May 10, 2019, https://harvardlawreview.org/2019/05/s-b-10-2017-2018-leg-reg-sess-cal-2018/.

27. "Essie Justice Group Withdraws Support for SB 10," Essie Justice Group, August 14, 2008, https://essiejusticegroup.org/2018/08/essie-justice-group-withdraws-support-for-sb-10/.

28. "California Proposition 25, Replace Cash Bail with Risk Assessments Referendum (2020)," Ballotpedia, https://ballotpedia.org/California_Proposition_25,_Replace_Cash_Bail_with_Risk_Assessments_Referendum_(2020).

29. Insha Rahman, *New York, New York: Highlights of the 2019 Bail Reform Law* (New York: Vera Institute of Justice, July 2019), https://www.vera.org/downloads/publications/new-york-new-york-2019-bail-reform-law-highlights.pdf.

30. "'Bail Reform' and Carceral Control: A Critique of New York's New Bail Laws," Survived & Punished NY, February 11, 2020 https://survivedandpunished.org/2020/02/11/bail-reform-carceral-control-a-critique-of-new-yorks-new-bail-laws/.

31. "Community Bail Funds," Brooklyn Community Bail Fund, https://medium.com/@bkbailfund/community-bail-funds-the-fight-for-freedom-17dc40311230.

32. Ibid.

33. Michael Rempel and Krystal Rodriguez, "Bail Reform Revisited: The Impact of New York's Amended Law," Center for Court Innovation, May 2020, https://www.courtinnovation.org/publications/bail-revisited-NYS.

34. See Kim Bellware, "Class, Race, and Geography Emerge as Flashpoints in New York's Bail Reform Debate," *Washington Post*, February 14, 2020, https://www.washingtonpost.com/nation/2020/02/15/new-york-bail-reform/. See also "Dear Members of the New York Press Club and Other Interested Journalists," open letter from criminal law experts at colleges and universities in New York and across the country, January 27, 2020. https://static1.squarespace.com/static/5e2b3dab8e27aa693a1bc79e/t/5e2b708b73a1536c466535a8/1579905163299/TAF_NYBailReform_SignOnLetter_04.pdf.

35. Pete Harckham, "Bail Reform Changes Included in New Budget," New York State Senate, April 6, 2020, https://www.nysenate.gov/newsroom/press-releases/pete-harckham/bail-reform-changes-included-new-budget.

36. For detailed information on the Arnold PSA, visit the Advancing Pretrial Policy & Research (APPR) website. APPR is supported by Arnold Ventures. The PSA node is found at https://advancingpretrial.org/psa/about/.

37. "The Use of Pretrial 'Risk Assessment' Instruments: A Shared Statement of Civil Rights Concerns," Leadership Conference on Civil & Human Rights, July 30, 2018, https://civilrights.org/2018/07/30/more-than-100-civil-rights-digital-justice-and-community-based-organizations-raise-concerns-about-pretrial-risk-assessment/. A pdf of the full statement is available here: http://civilrightsdocs.info/pdf/criminal-justice/Pretrial-Risk-Assessment-Full.pdf.

38. Julia Angwin, et al., "Machine Bias," ProPublica, May 23, 2016, https://www.propublica.org/article/machine-bias-risk-assessments-in-criminal-sentencing.

39. Julia Dressel and Hany Farid, "The Accuracy, Fairness, and Limits of Predicting Recidivism," *Science Advances* 4, no. 1 (January 17, 2018), (corrected March 30, 2018), https://advances.sciencemag.org/content/advances/4/1/eaao5580.full.

40. Marie Gottschalk, *Caught: The Prison State and the Lockdown of American Politics* (Princeton, NJ: Princeton University Press, 2015), 101–11.

41. Chelsea Barbaris, Karthik Dinakar, and Colin Doyle, "Technical Flaws of Pretrial Risk Assessments Raise Grave Concerns," MIT Media Lab, July 17, 2019, https://www.media.mit.edu/posts/algorithmic-risk-assessment/. A pdf of the full statement and list of signatories can be downloaded here: https://dam-prod.media.mit.edu/x/2019/07/16/TechnicalFlawsOfPretrial_ML%20site.pdf.

42. Sara Picard, et. al. *Beyond the Algorithm: Pretrial Reform, Risk Assessment, and Racial Fairness,* Center for Court Innovation, July 2019, https://www.courtinnovation.org/publications/beyond-algorithm. A pdf of the complete report, n.d., can be downloaded here: https://www.courtinnovation.org/sites/default/files/media/document/2019/Beyond_The_Algorithm.pdf.

43. Ethan Corey and Puck Lo, "The 'Failure to Appear' Fallacy, *The Appeal*, January 9, 2019, https://theappeal.org/the-failure-to-appear-fallacy/.

44. Pretrial Justice Institute, *Scan of Pretrial Practices 2019* (Washington, DC: Author, October 2, 2019), 25–31, https://university.pretrial.org/HigherLogic/System/DownloadDocumentFile.ashx?DocumentFileKey=24bb2bc4-84ed-7324-929c-d0637db43c9a&forceDialog=0.

45. Chelsea Barabas, Karthik Dinakar, and Colin Doyle, "The Problems with Risk Assessment Tools," *New York Times*, July 17, 2019, https://www.nytimes.com/2019/07/17/opinion/pretrial-ai.html.

46. See for example, Julie Pittman, "Released Into Shackles: The Rise of Immigrant E-Incarceration," *California Law Review*, Vol. 108, No. 2 (April 2020), *California Law Review* https://www.californialawreview.org/print/released-into-shackles/.

47. James Kilgore, "Let's Fight for Freedom from Electronic Monitors and E-Carceration," *Truthout*, September 4, 2019, https://truthout.org/articles/lets-fight-for-freedom-from-electronic-monitors-and-e-carceration/.

48. Albert Fox Cahn, "Ankle Monitors Can Hold Captives in Invisible Jails of Debt, Pain, and Bugged Conversations," NBC News Think, November 6, 2019, https://www.nbcnews.com/think/opinion/ankle-monitors-can-hold-captives-invisible-jails-debt-pain-bugged-ncna1076806.

49. Maya Schenwar and Victoria Law, *Prison by Any Other Name: The Harmful Consequences of Popular Reforms* (New York: The New Press, 2020), 27.

50. Kira Lerner, "Chicago Is Tracking Kids with GPS Monitors That Can Call and Record Them without Consent," *The Appeal*, April 8,

2019, https://theappeal.org/chicago-electronic-monitoring-wiretapping-juveniles/.

51. See, for example, the E-Cell House Arrest App for smartphones which requires biometric identification at E-cell.com, accessed July 17, 2020, https://e-cell.com/.

52. "Guidelines for Respecting the Rights of Individuals on Monitors," #Challenging Ecarceration Project and the Center for Media Justice, March 4, 2018, https://mediajustice.org/resource/electronic-monitoring-guidelines/.

53. MediaJustice, *No More Shackles: Ten Arguments against Pretrial Electronic Monitoring* (Oakland, CA: Author, 2019), 19, https://mediajustice.org/wp-content/uploads/2020/04/NoMoreShackles_PretrialReport_2019-final-draft.pdf.

54. Ibid., 6–11.

55. Pretrial Justice Institute, *Pretrial Scan 2019*, 40.

56. Ava Kaufman, "Digital Jail: How Electronic Monitoring Drives Defendants into Debt," ProPublica, July 3, 2019, https://www.propublica.org/article/digital-jail-how-electronic-monitoring-drives-defendants-into-debt.

57. Geoff Pender, "Contract with Company Connected to Epps Bribery Case Questioned," *Clarion Ledger*, April 24, 2017, https://www.clarionledger.com/story/news/politics/2017/04/24/mdoc-contract-questioned/100851862/.

58. Court Watch NOLA, *New Orleans Criminal District Court, Magistrate Court & Municipal Court 2018* (New Orleans: Author, 2018), 3, https://www.courtwatchnola.org/wp-content/uploads/2018-Annual-Report.pdf.

CHAPTER 5. COURTS, SENTENCING, AND "DIVERSION"

1. Alexi Jones, "Correctional Control 2018: Incarceration and Supervision by State," Prison Policy Initiative, 2018, https://www.prisonpolicy.org/reports/correctionalcontrol2018.html.

2. Ibid.

3. Nancy A. Heitzeg, "The Myth of 'Bipartisan Criminal Justice Reform': Mississippi Close-Up," *Truthout*, November 2014, https://truthout.org/articles/the-myth-of-bipartisan-criminal-justice-reform-mississippi-close-up/.

4. Ibid.

5. "Mississippi Takes Historic Step to Reform Criminal Justice System," Southern Poverty Law Center Blog, March 31, 2014, https://www.splcenter.org/news/2014/03/31/mississippi-takes-historic-step-reform-criminal-justice-system.

6. Heitzeg, "The Myth of 'Bipartisan Criminal Justice Reform.'"

7. "Mississippi's 2014 Corrections and Criminal Justice Reform," PEW Charitable Trusts, https://www.pewtrusts.org/-/media/assets/2014/09/pspp_mississippi_2014_corrections_justice_reform.pdf.

8. "Prison Reform Bill's Effectiveness Questioned," Mississippi NAACP, April 3, 2014, http://naacpms.org/prison-reform-bills-effectiveness-questioned/.

9. Human Rights Watch, *Profiting from Probation: America's Offender Funded Probation Program* (New York : Human Rights Watch, 2014), https://www.hrw.org/sites/default/files/reports/us0214_ForUpload_0.pdf.

10. Heitzeg, "The Myth of 'Bipartisan Criminal Justice Reform.'"

11. Julianne Hing, "The Shocking Details of a Mississippi School to Prison Pipeline," *Colorlines*, November 26, 2012, http://www.colorlines.com/articles/shocking-details-mississippi-school-prison-pipeline.

12. "The Lasting Legacy of Parchman Farm, the Prison Modeled after a Slave Plantation," *Innocence Project*, June 29, 2020, https://www.innocenceproject.org/parchman-farm-prison-mississippi-history/.

13. Jerry Mitchell, "Trump Hailed This States Reforms as a National Model—but the Numbers Reflect a Grim Reality," ProPublica, May 9, 2019, https://www.propublica.org/article/trump-hailed-mississippi-prison-reforms-national-model-but-the-numbers-reflect-grim-reality.

14. Ibid.

15. Debbie Elliot, "Mississippi Prison System Faces Investigation, Lawsuits after Rash of Inmate Deaths," MPR News, April 18, 2020, https://www.npr.org/2020/04/18/837855215/mississippi-prison-system-faces-investigation-lawsuits-after-rash-of-inmate-deat.

16. Ibid.

17. Associated Press, "Former Louisiana Warden Confirmed as Mississippi Prisons Leader," *Clarion Ledger*, June 17, 2020, https://www.clarionledger.com/story/news/2020/06/17/burl-cain-former-angola-prison-warden-new-mississippi-prison-leader/3210035001/.

18. Gordon Russell and Maya Lau, "The Fall of Burl Cain: How 1 Last Side Deal Led to Angola Warden's Undoing" *The Advocate*, December 15,

2015, https://www.nola.com/news/politics/article_987176f3-8571-543b-b331-186b8077a7cf.html.

19. Keisha Rowe, "MDOC: 2 Inmates Died This Week," *Clarion Ledger*, November 6, 2020, https://www.clarionledger.com/story/news/2020/11/06/mississippi-prison-crisis-2-inmates-separate-state-prisons-die/6193475002/; "Mississippi Prison COVID Timeline," fwd.us, November 2020, https://www.fwd.us/criminal-justice/mississippi/ms-covid19-timeline/.

20. "Lawsuit Filed against MDOC for Failure to Protect Prisoners from COVID-19," Mississippi Center for Justice, May 14, 2020, https://mscenterforjustice.org/lawsuit-filed-against-mdoc-for-failing-to-protect-prisoners-from-covid-19/.

21. Richard S. Frase, "Why Have U.S. State and Federal Jurisdictions Enacted Sentencing Guidelines?" Sentencing Guidelines Resource Center, Robina Institute, March 25, 2015, https://sentencing.umn.edu/content/why-have-us-state-and-federal-jurisdictions-enacted-sentencing-guidelines.

22. Ibid.

23. Ibid.

24. "Mandatory Minimums Were Once America's Law and Order Panacea: Here's Why It Is Not Working," FAMM, 2012 https://www.prisonpolicy.org/scans/famm/Primer.pdf.

25. Ibid,

26. Jerry J. Rachlinski, Sherri Johnson, Andrew J Wistrich, and Chris Guthrie, "Does Unconscious Racial Bias Affect Trial Judges?," *Cornell Law Faculty Publications* 786, https://scholarship.law.cornell.edu/facpub/786; "Judicial Bias: What Crosses the Line?," *Talk of the Nation*, NPR, July 19, 2012, https://www.npr.org/2012/07/19/157052848/laying-down-the-law-on-judicial-bias.

27. Richard S. Frase, "Prior Record Enhancements: High Costs, Uncertain Benefits," Sentencing Guidelines Resource Center, Robina Institute, November 28, 2017, https://sentencing.umn.edu/content/prior-record-enhancements-high-costs-uncertain-benefits.

28. Dr. James Austin and Lauren-Brooke Eisen, with James Cullen and Jonathan Frank, *How Many Americans Are Unnecessarily Incarcerated?* (New York: Brennan Center for Justice at New York University School of Law, 2016), https://www.brennancenter.org/sites/default/files/2019-08/Report_Unnecessarily_Incarcerated_0.pdf.

29. Ibid.

30. Ibid.

31. Ashley Polk, "Three Strikes Laws in Different States," LegalMatch, https://www.legalmatch.com/law-library/article/three-strikes-laws-in-different-states.html.

32. Ibid.

33. Ashley Nellis, *Still Life: America's Increasing Use of Life and Long-Term Sentences* (Washington, DC: Sentencing Project, 2017), https://www.sentencingproject.org/publications/still-life-americas-increasing-use-life-long-term-sentences/; Frase, "Prior Record Enhancements."

34. Josh Rosner, "Juvenile Life without Parole: An Overview," Sentencing Project, February 25, 2020, https://www.sentencingproject.org/publications/juvenile-life-without-parole/.

35. Nellis, Still Life.

36. Chiara Caraccio, "The Injustice of the Felony Murder Rule," Columbia Undergraduate Law Review Blog, November 16, 2016, https://blogs.cuit.columbia.edu/culr/2016/11/16/the-injustice-of-the-felony-murder-rule/.

37. Alexis Lee Watts, "In Depth: Sentencing Guideline Grids," Sentencing Guidelines Resource Center, Robina Institute, January 11, 2018, https://sentencing.umn.edu/content/depth-sentencing-guideline-grids.

38. Ibid.

39. Ibid.

40. Frase, "Prior Record Enhancements."

41. Ibid.; Rhys Hester, Richard S. Frase, Julian V. Roberts, and Kelly Lyn Mitchell, "Prior Record Enhancements at Sentencing: Unsettled Justifications and Unsettling Consequences," *Crime and Justice* 47, no. 1 (2018): 209–54.

42. Margaret Love and Davis L. Schlussel, *Pathways to Reintegration: Criminal Record Reforms in 2019* (Washington, DC: CCRC, February 2020), http://ccresourcecenter.org/wp-content/uploads/2020/02/Pathways-to-Reintegration_Criminal-Record-Reforms-in-2019.pdf.

43. Jones, *Correctional Control 2018.*

44. Ibid.

45. Schenwar and Law, *Prison by Any Other Name.*

46. Ibid.

47. Jones, *Correctional Control 2018.*

48. Ibid.; Human Rights Watch Report, *Profiting from Probation.*

49. Human Rights Watch Report, *Profiting from Probation.*

50. Michelle Phelps, "Mass Probation and Inequality: Race, Class, Gender and in Supervision and Revocation," in *Handbook on Punishment Decisions: Locations of Disparity*, ed. Jeffery T. Ulmer and Mindy S. Bradley (New York: Routledge 2018).

51. "PEW Issue Brief: Probation and Parole Systems Marked by High Stakes, Missed Opportunities," PEW Charitable Trusts, February 2018, https://www.pewtrusts.org/en/research-and-analysis/issue-briefs/2018/09/probation-and-parole-systems-marked-by-high-stakes-missed-opportunities.

52. Ibid.

53. Sarah Lustbader, "Are Problem-Solving Court Impeding Progress?" *The Appeal*, January 7, 2020, https://theappeal.org/are-problem-solving-courts-impeding-progress/.

54. Ibid.

55. Douglas Marlowe, Carolyn D. Hardin, and Carson L. Fox, *Painting the Current Picture: A National Report on Drug Courts and Other Problem-Solving Courts in the United States* (Washington, DC: National Drug Court Institute, 2016), https://www.researchgate.net/publication/331374798_Painting_the_Current_Picture_A_National_Report_on_Drug_Courts_and_Other_Problem-Solving_Courts_in_the_United_States.

56. Ibid.

57. Kerwin Kaye, *Enforcing Freedom: Drug Courts, Therapeutic Communities, and the Intimacies of the State* (New York: Columbia University Press, 2019)

58. Marlowe et al., *Painting the Current Picture.*

59. Ibid.

60. Issa Kohler-Hausmann, *Misdemeanorland: Criminal Courts and Social Control in an Age of Broken Windows Policing* (Princeton, NJ: Princeton University Press, 2018).

61. David Alan Sklansky "The Problems with Prosecutors," *Annual Review of Criminology* 2018, 1, no. 1, 451–69, https://www.annualreviews.org/doi/abs/10.1146/annurev-criminol-032317-092440; Joe Watson, "Study: 95 Percent of Elected Prosecutors Are White," *Prison Legal News*, February 2017, 44.

62. Sklansky, "The Problems with Prosecutors."

63. John Pfaff, *Locked In: The True Causes of Mass Incarceration—and How to Achieve Real Reform* (New York: Basic Books, 2017).

64. Michelle Alexander, "Go to Trail: Crash the Justice System," *New York Times*, March 10, 2012, https://www.nytimes.com/2012/03/11/opinion/sunday/go-to-trial-crash-the-justice-system.html; Danielle Dosch "Plea to Prison Pipeline: Assessing the Feasibility of Mass Plea Refusal," *The Review*, October 3, 2019, https://bpr.berkeley.edu/2019/10/03/plea-to-prison-pipeline-assessing-the-feasibility-of-mass-plea-refusal/

65. Sklansky, "The Problems with Prosecutors"; Pfaff, *Locked In*.

66. Jordan Smith, "The Power to Kill: What Happens When a Reform Prosecutor Stands Up to the Death Penalty," *The Intercept*, December 3, 2019, https://theintercept.com/2019/12/03/death-penalty-reform-prosecutors/.

67. Bryan Furst, *A Fair Fight: Achieving Indigent Defense Resource Parity* (New York: Brennan Center for Justice at New York University School of Law, 2019), https://www.brennancenter.org/sites/default/files/2019-09/Report_A%20Fair%20Fight.pdf.

68. Gideon v. Wainwright 372 US 335 (1963), https://www.oyez.org/cases/1962/155.

69. Furst, *A Fair Fight*.

70. Ibid.; Sklansky "The Problems with Prosecutors."

71. Daniel A. Medina, " The Progressive Prosecutors Blazing a New Path for the U.S. Justice System," *Guardian*, July 23, 2019, https://www.theguardian.com/us-news/2019/jul/23/us-justice-system-progressive-prosecutors-mass-incarceration-death-penalty.

72. Mark Berman and Tom Jackman, "After a Summer of Protest, Americans Vote for Policing and Criminal Justice Changes," *Washington Post*, November 14, 2020, https://www.washingtonpost.com/national/criminal-justice-election/2020/11/13/20186380-25d6-11eb-8672-c281c7a2c96e_story.html.

73. Mark Berman, "These Prosecutors Won Vowing to Fight the System. Now the System Is Fighting Back, *Washington Post*, November 9, 2019, https://www.washingtonpost.com/national/these-prosecutors-won-office-vowing-to-fight-the-system-now-the-system-is-fighting-back/2019/11/05/20d863f6-afc1-11e9-a0c9-6d2d7818f3da_story.html.

74. National Partnership for Pretrial Justice, "Unfair Fight: Public Defenders Nationwide Battle System with fewer Resources, Burdensome Caseloads", Arnold Ventures, November 30, 2020, https://www.arnoldventures.org/stories/an-unfair-fight-public-defenders-nationwide-battle-system-with-fewer-resources-burdensome-caseloads.

75. "Abolitionist Principles & Campaign Strategies for Prosecutor Organizing," Community Justice Exchange, Court Watch MA, Families for Justice as Healing, Project NIA, and Survived and Punished NY (Community Justice Exchange, n/d), https://www.communityjusticeexchange.org/abolitionist-principles (pdf available here).

76. Alexi Jones, "Reforms without Results: Why States Should Stop Excluding Violent Offenses from Criminal Justice Reforms," Prison Policy Initiative, April 2020, https://www.prisonpolicy.org/reports/violence.html.

77. Danielle Sered, *Until We Reckon: Violence, Mass Incarceration, and a Road to Repair* (New York: New Press, 2019).

78. Ibid.; Mariame Kaba and Shira Hassan, *Fumbling toward Repair* (New York: AK Press, 2019).

79. Ejeris Dixon and Leah Lakshmi Piepzna-Samarasinha, eds., *Beyond Survival Strategies and Stories from the Transformative Justice Movement* (New York: AK Press, 2020); Transform Harm, https://transformharm.org/.

CHAPTER 6. IMPRISONMENT AND RELEASE

1. Jackie Wang, *Carceral Capitalism* (South Pasadena, CA: Semiotext(e), 2018), 261.

2. Steve Kilar, Arthur Hirsch, and Scott Dance, "Charges Dropped in 2007 Bowling Brook Death," *Baltimore Sun*, March 28, 2012, https://www.baltimoresun.com/latest/bs-md-bowling-brook-charges-20120328-story.html.

3. Victoria Law, "Why Is California Keeping Kelly Savage in Prison for a Crime She Didn't Commit?," *Truthout*, November 29, 2014, https://truthout.org/articles/why-is-california-keeping-kelly-savage-in-prison-for-a-crime-she-didn-t-commit/.

4. Priscilla A. Ocen, "Awakening to a Mass-Supervision Crisis," *Atlantic*, December 26, 2019, https://www.theatlantic.com/politics/archive/2019/12/parole-mass-supervision-crisis/604108/.

5. Jared Ware, "South Carolina Prisoners in Inhumane Conditions Call for UN Intervention," *Shadowproof*, December 17, 2019, https://shadowproof.com/2019/12/17/south-carolina-prisoners-call-for-un-intervention-as-abusive-conditions-worsen/.

6. Jared Ware, "Interview: South Carolina Prisoners Challenge Narrative around Violence at Lee Correctional Institution," *Shadowproof*, May 3, 2018, https://shadowproof.com/2018/05/03/interview-south

-carolina-prisoners-challenge-narrative-around-violence-lee-correctional-institution/.

7. Brian Sonenstein, "All 50 States Report Prison Understaffing," *Shadowproof*, February 12, 2020, https://shadowproof.com/2020/02/12/all-50-states-report-prison-understaffing/.

8. Prison Policy Initiative and VOCAL-NY, Prison Policy Initiative, "Mapping Disadvantage: The Geography of Incarceration in New York State," Prison Policy Initiative, February 19, 2020, https://www.prisonpolicy.org/origin/ny/report.html.

9. See, for example, Dan Berger and Toussaint Losier, *Rethinking the American Prison Movement* (New York: Routledge, 2017).

10. Emily L. Thuma, *All Our Trials: Prisons, Policing, and the Feminist Fight to End Violence* (Champaign, IL: University of Illinois Press, 2019).

11. Martin Macias Jr., "LA County Strikes Down Plans for Women's and Mental Health Jail," Courthouse News Service, February 12, 2019, https://www.courthousenews.com/la-county-strikes-down-plans-for-womens-and-mental-health-jail/.

12. Heather Ann Thompson, "How a South Carolina Prison Riot Really Went Down," *New York Times*, April 28, 2018, https://www.nytimes.com/2018/04/28/opinion/how-a-south-carolina-prison-riot-really-went-down.html.

13. Margo Schlanger, "Trends in Prisoner Litigation as the PLRA Enters Adulthood," *UC Irvine Law Review* 5, no. 1 (2015): 153–79, https://repository.law.umich.edu/articles/1512/.

14. Jean Casella, "Charles Dickens on Solitary Confinement: 'Immense Torture and Agony,'" Solitary Watch, February 27, 2010, https://solitarywatch.org/2010/02/27/charles-dickens-on-solitary-confinement-immense-torture-and-agony/.

15. "FAQ," *Solitary Watch* (blog), January 31, 2012, https://solitarywatch.org/facts/faq/.

16. Albert Woodfox, *Solitary: My Story of Transformation and Hope* (New York: Grove Press, 2019).

17. "New Lawsuit Challenges Use of Solitary Confinement for Children in Florida," Southern Poverty Law Center, September 5, 2019, https://www.splcenter.org/presscenter/new-lawsuit-challenges-use-solitary-confinement-children-florida.

18. American Civil Liberties Union, *Still Worse Than Second Class: Solitary Confinement of Women in the United States* (New York: ACLU,

2019), 7, https://www.aclu.org/report/worse-second-class-solitary-confinement-women-united-states.

19. "Fact Sheet: Kids in Solitary Confinement in Jails and Juvenile Facilities," Stop Solitary for Kids, 2018, https://www.stopsolitaryforkids.org/wp-content/uploads/2018/08/One-Pager-Youth-Solitary-5-31-18.pdf.

20. Michael Barjas, "The Prison Inside Prison," *Texas Observer*, January 21, 2020, https://www.texasobserver.org/solitary-confinement-texas/.

21. Victoria Law, "Two Years after Pelican Bay Hunger Strike, What's Changed for People Inside the Prison?," *Truthout*, July 8, 2015, https://truthout.org/articles/two-years-after-pelican-bay-hunger-strike-what-s-changed-for-people-inside-the-prison/.

22. Joshua Manson, "Solitary Confinement Is Fueling New York's Prison Suicide Crisis," *Solitary Watch* (blog), May 29, 2020, https://solitarywatch.org/2020/05/29/solitary-confinement-is-fueling-new-yorks-prison-suicide-crisis/.

23. "Fact Sheet: Kids in Solitary Confinement."

24. Lauren Brinkley-Rubinstein et al., "Association of Restrictive Housing during Incarceration with Mortality after Release," *JAMA Network Open* 2, no. 10 (October 4, 2019): e1912516–e1912516, https://doi.org/10.1001/jamanetworkopen.2019.12516.

25. Brian Sonenstein, "Brief Exposure to Solitary Confinement May Increase Mortality after Prison," Shadowproof, February 13, 2020, https://shadowproof.com/2020/02/13/even-brief-exposure-to-solitary-confinement-may-increase-risk-of-death-after-prison/.

26. "Solitary Confinement Is Never the Answer: A Special Report on the Covid-19 Pandemic in Prisons and Jails, the Use of Solitary Confinement, and Best Practices for Saving the Lives of Incarcerated People and Correctional Staff," Unlock the Box, June 2020, https://static1.squarespace.com/static/5a9446a89d5abbfa67013da7/t/5ee7a602b4a0f009a9732079/1592239667348/June2020Report.pdf. See also Samara Fox, Ellen Gallagher, and J. Wesley Boyd, "When the Treatment Is Torture: ICE Must Stop Using Solitary Confinement for Covid-19 Quarantine," *STAT*, August 7, 2020, https://www.statnews.com/2020/08/07/ice-must-stop-using-solitary-confinement-for-covid-19-quarantine/.

27. "Fact Sheet on New Federal Laws Address Youth Solitary," Children's Law and Policy and Stop Solitary for Kids, January 8, 2019, https://www.stopsolitaryforkids.org/wp-content/uploads/2019/01/CCLP-Summary_-JJDPA-FSA_Federal-Laws-Affecting-Youth-Solitary_1-14-19.pdf.

28. Victoria Law, "Even When You Change Its Name, Solitary Confinement Is Torture," *Truthout*, January 14, 2020, https://truthout.org/articles/even-when-you-change-its-name-solitary-confinement-is-torture/.

29. Adrian Walker, "There Was a Consensus to Reduce Solitary Confinement. But It Hasn't Translated into Action - *Boston Globe*," February 26, 2019, https://www.bostonglobe.com/metro/2019/02/26/there-was-consensus-reduce-solitary-confinement-but-hasn-translated-into-action/v4Ytxvy4fZ6xukk0ZfjIRK/story.html.

30. Ramona R. Rantala, *Sexual Victimization Reported by Adult Correctional Authorities, 2012–2015* (Washington, DC: US Department of Justice, July 2018), https://www.ojp.gov/library/abstracts/sexual-victimization-reported-adult-correctional-authorities-2012-2015.

31. Michael Cox, email statement to Whitlock, March 21, 2020.

32. Romy Ellenbogen, "Rape Is Rampant at This Women's Prison. Anyone Who Complains Is Punished, Lawsuit Says," *Miami Herald*, December 4, 2019, https://www.miamiherald.com/news/special-reports/florida-prisons/article237797554.html.

33. United States Department of Justice, Civil Rights Division, United States Attorney's Office, District of New Jersey, *Investigation of the Edna Mahan Correctional Facility for Women* (Union Township, NJ: US Department of Justice, April 2020), https://www.justice.gov/opa/pressrelease/file/1268391/download.

34. Valdya Guillapalli, "Sexual Abuse in Youth Detention Facilities, *The Appeal*, January 13, 2020, https://theappeal.org/sexual-abuse-in-youth-detention-facilities/.

35. Su'ganni (Aaron Lester) Tiuza, "A Report of Dehumanization, Criminalization, and Hostility Towards LGBT+ Prisoners: A Narrative of LGBT+ Massachusetts Prisoners' Experiences," January 2020. This report was given to Whitlock by Michael Cox. The authors were granted permission by Tiuza to give his name.

36. Malika Saada Saar, Rebecca Epstein, Lindsay Rosenthal, and Yasmin Vafa, *The Sexual Abuse to Prison Pipeline: The Girls' Story* (Washington, DC: Human Rights Project for Girls (Rights4Girls), Georgetown University Law Center, Center on Poverty and Inequality, and Ms. Foundation for Women, 2015), https://www.law.georgetown.edu/poverty-inequality-center/wp-content/uploads/sites/14/2019/02/The-Sexual-Abuse-To-Prison-Pipeline-The-Girls%E2%80%99-Story.pdf.

37. Andrea J. Ritchie, "How Some Cops Use the Badge to Commit Sex Crimes," *Washington Post*, January 12, 2018, https://www.washingtonpost

.com/outlook/how-some-cops-use-the-badge-to-commit-sex-crimes/2018/01/11/5606fb26-eff3-11e7-b390-a36dc3fa2842_story.html.

38. Dan Manville, “Federal Legal Standards for Prison Medical Care,” *Prison Legal News*, May 15, 2003, https://www.prisonlegalnews.org/news/2003/may/15/federal-legal-standards-for-prison-medical-care/.

39. See, for example, Colleen Walsh, “In Prisons, a Looming Coronavirus Crisis,” *Harvard Gazette* (blog), April 2, 2020, https://news.harvard.edu/gazette/story/2020/04/harvard-professors-call-to-help-incarcerated-population/.

40. Brendan Saloner et al., “COVID-19 Cases and Deaths in Federal and State Prisons,” *JAMA*, July 8, 2020, https://doi.org/10.1001/jama.2020.12528.

41. “Failing Grades: States’ Responses to COVID-19 in Jails and Prisons,” American Civil Liberties Union and Prison Policy Initiative, June 25, 2020, https://www.prisonpolicy.org/reports/failing_grades.html.

42. Emily Kassie and Barbara Marcolini, “‘It Was Like a Time Bomb’: How ICE Helped Spread the Coronavirus,” *New York Times*, July 10, 2020, https://www.nytimes.com/2020/07/10/us/ice-coronavirus-deportation.html?smid=fb-share.

43. Connor Sheets, “These Sheriffs Release Sick Inmates to Avoid Paying Their Hospital Bills,” ProPublica, September 30, 2019, https://www.propublica.org/article/these-sheriffs-release-sick-inmates-to-avoid-paying-their-hospital-bills?token=lZ_nPrh6oVJEnMzcTH1Jr59Ibe3K8XZC.

44. The Pew Charitable Trusts, *State Prisons and the Delivery of Hospital Care* (Philadelphia: Author, July 2018), https://www.pewtrusts.org/-/media/assets/2018/07/prisons-and-hospital-care_report.pdf.

45. US Department of Justice, Office of Justice Programs, National Institute of Justice, *Implementing Telemedicine in Correctional Facilities* (Washington, DC: US Department of Justice, May 2002), https://www.ncjrs.gov/pdffiles1/nij/190310.pdf.

46. “Incarceration Shortens Life Expectancy,” Prison Policy Initiative, June 26, 2017, https://www.prisonpolicy.org/blog/2017/06/26/life_expectancy/.

47. “Deaths in State Prisons Are on the Rise, New Data Shows: What Can Be Done?,” Prison Policy Initiative, February 13, 2020, https://www.prisonpolicy.org/blog/2020/02/13/prisondeaths/.

48. See, for example, “Documenting and Addressing the Health Impacts of Carceral Systems,” Supplement 1 2020, *American Journal of Public*

Health 110, no. S1 (January 2020), https://ajph.aphapublications.org/toc/ajph/110/S1.

Articles explore the relationships among health inequity and mass incarceration, with special attention to racism, gender, and poverty.

49. "BJS Data Shows Graying of Prisons," Prison Policy Initiative, May 16, 2016, https://www.prisonpolicy.org/blog/2016/05/19/bjsaging/.

50. "The Prevalence and Severity of Mental Illness among California Prisoners on the Rise," Stanford Justice Advocacy Project, 2017, accessed May 15, 2020, https://www-cdn.law.stanford.edu/wp-content/uploads/2017/05/Stanford-Report-FINAL.pdf.

51. Sharon Cohen and Nora Eckert, "Many US Jails Fail to Stop Inmate Suicides," Associated Press, June 18, 2019, https://apnews.com/94aa300b102546259355f52c306e0748.

52. Samantha Melamed, "Pennsylvania Prison Suicides Are at an All-Time High," *Philadelphia Inquirer*, February 20, 2020, https://www.inquirer.com/news/graterford-prison-suicide-pennsylvania-lawsuits-correct-care-solutions-mhm-20200220.html.

53. Lori Goshin, D. R. Gina Sissoko, Kristi L. Stringer, Carolyn Sufrin and Lorraine Byrnes, "Stigma and US Nurses' Intentions to Provide the Standard of Maternal Care to Incarcerated Women, 2017," in "Documenting and Addressing the Health Impacts of Carceral Systems," ed. David H. Cloud et al., supplement, *American Journal of Public Health* 110, no. S1 (2020): S93–S99.

54. Laurie Teresa Yearwood, "Pregnant and Shackled: Why Inmates Are Still Giving Birth Cuffed and Bound," *The Guardian*, January 24, 2020, https://www.theguardian.com/us-news/2020/jan/24/shackled-pregnant-women-prisoners-birth.

55. American Civil Liberties Union, *Still Worse*, 14.

56. Candice Bernd, Zoe Loftus-Ferren, and Maureen Nandini Mitra, "America's Toxic Prisons: The Environmental Injustices of Mass Incarceration," a special report by *Earth Island Journal* and *Truthout*, June 1, 2017, https://truthout.org/articles/america-s-toxic-prisons-the-environmental-injustices-of-mass-incarceration/

57. Adam D. Reich and Seth J. Prins, "The Disciplining Effect of Mass Incarceration on Labor Organization," *American Journal of Sociology* 125, no. 5 (March 1, 2020): 1303–44, https://doi.org/10.1086/709016.

58. "How Much Do Incarcerated People Earn in Each State?" Prison Policy Initiative, April 10, 2017, https://www.prisonpolicy.org/blog/2017/04/10/wages/.

59. "Prison Industry Enhancement Certification Program," Bureau of Justice Assistance, Program Brief, August 2018, https://bja.ojp.gov/sites/g/files/xyckuh186/files/Publications/PIECP-Program-Brief_2018.pdf.

60. "Is Charging Inmates to Stay in Prison Smart Policy?" Brennan Center for Justice, September 9, 2019, https://www.brennancenter.org/our-work/research-reports/charging-inmates-stay-prison-smart-policy.

61. For reports on ways in which incarcerated people, their families, and friends are exploited, see Prison Policy Initiative's "Exploitation" resources hub, accessed May 14, 2020, https://www.prisonpolicy.org/exploitation.html. See also "The Steep Cost of Medical Co-Pays in Prison Puts Health at Risk," Prison Policy Initiative, April 19, 2017, https://www.prisonpolicy.org/blog/2017/04/19/copays/.

62. Katti Gray, "The Run-On Sentence: Eddie Ellis on Life after Prison," *The Sun*, July 2013, https://thesunmagazine.org/issues/451/the-run-on-sentence.

63. The Collateral Consequences Resource Center is the best available resource for learning about and researching collateral consequences of incarceration. Accessed May 10, 2020, https://ccresourcecenter.org/about-the-collateral-consequences-resource-center/.

64. "Getting Back on Course: Educational Exclusion and Attainment among Formerly Incarcerated People," Prison Policy Initiative, October 2018, https://www.prisonpolicy.org/reports/education.html.

65. Christopher Zoukis, "Pell Grants for Prisoners: New Bill Restores Hope of Reinstating College Programs," *Prison Legal News*, July 31, 2015, https://www.prisonlegalnews.org/news/2015/jul/31/pell-grants-prisoners-new-bill-restores-hope-reinstating-college-programs/.

66. Vontrese R. Deeds Pamphile, "How School Closures Can Hurt Students by Disrupting Urban Educational Communities," Scholars Strategy Network, June 19, 2014, https://scholars.org/contribution/how-school-closures-can-hurt-students-disrupting-urban-educational-communities.

67. The Times Editorial Board, "Inmates Risking Their Lives to Fight California's Wildfires Deserve a Chance at Full-Time Jobs, *The Los Angeles Times*, November 1, 2019, https://www.latimes.com/opinion/story/2019-11-01/california-inmate-firefighters.

68. Kayla Galloway, "Gov. Gavin Newsom Signs Bill to Allow Inmate Firefighters to Work Professionally after Serving Prison Time," *ABC Eyewitness News*, Los Angeles, California, September 11, 2020, https://abc7.com/inmate-firefighters-california-incarcerated-cdcr-gavin-newsom/6419175/.

69. Alexandra Cox, "The New Economy and Youth Justice." *Youth Justice*, November 6, 2020, https://doi.org/10.1177/1473225420971043.

70. Terry-Ann Craigie, "Employment after Incarceration: Ban the Box and Racial Discrimination, Brennan Center for Justice, October 13, 2017, https://www.brennancenter.org/our-work/analysis-opinion/employment-after-incarceration-ban-box-and-racial-discrimination.

71. Rebecca Beitsch, "'Ban the Box' Laws May Be Harming Young Black Men Seeking Jobs," The Pew Charitable Trusts, August 22, 2017, https://www.pewtrusts.org/en/research-and-analysis/blogs/stateline/2017/08/22/ban-the-box-laws-may-be-harming-young-black-men-seeking-jobs.

72. Nicole D. Porter, "Voting in Jails," The Sentencing Project, May 7, 2020 https://www.sentencingproject.org/publications/voting-in-jails/.

73. Morgan McLeod, *Expanding the Vote: Two Decades of Felony Disenfranchisement* (Washington, DC: The Sentencing Project, October 17, 2018), https://www.sentencingproject.org/publications/expanding-vote-two-decades-felony-disenfranchisement-reforms/.

74. "Can't Pay, Can't Vote: A National Survey on the Modern-Day Poll Tax," Georgetown Law Civil Rights Clinic and Campaign Legal Center, July 25, 2019, https://www.law.georgetown.edu/news/too-poor-to-vote-civil-rights-clinic-campaign-legal-center-release-cant-pay-cant-vote/.

75. "The Myth of Voter Fraud," The Brennan Center for Justice, accessed June 5, 2020, https://www.brennancenter.org/issues/ensure-every-american-can-vote/vote-suppression/myth-voter-fraud.

76. "The New Voter Suppression," The Brennan Center for Justice, January 16, 2020, https://www.brennancenter.org/our-work/research-reports/new-voter-suppression.

77. "Grading the Parole Release Systems of All 50 States," Prison Policy Initiative, February 26, 2019, https://www.prisonpolicy.org/reports/grading_parole.html.

78. Leadership Conference on Civil and Human Rights, et. al., Comment Letter to Department of Justice on PATTERN First Step Act, September 3, 2019, https://civilrights.org/resource/comment-letter-to-department-of-justice-on-pattern-first-step-act/.

CHAPTER 7. THRESHOLD

1. Ruth Delaney, Ram Subramanian, Alison Shames, and Nicholas Turner, *Reimagining Prison* (Brooklyn, NY: Vera Institute of Justice, October 2018), xii, https://www.vera.org/downloads/publications/Reimagining-Prison_FINAL3_digital.pdf.

2. For a useful discussion of racial capitalism and its production of social separateness, see Jodi Malamed, "Racial Capitalism," *Critical*

Ethnic Studies 1, no. 1 (Spring 2015): 76–85, https://www.jstor.org/stable/10.5749/jcritethnstud.1.1.0076?seq=1.

3. Vera Institute, *Reimagining Prison*, 1–36.

4. "Arnold Ventures Dedicates $17 Million to Support Fundamental Prison Reform," Arnold Ventures, Press Release, May 15, 2019, https://www.arnoldventures.org/newsroom/arnold-ventures-dedicates-17-million-to-support-fundamental-prison-reform/.

5. Ruth Wilson Gilmore and James Kilgore, "The Case for Abolition," The Marshall Project, June 19, 2019, https://www.themarshallproject.org/2019/06/19/the-case-for-abolition.

6. Ian MacDougall, "New York City Paid McKinsey Millions to Stem Jail Violence. Instead, Violence Soared," ProPublica, December 10, 2019, https://www.propublica.org/article/new-york-city-paid-mckinsey-millions-to-stem-jail-violence-instead-violence-soared.

7. Alexandra Cox, "Youth Incarceration Comes to North Country," *Adirondack Daily Enterprise*, March 29, 2018, https://www.adirondackdailyenterprise.com/opinion/guest-commentary/2018/03/youth-incarceration-comes-to-the-north-country/.

8. Alexandra Cox, *Trapped in a Vice: The Consequences of Confinement for Young People* (New Brunswick, NJ: Rutgers University Press, 2017), 162.

9. John Arnold's Twitter thread on Pell Grants and prison conditions can be found at https://twitter.com/JohnArnoldFndtn/status/1215649919119380481.

10. Brett Story, dir. *The Prison in Twelve Landscapes*, documentary website, accessed July 2, 2020, https://www.prisonlandscapes.com/.

11. Brett Story, *Prison Land: Mapping Carceral Power across Neoliberal America* (Minneapolis: University of Minnesota Press, 2019).

12. Liat Ben-Moshe, *Decarcerating Disability: Deinstitutionalization and Prison Abolition* (Minneapolis: The University of Minnesota Press, 2020).

13. Chuck Collins, Omar Ocampo, and Sophia Paslaski, *Billionaire Bonanza 2020: Wealth Windfalls, Tumbling Taxes, and Pandemic Profiteers* (Washington, DC: Institute for Policy Studies, April 23, 2020), 4, https://ips-dc.org/wp-content/uploads/2020/04/Billionaire-Bonanza-2020.pdf. See also updates at inequality.org, accessed July 16, 2020, https://inequality.org/billionaire-bonanza-2020-updates/.

14. Cameron Peters, "A Detailed Timeline of All the Ways Trump Failed to Respond to the Coronavirus," *Vox*, June 8, 2020, https://www.vox.com/2020/6/8/21242003/trump-failed-coronavirus-response.

15. Andre Perry and Natalie Hopkinson, "Black Businesses Left Behind in Covid-19 Relief," *Bloomberg CityLab,* March 30, 2020, https://www.bloomberg.com/news/articles/2020-03-30/black-businesses-left-behind-in-covid-19-relief.

16. Larry Buhl, "Betsy DeVos Directs COVID-19 Relief Funds to Private and Charter Schools," *Capital and Main*, May 27, 2020, https://capitalandmain.com/betsy-devos-directs-covid-19-relief-funds-private-charter-schools-0527.

17. Jessica Silver- Greenberg, Jesse Drucker, and David Enrich, "Hospitals Got Bailouts and Furloughed Thousands While Paying C.E.O.s Billions," *New York Times*, June 8, 2020, https://www.nytimes.com/2020/06/08/business/hospitals-bailouts-ceo-pay.html?login=email&auth=login-email.

18. See, for example, Amy Goodman, "Mike Davis: Workers Face 'Sophie's Choice' Between Income & Health as 50 States Reopen Amid Pandemic." Interview with Mike Davis, *Democracy Now!* video, 59:02, May 22, 2020, https://www.democracynow.org/2020/5/22/historian_mike_davis_increased_inequality_coronavirus.

19. Alice Speri, "New York City and Los Angeles Slash Budgets—But Not for Police," *The Intercept*, May 22, 2020, https://theintercept.com/2020/05/22/la-budget-nyc-police/.

20. David Marans, "Andrew Cuomo Uses Budget to Cut Medicaid, Settle Political Scores," *HuffPost*, April 3, 2020, https://www.huffpost.com/entry/governor-andrew-cuomo-new-york-budget-cuts-medicaid-coronavirus-pandemic_n_5e86b371c5b6a9491833f612.

21. Valerie Strauss, "Cuomo Questions Why School Buildings Still Exist—and Says New York Will Work with Bill Gates to 'Reimagine Education," May 6, 2020, *Washington Post*, https://www.washingtonpost.com/education/2020/05/06/cuomo-questions-why-school-buildings-still-exist-says-new-york-will-work-with-bill-gates-reimagine-education/.

22. Alice Speri, "New York City." Vitale is quoted in the article.

23. Melina Abdullah, Jane Nguyen, Jacob Woocher, and Pastor Eddie Anderson, "The L.A. Mayor's 'Unacceptable' Budget Would Deprive Those in Need and Accelerate the City's Slide toward a Police State," *The Appeal,* May 21, 2020, https://theappeal.org/the-la-mayors-unacceptable-budget-would-deprive-those-in-need-and-accelerate-the-citys-slide-toward-a-police-state/.

24. Dana Rubenstein and Jeffery C. Mayes, "Nearly $1 Billion Is Shifted from Police in Budget That Pleases No One," *New York Times*, June 30,

2020, https://www.nytimes.com/2020/06/30/nyregion/nypd-budget.html.

25. David Zahniser, Dakota Smith, and Emily Alpert Reyes, "Los Angeles Cuts LAPD Spending, Taking Police Staffing to Its Lowest Level in 12 Years," *Los Angeles Times*, https://www.latimes.com/california/story/2020-07-01/lapd-budget-cuts-protesters-police-brutality.

26. Jaclyn Cosgrove, "L.A. County Voters Approve Measure J, Providing New Funding for Social Services," *Los Angeles Times*, November 3, 2020, *Los Angeles Times*, https://www.latimes.com/california/story/2020-11-03/2020-la-election-tracking-measure-j.

27. "'Bail Reform' and Carceral Control: A Critique of New York's New Bail Laws," Survived & Punished NY, February 11, 2020, https://survivedandpunished.org/2020/02/11/bail-reform-carceral-control-a-critique-of-new-yorks-new-bail-laws/.

28. Joshua Liefer, "The Only Way to Fight Antisemitism Is Solidarity and Compassion—Not Division," *The Guardian*, December 30, 2019, https://www.theguardian.com/commentisfree/2019/dec/30/antisemitism-attacks-monsey-new-york-joshua-leifer.

29. Everett C. Hughes, "Good People and Dirty Work," in *On Work, Race, and the Sociological Imagination*, ed. Lewis A. Closer (Chicago: University of Chicago Press, 1944), 184.

30. Derecka Purnell, "How I Became a Police Abolitionist," *Atlantic*, July 6, 2020, https://www.theatlantic.com/ideas/archive/2020/07/how-i-became-police-abolitionist/613540/.

31. Aishah Shahida Simmons, ed. *Love WITH Accountability: Digging Up the Roots of Child Sexual Abuse* (Chico, CA: AK Press, 2019), https://www.akpress.org/love-with-accountability.html.

32. Ejeris Dixon and Leah Lakshmi Piepzna-Samarasinha, eds., *Beyond Survival: Strategies and Stories from the Transformative Justice Movement* (Chico, CA: AK Press, 2020). https://www.akpress.org/beyond-survival.html.

33. Angela K. Evans, "Building Power: How Healing Justice Imagines the World," *Boulder Weekly*, October 29, 2020, https://www.boulderweekly.com/entertainment/arts-culture/building-power/.

34. Dean Spade, *Mutual Aid: Building Solidarity during This Crisis (and the Next)* (Brooklyn, NY: Verso, 2020).

35. Mariame Kaba, "Police Reforms You Should Always Oppose," *Truthout*, December 7, 2014, https://truthout.org/articles/police-reforms-you-should-always-oppose/.

36. Mariame Kaba, *We Do This 'til We Free Us: Abolitionist Organizing and Transforming Justice* (Chicago: Haymarket Books, 2021).

37. 8 to Abolition's website is https://www.8toabolition.com/.

38. Mariame Kaba and Kelley Hayes, "A Jailbreak of the Imagination: Seeing Prisons for What They Are and Demanding Transformation," *Truthout*, May 3, 2018, https://truthout.org/articles/a-jailbreak-of-the-imagination-seeing-prisons-for-what-they-are-and-demanding-transformation/.

39. Rose Braz and Craig Gilmore, "Joining Forces: Prison and Environmental Justice in Recent California Organizing," *Radical History Review*, 96 (Fall 2006): 95–111. This article can be found online at the Real Prisons Project at http://realcostofprisons.org/materials/Joining_Forces_Braz.pdf. See also Louis Sahagun, "The Mothers of East L.A. Transform Themselves and Their Neighborhood," *Los Angeles Times*, August 13, 1989, https://www.latimes.com/archives/la-xpm-1989-08-13-me-816-story.html.

Index

Founded in 1893,
UNIVERSITY OF CALIFORNIA PRESS
publishes bold, progressive books and journals on topics in the arts, humanities, social sciences, and natural sciences—with a focus on social justice issues—that inspire thought and action among readers worldwide.

The UC PRESS FOUNDATION
raises funds to uphold the press's vital role as an independent, nonprofit publisher, and receives philanthropic support from a wide range of individuals and institutions—and from committed readers like you. To learn more, visit ucpress.edu/supportus.